Translated the three
Olynthiacs in 1885-6

Teacher, Rev. Fath. Mor
and had four monthly exam
nations.

THE

OLYNTHIACS

OF

DEMOSTHENES.

With Notes

FOR SCHOOLS AND COLLEGES.

By W. S. TYLER,

WILLISTON PROFESSOR OF GREEK IN AMHERST COLLEGE.

———

BOSTON:
JOHN ALLYN, PUBLISHER.
1882.

Copyright, 1875.
By JOHN ALLYN.

University Press : John Wilson & Son,
Cambridge.

PREFACE.

THIS edition of the Olynthiacs of Demosthenes is intended, as announced in the title-page, for schools and colleges, and is meant especially for the use of students in these institutions. In an age when, relatively and more emphatically than ever before, "life is short and art is long," and when, next to mathematics, perhaps, Greek is usually one of the first studies to be retrenched, other things being equal, that commentary will be the best on a Greek classic which gives the most *needed* guidance and assistance, and takes the least time in giving it. In such an age brevity and conciseness are demanded, and may well be regarded as prime qualities in helps to classical study. Notes on the Olynthiacs of Demosthenes ought especially to have something of the compactness of the Orations themselves. I have therefore aimed to help the student only where he needs help, to dispense with all superfluous and all *useless* comment which includes all notes that are *certain not to be used*, and to condense the entire book within the smallest possible compass. At the same time I have endeavored to point to the sources — grammars, lexicons, dictionaries, histories, and editions — from which, if he has the time and the inclination, the student may derive further knowledge or illustration, thus choosing to be a finger-board to guide

his studies rather than a pack-horse or pony to carry him
over the road, and deeming it far better that he should be
taught and led to do the work wisely and well himself than
to have it done for him. With this view I have referred
him or left him to go to the dictionary, which every student should have continually by him and should form the
habit of consulting, for the geography of places and even
for the knowledge of antiquities, except when it was essential to the understanding of the passage, or perchance the
point was involved in some special difficulty or uncertainty.
If any should question the necessity of so copious an introduction, or its consistency with the brevity which has
been studied in the notes, I have only to say, that regard-
ing a pretty familiar acquaintance with the occasion and the
circumstances as the first requisite to the interpretation or
the appreciation of any work, I hoped that all this introductory matter would conduce directly to the understanding
of the orations and to a fuller sympathy with the orator
and the actors.

The text of this edition follows mainly that of Bekker's
stereotype edition. I have not hesitated, however, to depart from it, whenever there seemed to be sufficient reasons,
which have usually been stated in the notes. The editions
and commentaries which I have most frequently consulted
are those of J. H. Reiske, corrected and enlarged by G. H.
Schäfer, London, 1823 ; W. Dindorf, Oxford, 1849, itself
a *library* of notes and comments on Demosthenes ; K. H.
Frötscher and K. H. Funkhänel, Leipsic, 1834 ; J. H.
Vömel, Halle, 1856 ; A. Westermann, Leipsic, 1851 ; F.
Franke, Leipsic, 1871 ; C. Rehdantz, Leipsic, 1873 ; R.
Whiston, London, 1859 ; and G. H. Heslop, Oxford, 1872.
I have usually compared them all in reference to difficult
and disputed passages. I have found the notes of Whiston,

Franke, and Rehdantz particularly sensible and suggestive. When I have thought the renderings in any of these editions particularly just and happy, I have often quoted them and given credit accordingly ; and I am indebted to them for suggestion and confirmation in other instances in which I can only make this general acknowledgment. In my own renderings I have tried to follow the rule which I inculcate in my classes of giving as close and exact a translation as can be given in good idiomatic English, aiming *as far as possible* to make Demosthenes speak an English as compact, clear, pointed, and energetic as his own Greek, and believing, as I do with all my heart, that there can be no better discipline for the faculties of reason and speech in the schools than that which may be acquired by a faithful representation, a genuine *reproduction,* in our vernacular, if only that might be hoped for, of the Orations of Demosthenes.

W. S. TYLER.

AMHERST COLLEGE, April 20, 1875.

Phila.13, Charleston 2,

Phila 1 Athletic 2

Phila. 8, Athletic 3

Phila 6 New York 3
Phila 12 Washington 3
Phila. 13 Boston 4

ing in the early history of Greece that more fatal overthrow which shortly preceded the subversion of Grecian liberty. Repeopled by Chalcidic Greeks, who had settled in the neighborhood from Chalcis, a colony of Athens in Eubœa, Olynthus now came more directly into the circle of Grecian states and entered upon a new career of diversified and eventful history. We cannot follow it in detail. Concisely it is as follows: Originally by descent and by natural affinity allied to Athens, but in the Peloponnesian War taking sides with Sparta, and thus securing an acknowledged independence; usually on friendly terms with the earlier kings of Macedon, but gradually growing rich and powerful at their expense, now by inducing Pella, their chief city, to join the Olynthiac confederacy, and now through the voluntary cession of Lower Macedonia on the Thermaic Gulf by King Amyntas to save it from the Illyrians; attracting most of the Chalcidic cities to its alliance by the liberality of its international principles and political spirit, but by this very prosperity awakening the envy and jealousy of Acanthus and Apollonia, and provoking them to join with Macedon in calling for the armed intervention of Sparta; successfully resisting for a time the Lacedæmonians at the height of their power in a four years' war and inflicting upon them a terrible defeat in which they lost their general, but compelled by famine to sue for peace and submit to their hegemony; on the decline of that hegemony, reuniting all the Chalcidians under its own supremacy, and even wresting Amphipolis from the Athenians, but in turn stripped by them of Methone, Potidæa, Toronea, and several other towns in the vicinity; courted, flattered, and sought as an ally, both by Athens and by Philip, and vibrating now towards the one and now towards the other of these great powers, but attacked violently at length by all the forces of the latter and imperfectly succored and sustained by the former — Olynthus was finally betrayed into the hands of Philip, the city was destroyed, and the inhabitants, men, women, and children, were sold into slavery. The fall of Olynthus completed the conquest of the thirty-two Chalcidic cities, whose destruction was so complete that Demosthenes says in his third Philippic, five years afterwards, that their sites could hardly be found, and it might be supposed that they had never been inhabited.

A fuller history of the period after the accession of Philip to the throne may shed light on the relations of the Olynthians, Athenians, and Macedonians at the time of the Olynthian War, and may help the reader to a better understanding of the Olynthiac orations. Whiston has given it concisely and with careful reference to authorities : " This event (the accession of Philip) soon changed the position of affairs. The Athenians at first supported a rival, Argæus, in his claims to the throne, with a view of recovering Amphipolis (Diod., XVI. 3), and a portion of their forces, principally mercenaries, actually marched from Methone on the coast for thirty miles inland, where, with Argæus himself, they were attacked by Philip and obliged to surrender (c. Aristoc., § 144). But it was not Philip's policy to make enemies, so he allowed them to depart, and sent an embassy to Athens, with proposals of peace and friendship, professing also to give up all claims of his own to Amphipolis (Diod,. XVI. 3, 4 ; Grote, XI. 301), which, according to Diodorus, had already been evacuated by the Macedonian troops posted there by Philip's predecessor, Perdiccas (Grote, X. 516), to protect it against the Athenians (B. C. 359 – 58). Nevertheless, from whatever cause (Grote, XI. 306), the Athenians did not themselves make any attempt to occupy it : and Philip, as soon as he could, resolved to take advan-

tage of their remissness by attacking it himself, while he
deluded them with the assurance that he intended to restore
it to them after capturing it (c. Aristoc., 138 ; De Halon., 28).
But this promise he did not fulfil, and the Olynthians,
alarmed at the conquest and the rapid extension of his
power, thereupon sent to Athens to negotiate an alliance
(Olynth., II. 20), but without success, for the Athenians
still trusted the continued assurances of Philip. Repulsed
in that quarter, they readily accepted the alliance which
that politic monarch offered them, and received from him
the cession of Potidæa, taken from the Athenians (B. C.
357) by their combined forces (Phil., II. 22 ; Grote, XI.
335). And even before this he had ceded to them the district and city of Anthemus, so that he effectually secured
their friendship to himself and their hostility against
Athens, while, without any formal declaration of war, he
was commencing that series of aggressions which led to what
was called the war of Amphipolis, and continued between
the Athenians and himself for twelve years, till the peace
of B. C. 346 (Fal. Leg. *passim*). But Philip and the Olynthians were too near neighbors to continue friends, their
independence and progress being manifestly inconsistent
with his ambitious aggrandizement. As his power and
conquests extended, their conviction of this fact appears to
have become more decided, for we read (c. Aristoc., 129) that
in B. C. 352 – 51, probably after Philip's victories in Thessaly, they had again become the friends, though not as yet
allies, of Athens. This change in their sentiments Philip
appears to have considered, and perhaps with satisfaction, a
sufficient reason for hostilities. Accordingly soon afterwards (Phil., I. 20) his troops invaded their territory, and in
B. C. 350 – 49 (Grote, XI. 449), after recovering from an
illness in Thrace, he commenced serious operations against

them by marching into Chalcidice. The *immediate cause* of this attack is stated by Justin (VIII. 3) to have been their reception and protection of his two half-brothers, a brother of whom he had already put to death, and who themselves escaped, for a time, the same fate by flight. But this doubtless was only a pretext, not the real cause of his hostility, nor do we even know when it was first put forward. This attack was preceded by his previous reduction of several other Chalcidian towns, till the progress of his conquests and their proximity to themselves at last induced the Olynthians to send to Athens with proposals for an alliance, and to solicit its active co-operation against him. This proposition was favorably received, as the Olynthians would naturally expect; for not long before the Athenians themselves had expressed a wish that Olynthus might be induced to act against Philip (Olyn., I. 7). The assembly which was called to consider it was almost unanimous in voting that assistance should be sent, though Demades (Suidas s. v.) opposed it. But the conclusion of an alliance was a very different thing with the Athenians from active co-operation with their allies, and therefore it was that Demosthenes delivered his three Olynthiac orations one after the other, pressing upon his reluctant fellow-citizens the duty of vigorous action as well as wise determination. After his second speech, as it would seem, two thousand *mercenaries* were despatched under the command of Chares (Dionys., Epis. I. ad Amm. IX.) and some successes were achieved by him. The news created much exultation at Athens, and the people began to fancy, not only that they had rescued Olynthus, but that there was a fair prospect of their punishing and humbling Philip (τοὺς λόγους περὶ τοῦ τιμωρήσασθαι Φίλιππον ὁρῶ γιγνομένους). To combat this delusion, to exhort his fellow-countrymen to

1*

still greater and personal exertions, — possibly, too, in consequence of a second embassy from Olynthus, — Demosthenes delivered his third Olynthiac. One specific measure which he then recommended was an expedition of Athenian citizens instead of foreign mercenaries. This plan, however, was not then adopted, nor do we know for certain whether the oration (delivered towards the end of B. C. 350) was productive of any immediate and practical results, for soon afterwards the Athenian forces were engaged in Euboea in putting down a revolt, probably instigated by Philip himself (De Pace, 5). From Euboea, in the first half of B. C. 349, a cavalry force of Athenian citizens crossed over to Olynthus, and Philochorus, an author quoted by Dionysius of Halicarnassus (Epis. I. ad Amm. IX.), states that Chares was despatched with a body of two thousand hoplites and three hundred horsemen, all citizens. This force, however, of Athenian citizens, as Mr. Grote suggests (XI. 467), was not sent till the latter part of the war, which continued two years and a half. We are further assured by Demosthenes (Fal. Leg., 301) that from first to last the Athenians despatched no less than ten thousand mercenaries and four thousand native troops and fifty triremes to assist their allies. But all to no purpose ; their troops were badly commanded, and no really efficient aid was given till it was too late ; and Olynthus finally fell by treachery into Philip's hands (B. C. 347)."

Such is the narrative which Whiston, following the lead of Grote, gives of the efforts of the Athenians to aid Olynthus, and such all that can be *known* with *certainty* of the effect of the Olynthiacs of Demosthenes on these transactions. The more common account, adopted by Becker in his " Demosthenes as Statesman and Orator," Thirlwall in his " History of Greece," etc., and generally accepted previous

to the appearance of Grote's History, ascribes to the Olynthiac orations a more direct and controlling influence in the
Olynthian War. In brief it is as follows : the three Olynthiac orations were occasioned by three successive embassies
from Olynthus asking military aid against the encroachments of Philip, and were followed by three successive
expeditions sent out from Athens for that purpose. The
first embassy, opposed by Demades, Eubulus, and others,
was warmly supported by Demosthenes, and a force of two
thousand mercenaries, under Chares, was sent for their
relief. But after skirmishing about the coast of Pallene
and capturing a few scattering bands of Macedonians, they
returned in triumph to Athens. Beaten in two engagements and driven within their walls, the Olynthians now
sent a second embassy. Demosthenes, in a second oration,
exerted all his energies to rouse the Athenians to exertions
worthy of the interests at stake and their former glory ;
and the people sent a force of four thousand mercenaries
and one hundred and fifty horse under Charidemus. The
Olynthians sallied forth to meet them, and were repulsed ;
and then the mercenaries resolved themselves into a band
of freebooters and plundered the territory which they were
sent to protect. A third embassy now entreated for an
army of citizens ; and Demosthenes seconded their request
in a third oration of still greater urgency and eloquence.
They accordingly voted an army of two thousand infantry
and three hundred cavalry consisting of citizen soldiers,
and summoned all Greece to resist the encroachments of
the common enemy.

Grote does not deny the sending of the three expeditions
mentioned by Dionysius on the authority of Philochorus,
but he finds insuperable objections against associating them
with the three orations of Demosthenes and supposing

them, as Dionysius does, to constitute the whole Olynthian
War. "The Olynthian War," he says, "began in 350 B. C.,
and the three Olynthiacs of Demosthenes refer, in my judgment, to the first months of the war. But it lasted until the
early spring of 347 B. C., so that the armaments mentioned by Philochorus may have occurred during the last
half of the war. I cannot but think that Dionysius, being
satisfied with finding *three* expeditions to Olynthus which
might be attached as results to the *three* orations of Demosthenes, has too hastily copied out the three from Philochorus,
and has assigned the date of 349 – 48 B. C. to the three *orations*, simply because he found that date given to the three *expeditions* by Philochorus " (Grote, XI. p. 467). The principal
reason for separating the three expeditions from the three
orations is found in the history of the Athenian expedition to
Euboea. At the time when the third Olynthiac was delivered,
no expedition of Athenian *citizens* had been sent to the aid
of Olynthus. But Athenian citizens *were* sent thither, as
above stated, from Euboea during the first half of 349 B. C.
The inference is that the orations were all delivered prior
to that sending. The simple fact that the Olynthiacs make
no allusion to the Euboean expedition certainly favors the
opinion that the orations preceded that agitating and important expedition (Grote, XI. p. 469). The question cannot
be settled, although that question carries with it another,
namely, the date of the Olynthiacs, which Grote, followed
by Whiston, assigns to 350 B. C., but which is more commonly assigned to 349 – 48 B. C.

There is another vexed question which is more insoluble
than these, and that relates to the order in which the three
orations were delivered. In all the manuscripts as well as
principal editions they are arranged in the order in which
they are now numbered. But Dionysius cites them by

their first words in such a manner as to indicate that he reckoned the first as last, and the second and third as first and second. And Grote accedes to the arrangement of Dionysius so far as to place the second first, but he regards the first as belonging in the second place, and holds the third as still entitled to the place which it has always occupied. The *presumption* is certainly in favor of the order which they occupy in the manuscripts ; and the preponderance of authority is in favor of the same arrangement, which had the unanimous sanction of the ancient scholiasts, grammarians, and rhetoricians, and also meets the approval of the majority of modern scholars. Petrenz, in his dissertations (1833 and 1834), has thoroughly canvassed the internal evidence, and presented in a clear and strong light the arguments in favor of the traditional order. Dindorf considers the argument conclusive, and has prefixed a summary of it to his notes on the Olynthiacs. Westermann has reached the same conclusion in the first part of his *Quæstiones Demosthenicæ* where he has devoted an elaborate treatise of eighty-four pages to this question. Schaefer, Böhnecke, Vömel, Rehdantz, and Kennedy also defend the order in which they are edited. Thirlwall advocates the Dionysian order. Grote, followed by Whiston, as we have seen, and by Müller, in his " History of Greek Literature," agrees with Dionysius in placing the second first, but adheres to the common opinion in retaining the third as the last. This last point may be regarded as substantially settled by the almost unanimous verdict of competent judges. Thirlwall now stands almost alone in opposition to the spontaneous conviction or feeling that the third oration alone was worthy to be and must in fact have been the last oration of Demosthenes on the subject of Olynthus. The order of the other two still remains and is likely always to remain *sub judice.* The order of the manuscripts cannot be allowed to *settle* the question of the chronological order, for on that principle the first Philippic which follows them in the manuscripts would precede them, since, by common consent, it was delivered prior to them. The argument from the contents of the two orations is so plausible on both sides that the advocate of either seems to have carried his point, till "his neighbor cometh and searcheth him," and is so far from conclusive that the very same acknowledged characteristic, as, for example, the particular and specially *Olynthiac* character of the first oration as compared with the confessedly general and *Philippic* cast of the second, has been adduced as an argument on both sides. Fortunately the value and interest of the orations do not depend on a knowledge of their chronological order ; hence some of the best recent editions, as, for instance, those of Franke, Rehdantz, and Heslop, either ignore the question or barely allude to it. Readers who are interested in it will do well to consult Grote's Appendix to Chap. LXXXVIII. Vol. XI. ; Thirlwall's Appendix to Vol. II. p. 501, Amer. ed. ; Whiston's Excursus, Vol. I. p. 68 ; and above all the dissertations of Petrenz, in Dindorf's Prolegomena to the Olynthiac Orations, Vol. I. pp. 8 – 22, and Westermann's treatise De Or. Ol. Demos. Ordine.

The Olynthiacs were called Philippics by Dionysius of Halicarnassus, who reckoned as such twelve orations all bearing more or less directly against Philip and all delivered in the course of about as many years (B. C. 352 – 340), and who numbered the Olynthiacs as the second, third, and fourth in the series.

Lasthenes and Euthycrates, of whom the former led the cavalry in the last battle before Olynthus and betrayed them into the hands of Philip, have been immortalized as

traitors by Demosthenes (De Cherson., 40; De Cor., 48).
The strong language of the orator in the former of these
passages has been understood to imply that they were put
to death. But the latter passage explains his meaning (see
note on De Cor., 48). The real state of the case is more
truly indicated by one of Plutarch's anecdotes which represents them as complaining that some of Philip's courtiers
had called them traitors. "The Macedonians," he is said
to have replied, "are blunt, rough folks: they call a spade
a spade." Nothing worse appears to have befallen them
than the disappointment of their ambitious aims, in the
utter ruin of the city where they had probably hoped to rule,
and the condition of exiles with the consciousness that they
were abhorred by the friends of their country and despised
by its enemies. (See Thirlwall, Vol. II. p. 209.)

ANALYSIS OF THE OLYNTHIACS.

One characteristic of these orations which cannot but
strike the modern reader is their brevity. The text in this
edition, as the reader will see, occupies only about ten pages
for each, and only a little over thirty pages in all. Mr.
Kennedy's translation of the orations fills a little over
twenty pages in Bohn's edition, giving an average of less
than seven pages to each. A modern orator would have
occupied five or ten times the space, without after all saying so much as our orator has said that was directly to the
point, and adapted simply to accomplish his object. Di-
rectness, simplicity, plainness, and clearness are also equally
characteristic of these orations. They are masterpieces of
art, and yet it is the art which conceals art. They are
highly artistic, but at the farthest possible remove from all
that is artificial. These qualities will be fully appreciated

only after a repeated reading of the orations. But the following analysis may serve to illustrate them and may also aid the reader's perception and remembrance of the plan and principal contents.

FIRST OLYNTHIAC.

The exordium, comprised in a single section, we might say in a single sentence, simply presents in a clear and striking light the reason why the people should give the orator, in common with other speakers, an attentive hearing. The second paragraph, consisting of the next eleven sections (2 – 12), states with equal clearness and conciseness the orator's advice to send immediate succor to Olynthus and his reasons for it, in which he skilfully mingles encouragement drawn from the spontaneous offer of so important and so natural an ally with warnings from the perpetual encroachments of the crafty and despotic Philip, and reproofs for their own negligence of the past and present, and fond but false hopes for the future. The next two sections (14, 15) exhibit forcibly in the light of the past the bankruptcy and ruin which must inevitably result from a continuance in the same course. The next three sections (16 – 18) develop in a manner worthy of the chief statesman as well as the first orator of Athens his definite plan for the relief of Olynthus, which is twofold : first, to send troops to protect the Chalcidic cities ; and, second, to despatch another armament, partly naval and partly military, to ravage the territory of Philip. The next two sections (19, 20) relate to ways and means, and show how the Athenians can have money enough by a temporary appropriation of the theoric fund if they will ; if they will not, by an extraordinary war-tax. Sections 21 – 24 are intended to encourage and stimulate

the people by an examination of the critical and uncertain
state of Philip's affairs, owing especially to the fickleness
and jealousy of the Thessalians and the free and independent spirit of the Pæonians and Illyrians. In the next
three sections (25 – 27) the orator assures the Athenians
that they must take their choice, and now it is in their
power to choose, between meeting Philip at Olynthus and
fighting him at their own gates, and that in the latter case
the damage to the agricultural population alone in a single
campaign would exceed the whole expense of their late ten
years' war for the possession of Amphipolis. The conclusion — a single section and sentence like the exordium —
summons all classes, rich and poor, soldiers and orators, to
rally for the common weal which was no less the private
interest of them all, and ends with a brief prayer — only
five words — for a prosperous issue.

SECOND OLYNTHIAC.

The second Olynthiac is, as we have already intimated,
less distinctively Olynthiac and more Philippic than the first.
From this fact Grote draws an argument in favor of his
hypothesis, that the second oration was delivered first, for
the general purpose of rousing the indignation and hostility
of the Athenians against Philip, before the question of suc-
coring Olynthus had come before them with any urgency.
But the Greek Argument or Hypothesis prefixed to the
Greek text of the second Olynthiac explains this *Philippic*
cast of the oration by their fear and dread of Philip, which
it is now the orator's chief object to remove. " The Athenians had given a favorable reception to the Olynthian embassy and resolved to send them aid. And while they are
procrastinating and dreading an encounter with so formida-

ble an enemy as Philip, Demosthenes comes forward and endeavors to encourage them by showing how weak Philip really is : for he is an object of suspicion and distrust to his allies, and the Macedonians in themselves are anything but a great power." Such is the occasion of the oration as given in the ΥΠΟΘΕΣΙΣ and accepted by Petrenz, Westermann, and other advocates of the received order of the Olynthiacs. The first two sections constitute the exordium. The orator begins with the topic which was especially adapted to encourage the δεισιδαιμονέστεροι Ἀθηναῖοι, namely, the good-will of the gods manifested to them in all their history, but conspicuously manifest in the raising up at this crisis of an ally so near, of such considerable resources, and so irreconcilable to Philip ; and he exhorts them not to be so base as, with their towns and fortresses, to give up also the allies and opportunities furnished them by the blessing of heaven. The next two sections (3, 4) contain the *statement* of his object, which is not to set forth the power and success of Philip, and thus rouse them to do their duty, but to show his true character, his essential weakness in himself, and the only source of his accidental strength, which was not in himself but in Athens. The next paragraph (§§ 5 – 8) convicts Philip of faithlessness and perjury by repeated instances in his dealings with the Olynthians and Thessalians as well as the Athenians, and predicts that he will fall by the very means by which he has risen ; that the very men who have lifted him up when they thought he would further their own interests, would pull him down now that he was proved to be doing everything for himself. The two following sections (9, 10) insist on the necessary instability of all mere material resources, towns, fortresses, harbors, and the like, and the utter impossibility of building an enduring empire on the foundation of injustice, falsehood, and perjury. This is followed by a brief statement (11 – 13) of his advice, which is to send immediate succor to the Olynthians, to inform the Thessalians of this purpose and invite their co-operation, and, above all, to stop talking, in which their superiority was already too conspicuous, and begin to pay war-taxes, serve in the armies, and do their whole duty. The orator then proceeds (14 – 21) to expose analytically and at length the inherent weakness of Philip and his empire : he and his subjects have diametrically opposite interests ; *their* peace and prosperity are irreconcilable with the military glory which is *his* passion ; his troops have a reputation far beyond their deserts ; he is jealous and envious of his best officers and dismisses them ; and the rest, his favorites, are intemperate, licentious, drunkards and brigands, like himself ; his foreign wars have only weakened his resources, and a war on his frontiers will expose the rottenness of his power, as sickness brings out all the infirmities, wounds, and fractures of the natural body. True (22 – 29) Philip has been a fortunate man, and fortune is everything in human affairs. But he owes his success to his ceaseless toil and sleepless vigilance. Be as watchful and energetic as he is, nay, act as vigorously for your own rights and interests as you have often acted for those of the other Grecian states, and you are far more likely to enjoy the smiles of fortune and the blessing of heaven than Philip. Do your own duty in person ; see with your own eyes that your generals do theirs ; let your "classes" (συμμορίαι) pay war-taxes as they did in the good old times, and not, as they do now, manage politics, with an orator to preside on either side, a general under him, the three hundred to shout applause, and the rest of you attaching yourselves now to this party and now to that. In conclusion, then (30, 31), you must have done with all this ; you must equalize the privi-

(6 – 9) he exhorts them not to lose the opportunity now afforded by the war of Olynthus against Philip, which they had taken so much pains to foment, and warns them of the disgrace and danger that must result from such neglect. And now coming to the question of ways and means, he advances boldly (10 – 13) to the recommendation or demand which, unpopular and even odious as it is to the Athenian populace, is the orator's main counsel and reliance, namely, that they should annul the existing laws in regard to the theoric fund, which cut the very sinews of war, partly by distributing to those who stayed at home the money which should support the army abroad, and partly by shielding from deserved punishment those who shirk the service. Then he returns (14 – 20) to the necessity of carrying their resolves into execution, reminds them of the obvious fact that resolutions never execute themselves ; that action, though posterior in order of time to speaking and voting, is prior and superior in efficiency ; and now there is an imperative necessity, not for mutual censure and recrimination, not for vows, prayers, and good wishes, and not even for wise counsels, so much as for immediate vigorous action. It is no new thing for Athenian citizens to serve in the armies and sacrifice their private interest and pleasure to the public good (21 – 29); this was just what their ancestors did when they won such victories and reared such monuments ; when they ruled over willing Greece, and at the same time deposited millions in the Athenian treasury ; when they reared public edifices which were the admiration and envy of the world, while the private residences of Aristides, Miltiades, and the other leading men were no more imposing than those of their neighbors. How unlike to all this were the manners and the measures of the present rulers, and how different the results ! The radical cause of the difference (30 – 32) is,

that the people and their rulers have changed places ; that whereas the people were formerly the masters and the rulers their servants, now, on the other hand, the rulers are the masters, and the people, their humble servants, are delighted if they distribute among them the theoric fund and exhibit the Boëdromia for their entertainment. The only way to honor and save their country (33 – 36) is to act worthy of themselves and their ancestors ; to break away from this degrading and demoralizing servitude ; to give up this life of shows and this living on a miserable pittance of show-money, or rather to receive the money, and, serving in person in the army, to subsist themselves and carry on the war by that means, and thus, without taking away the rights or adding to the duties of Athenian citizens, only equalizing the burdens and systematizing the service, to stand at the post bequeathed to them by their ancestors, and do for themselves what they so highly honor in others. The oration ends, where it begins, with the gods, in a brief and simple prayer that they may choose such measures as will conduce to the prosperity of the state and the well-being of all the people.

How Bulwer could ever have persuaded himself — to say nothing of his readers — that such orations as these were suited to amuse and captivate the theatre-going Athenians, but not to convince and persuade a modern audience, is beyond my comprehension. They are wonderfully plain, simple, direct, straightforward, business-like, and statesman-like. There is not a word in them for the mere purpose of tickling the ear, affording amusement, or creating a sensation. There is not a figure or an illustration merely for the sake of ornament. They are the perfection of good common sense, plain matter of fact, forcible thought, and conclusive reasoning, or rather unquestionable *reason*, animated

by suitable feeling and expressed in a style of absolute fitness and transparent clearness ; and such orations, while
they were especially adapted to move and win those to
whom they were immediately addressed, are at the same
time suited to convince and persuade intelligent hearers and
readers in every age. The sufficient proof of this is found
in the fact that cultivated readers in all ages, in spite of
changing and adverse circumstances, *have* given them a verdict of unanimous approval.

ΔΗΜΟΣΘΕΝΟΥΣ

ΟΛΥΝΘΙΑΚΟΣ Α.

Ἀντὶ πολλῶν ἄν, ὦ ἄνδρες Ἀθηναῖοι, χρημάτων ὑμᾶς ἑλέσθαι νομίζω, εἰ φανερὸν γένοιτο τὸ μέλλον συνοίσειν τῇ πόλει περὶ ὧν νυνὶ σκοπεῖτε. ὅτε τοίνυν τοῦθ᾽ οὕτως ἔχει, προσήκει προθύμως ἐθέλειν ἀκούειν τῶν βουλομένων συμβουλεύειν· οὐ γὰρ μό- 5 νον εἴ τι χρήσιμον ἐσκεμμένος ἥκει τις, τοῦτ᾽ ἂν ἀκούσαντες λάβοιτε, ἀλλὰ καὶ τῆς ὑμετέρας τύχης ὑπολαμβάνω πολλὰ τῶν δεόντων ἐκ τοῦ παραχρῆμα ἐνίοις ἂν ἐπελθεῖν εἰπεῖν, ὥστ᾽ ἐξ ἁπάντων ῥᾳδίαν τὴν τοῦ συμφέροντος ὑμῖν αἵρεσιν γενέσθαι. 10

Ὁ μὲν οὖν παρὼν καιρός, ὦ ἄνδρες Ἀθηναῖοι, 2 μόνον οὐχὶ λέγει φωνὴν ἀφιεὶς ὅτι τῶν πραγμάτων ὑμῖν ἐκείνων αὐτοῖς ἀντιληπτέον ἐστίν, εἴπερ ὑπὲρ σωτηρίας αὐτῶν φροντίζετε· ἡμεῖς δ᾽ οὐκ οἶδ᾽ ὅντινά μοι δοκοῦμεν ἔχειν τρόπον πρὸς αὐτά. ἔστι δὴ τά 15 γ᾽ ἐμοὶ δοκοῦντα ψηφίσασθαι μὲν τὴν βοήθειαν, καὶ παρασκευάσασθαι τὴν ταχίστην ὅπως ἐνθένδε βοη- θήσετε καὶ μὴ πάθητε ταὐτὸν ὅπερ καὶ πρότερον, πρεσβείαν δὲ πέμπειν ἥτις ταῦτ᾽ ἐρεῖ καὶ παρέσται

1

A

3 τοῖς πράγμασιν· ὡς ἔστι μάλιστα τοῦτο δέος, μὴ
πανοῦργος ὢν καὶ δεινὸς ἄνθρωπος πράγμασι χρῆσθαι, τὰ μὲν εἴκων, ἡνίκα ἂν τύχῃ, τὰ δ᾽ ἀπειλῶν
(ἀξιόπιστος δ᾽ ἂν εἰκότως φαίνοιτο), τὰ δ᾽ ἡμᾶς
5 διαβάλλων καὶ τὴν ἀπουσίαν τὴν ἡμετέραν, τρέψη-
ται καὶ παρασπάσηταί τι τῶν ὅλων πραγμάτων.
4 οὐ μὴν ἀλλ᾽ ἐπιεικῶς, ὦ ἄνδρες Ἀθηναῖοι, τοῦθ᾽, ὃ
δυσμαχώτατόν ἐστι τῶν Φιλίππου πραγμάτων, καὶ
βέλτιστον ὑμῖν· τὸ γὰρ εἶναι πάντων ἐκεῖνον ἕνα
10 ὄντα κύριον καὶ ῥητῶν καὶ ἀπορρήτων, καὶ ἅμα
στρατηγὸν καὶ δεσπότην καὶ ταμίαν, καὶ πανταχοῦ
αὐτὸν παρεῖναι τῷ στρατεύματι, πρὸς μὲν τὸ τὰ τοῦ
πολέμου ταχὺ καὶ κατὰ καιρὸν πράττεσθαι πολλῷ
προέχει, πρὸς δὲ τὰς καταλλαγάς, ἃς ἂν ἐκεῖνος
15 ποιήσαιτο ἄσμενος πρὸς Ὀλυνθίους, ἐναντίως ἔχει.
5 δῆλον γάρ ἐστι τοῖς Ὀλυνθίοις ὅτι νῦν οὐ περὶ
δόξης οὐδ᾽ ὑπὲρ μέρους χώρας πολεμοῦσιν, ἀλλ᾽
ἀναστάσεως καὶ ἀνδραποδισμοῦ τῆς πατρίδος, καὶ
ἴσασιν ἅ τ᾽ Ἀμφιπολιτῶν ἐποίησε τοὺς παραδόντας
20 αὐτῷ τὴν πόλιν καὶ Πυδναίων τοὺς ὑποδεξαμένους·
καὶ ὅλως ἄπιστον, οἶμαι, ταῖς πολιτείαις ἡ τυραννίς,
6 ἄλλως τε κἂν ὅμορον χώραν ἔχωσι. ταῦτ᾽ οὖν
ἐγνωκότας ὑμᾶς, ὦ ἄνδρες Ἀθηναῖοι, καὶ τἄλλ᾽ ἃ
προσήκει πάντα ἐνθυμουμένους, φημὶ δεῖν ἐθελῆσαι
25 καὶ παροξυνθῆναι καὶ τῷ πολέμῳ προσέχειν, εἴπερ
ποτέ, καὶ νῦν, χρήματα εἰσφέροντας προθύμως καὶ
αὐτοὺς ἐξιόντας καὶ μηδὲν ἐλλείποντας. οὐδὲ γὰρ

κατεστήσαμεν τηλικοῦτον ἡλίκος οὐδείς πω βασιλεὺς γέγονε Μακεδονίας. νυνὶ δὴ καιρὸς ἥκει τις
οὗτος ὁ τῶν Ὀλυνθίων αὐτόματος τῇ πόλει, ὃς οὐδε-
10 νός ἐστιν ἐλάττων τῶν προτέρων ἐκείνων. καὶ
5 ἔμοιγε δοκεῖ τις ἄν, ὦ ἄνδρες Ἀθηναῖοι, δίκαιος λο-
γιστὴς τῶν παρὰ τῶν θεῶν ἡμῖν ὑπηργμένων κατα-
στάς, καίπερ οὐκ ἐχόντων ὡς δεῖ πολλῶν, ὅμως
μεγάλην ἂν ἔχειν αὐτοῖς χάριν, εἰκότως· τὸ μὲν γὰρ
πολλὰ ἀπολωλεκέναι κατὰ τὸν πόλεμον τῆς ἡμετέ-
10 ρας ἀμελείας ἄν τις θείη δικαίως, τὸ δὲ μήτε πάλαι
τοῦτο πεπονθέναι πεφηνέναι τέ τινα ἡμῖν συμμα-
χίαν τούτων ἀντίρροπον, ἂν βουλώμεθα χρῆσθαι,
τῆς παρ᾽ ἐκείνων εὐνοίας εὐεργέτημ᾽ ἂν ἔγωγε θείην.
11 ἀλλ᾽ οἶμαι, παρόμοιόν ἐστιν ὅπερ καὶ περὶ τῆς τῶν
15 χρημάτων κτήσεως· ἂν μὲν γάρ, ὅσα ἄν τις λάβῃ,
καὶ σώσῃ, μεγάλην ἔχει τῇ τύχῃ τὴν χάριν, ἂν δ
ἀναλώσας λάθῃ, συνανάλωσε καὶ τὸ μεμνῆσθαι τὴν
χάριν. καὶ περὶ τῶν πραγμάτων οὕτως οἱ μὴ χρη-
σάμενοι τοῖς καιροῖς ὀρθῶς, οὐδ᾽ εἰ συνέβη τι παρὰ
20 τῶν θεῶν χρηστόν, μνημονεύουσι· πρὸς γὰρ τὸ
τελευταῖον ἐκβὰν ἕκαστον τῶν πρὶν ὑπαρξάντων
κρίνεται. διὸ καὶ σφόδρα δεῖ τῶν λοιπῶν ἡμᾶς, ὦ
ἄνδρες Ἀθηναῖοι, φροντίσαι, ἵνα ταῦτ᾽ ἐπανορθωσάμενοι τὴν ἐπὶ τοῖς πεπραγμένοις ἀδοξίαν ἀποτριψώ-
12 μεθα. εἰ δὲ προησόμεθα, ὦ ἄνδρες Ἀθηναῖοι, καὶ
26 τούτους τοὺς ἀνθρώπους, εἶτ᾽ Ὄλυνθον ἐκεῖνος κατα-
στρέψεται, φρασάτω τις ἐμοὶ τί τὸ κωλῦον ἔτ᾽ αὐτὸν

ἔσται βαδίζειν ὅποι βούλεται.   ἆρα λογίζεταί τις
ὑμῶν, ὦ ἄνδρες Ἀθηναῖοι, καὶ θεωρεῖ τὸν τρόπον
δι᾽ ὃν μέγας γέγονεν ἀσθενὴς ὢν τὸ κατ᾽ ἀρχὰς Φίλιππος; τὸ πρῶτον Ἀμφίπολιν λαβών, μετὰ ταῦτα
Πύδναν, πάλιν Ποτίδαιαν, Μεθώνην αὖθις, εἶτα 5
Θετταλίας ἐπέβη·   μετὰ ταῦτα Φεράς, Παγασάς, 13
Μαγνησίαν, πάνθ᾽ ὃν ἐβούλετο εὐτρεπίσας τρόπον
ᾤχετ᾽ εἰς Θρᾴκην· εἶτ᾽ ἐκεῖ τοὺς μὲν ἐκβαλὼν τοὺς
δὲ καταστήσας τῶν βασιλέων ἠσθένησε· πάλιν
ῥαΐσας οὐκ ἐπὶ τὸ ῥαθυμεῖν ἀπέκλινεν, ἀλλ᾽ εὐθὺς 10
Ὀλυνθίοις ἐπεχείρησεν· τὰς δ᾽ ἐπ᾽ Ἰλλυριοὺς καὶ
Παίονας αὐτοῦ καὶ πρὸς Ἀρύμβαν καὶ ὅποι τις ἂν
εἴποι παραλείπω στρατείας.

Τί οὖν τις ἂν εἴποι ταῦτα λέγεις ἡμῖν νῦν; ἵνα 14
γνῶτε, ὦ ἄνδρες Ἀθηναῖοι, καὶ αἴσθησθε ἀμφότερα, 15
καὶ τὸ προΐεσθαι καθ᾽ ἕκαστον ἀεί τι τῶν πραγμάτων ὡς ἀλυσιτελές, καὶ τὴν φιλοπραγμοσύνην ᾗ
χρῆται καὶ συζῇ Φίλιππος, ὑφ᾽ ἧς οὐκ ἔστιν ὅπως
ἀγαπήσας τοῖς πεπραγμένοις ἡσυχίαν σχήσει.   εἰ
δ᾽ ὁ μὲν ὡς ἀεί τι μεῖζον τῶν ὑπαρχόντων δεῖ 20
πράττειν ἐγνωκὼς ἔσται, ὑμεῖς δὲ ὡς οὐδενὸς ἀντιληπτέον ἐρρωμένως τῶν πραγμάτων, σκοπεῖσθε εἰς
τί ποτ᾽ ἐλπὶς ταῦτα τελευτῆσαι.   πρὸς θεῶν, τίς 15
οὕτως εὐήθης ἐστὶν ὑμῶν ὅστις ἀγνοεῖ τὸν ἐκεῖθεν πόλεμον δεῦρο ἥξοντα, ἂν ἀμελήσωμεν; ἀλλὰ 25
μὴν εἰ τοῦτο γενήσεται, δέδοικα, ὦ ἄνδρες Ἀθηναῖοι,
μὴ τὸν αὐτὸν τρόπον, ὥσπερ οἱ δανειζόμενοι ῥᾳδίως

τότε ἤλπιζε τὰ πράγματα ἀναιρήσεσθαι, κᾆτα διέψευσται.   τοῦτο δὴ πρῶτον αὐτὸν ταράττει παρὰ
γνώμην γεγονός, καὶ πολλὴν ἀθυμίαν αὐτῷ παρέχει,
22 εἶτα τὰ τῶν Θετταλῶν.   ταῦτα γὰρ ἄπιστα μὲν ἦν
5 δήπου φύσει καὶ ἀεὶ πᾶσιν ἀνθρώποις, κομιδῇ δ',
ὥσπερ ἦν, καὶ ἔστι νῦν τούτῳ.   καὶ γὰρ Παγασὰς
ἀπαιτεῖν αὐτόν εἰσιν ἐψηφισμένοι, καὶ Μαγνησίαν
κεκωλύκασι τειχίζειν.   ἤκουον δ' ἔγωγε τινῶν ὡς
οὐδὲ τοὺς λιμένας καὶ τὰς ἀγορὰς ἔτι δώσοιεν αὐτῷ
10 καρποῦσθαι· τὰ γὰρ κοινὰ τὰ Θετταλῶν ἀπὸ τούτων δέοι διοικεῖν, οὐ Φίλιππον λαμβάνειν.   εἰ δὲ
τούτων ἀποστερηθήσεται τῶν χρημάτων, εἰς στενὸν
κομιδῇ τὰ τῆς τροφῆς τοῖς ξένοις αὐτῷ καταστήσε-
23 ται.   ἀλλὰ μὴν τόν γε Παίονα καὶ τὸν Ἰλλυριὸν
15 καὶ ἁπλῶς τούτους ἅπαντας ἡγεῖσθαι χρὴ αὐτονό-
μους ἥδιον ἂν καὶ ἐλευθέρους ἢ δούλους εἶναι· καὶ
γὰρ ἀήθεις τοῦ κατακούειν τινός εἰσι, καὶ ἄνθρωπος
ὑβριστής, ὥς φασιν.   καὶ μὰ Δί' οὐδὲν ἄπιστον
ἴσως· τὸ γὰρ εὖ πράττειν παρὰ τὴν ἀξίαν ἀφορμὴ
20 τοῦ κακῶς φρονεῖν τοῖς ἀνοήτοις γίγνεται, διόπερ
πολλάκις δοκεῖ τὸ φυλάξαι τἀγαθὰ τοῦ κτήσασθαι
24 χαλεπώτερον εἶναι.   δεῖ τοίνυν ὑμᾶς, ὦ ἄνδρες Ἀθηναῖοι, τὴν ἀκαιρίαν τὴν ἐκείνου καιρὸ ὑμέτερον νομί-
σαντας ἑτοίμως συνάρασθαι τὰ πράγματα, καὶ
25 πρεσβευομένους ἐφ' ἃ δεῖ καὶ στρατευομένους αὐτοὺς
καὶ παροξύνοντας τοὺς ἄλλους ἅπαντας, λογιζομένους, εἰ Φίλιππος λάβοι καθ' ἡμῶν τοιοῦτον καιρὸν

τότε ἤλπιζε τὰ πράγματα ἀναιρήσεσθαι, κᾆτα διέψευσται.   τοῦτο δὴ πρῶτον αὐτὸν ταράττει παρὰ
γνώμην γεγονός, καὶ πολλὴν ἀθυμίαν αὐτῷ παρέχει,
22 εἶτα τὰ τῶν Θετταλῶν.   ταῦτα γὰρ ἄπιστα μὲν ἦν
5 δήπου φύσει καὶ ἀεὶ πᾶσιν ἀνθρώποις, κομιδῇ δ',
ὥσπερ ἦν, καὶ ἔστι νῦν τούτῳ.   καὶ γὰρ Παγασὰς
ἀπαιτεῖν αὐτόν εἰσιν ἐψηφισμένοι, καὶ Μαγνησίαν
κεκωλύκασι τειχίζειν.   ἤκουον δ' ἔγωγε τινῶν ὡς
οὐδὲ τοὺς λιμένας καὶ τὰς ἀγορὰς ἔτι δώσοιεν αὐτῷ
10 καρποῦσθαι· τὰ γὰρ κοινὰ τὰ Θετταλῶν ἀπὸ τούτων δέοι διοικεῖν, οὐ Φίλιππον λαμβάνειν.   εἰ δὲ
τούτων ἀποστερηθήσεται τῶν χρημάτων, εἰς στενὸν
κομιδῇ τὰ τῆς τροφῆς τοῖς ξένοις αὐτῷ καταστήσε-
23 ται.   ἀλλὰ μὴν τόν γε Παίονα καὶ τὸν Ἰλλυριὸν
15 καὶ ἁπλῶς τούτους ἅπαντας ἡγεῖσθαι χρὴ αὐτονό-
μους ἥδιον ἂν καὶ ἐλευθέρους ἢ δούλους εἶναι· καὶ
γὰρ ἀήθεις τοῦ κατακούειν τινός εἰσι, καὶ ἄνθρωπος
ὑβριστής, ὥς φασιν.   καὶ μὰ Δί' οὐδὲν ἄπιστον
ἴσως· τὸ γὰρ εὖ πράττειν παρὰ τὴν ἀξίαν ἀφορμὴ
20 τοῦ κακῶς φρονεῖν τοῖς ἀνοήτοις γίγνεται, διόπερ
πολλάκις δοκεῖ τὸ φυλάξαι τἀγαθὰ τοῦ κτήσασθαι
24 χαλεπώτερον εἶναι.   δεῖ τοίνυν ὑμᾶς, ὦ ἄνδρες Ἀθηναῖοι, τὴν ἀκαιρίαν τὴν ἐκείνου καιρὸν ὑμέτερον νομί-
σαντας ἑτοίμως συνάρασθαι τὰ πράγματα, καὶ
25 πρεσβευομένους ἐφ' ἃ δεῖ καὶ στρατευομένους αὐτοὺς
καὶ παροξύνοντας τοὺς ἄλλους ἅπαντας, λογιζομένους, εἰ Φίλιππος λάβοι καθ' ἡμῶν τοιοῦτον καιρὸν

καὶ πόλεμος γένοιτο πρὸς τῇ χώρᾳ, πῶς ἂν αὐτὸν
οἴεσθε ἑτοίμως ἐφ' ὑμᾶς ἐλθεῖν. εἶτ' οὐκ αἰσχύ-
νεσθε, εἰ μηδ' ἃ πάθοιτ' ἄν, εἰ δύναιτ' ἐκεῖνος,
ταῦτα ποιῆσαι καιρὸν ἔχοντες οὐ τολμήσετε;

Ἔτι τοίνυν, ὦ ἄνδρες Ἀθηναῖοι, μηδὲ τοῦθ' ὑμᾶς 25
λανθανέτω, ὅτι νῦν αἵρεσις ἔστιν ὑμῖν πότερ' ὑμᾶς 6
ἐκεῖ χρὴ πολεμεῖν ἢ παρ' ὑμῖν ἐκεῖνον. ἐὰν μὲν
γὰρ ἀντέχῃ τὰ τῶν Ὀλυνθίων, ὑμεῖς ἐκεῖ πολεμή-
σετε καὶ τὴν ἐκείνου κακῶς ποιήσετε, τὴν ὑπάρχου-
σαν καὶ τὴν οἰκείαν ταύτην ἀδεῶς καρπούμενοι· ἂν 10
δ' ἐκεῖνα Φίλιππος λάβῃ, τίς αὐτὸν ἔτι κωλύσει
δεῦρο βαδίζειν; Θηβαῖοι; μὴ λίαν πικρὸν εἰπεῖν 26
ᾖ, καὶ συνεισβαλοῦσιν ἑτοίμως. ἀλλὰ Φωκεῖς; οἱ
τὴν οἰκείαν οὐχ οἷοί τε ὄντες φυλάττειν, ἐὰν μὴ
βοηθήσηθ' ὑμεῖς. ἢ ἄλλος τις; ἀλλ' ὦ τᾶν οὐχὶ 15
βουλήσεται. τῶν ἀτοπωτάτων μέντ' ἂν εἴη, εἰ ἃ
νῦν ἄνοιαν ὀφλισκάνων ὅμως ἐκλαλεῖ, ταῦτα δυνη-
θεὶς μὴ πράξει. ἀλλὰ μὴν ἡλίκα γ' ἐστὶ τὰ διά- 27
φορα ἐνθάδε ἢ ἐκεῖ πολεμεῖν, οὐδὲ λόγου προσδεῖν
ἡγοῦμαι. εἰ γὰρ ὑμᾶς δεήσειεν αὐτοὺς τριάκοντα 20
ἡμέρας μόνας ἔξω γενέσθαι καὶ ὅσα ἀνάγκη στρα-
τοπέδῳ χρωμένους τῶν ἐκ τῆς χώρας λαμβάνειν,
μηδενὸς ὄντος ἐν αὐτῇ πολεμίου λέγω, πλέον ἂν
οἶμαι ζημιωθῆναι τοὺς γεωργοῦντας ὑμῶν ἢ ὅσα εἰς
ἅπαντα τὸν πρὸ τοῦ πόλεμον δεδαπάνησθε. εἰ δὲ δὴ 25
πόλεμός τις ἥξει, πόσα χρὴ νομίσαι ζημιώσεσθαι;
καὶ προσέσθ' ἡ ὕβρις καὶ ἔτι ἡ τῶν πραγμάτων

αἰσχύνη, οὐδεμιᾶς ἐλάττων ζημίας τοῖς γε σώ-
φροσιν.

28   Πάντα δὴ ταῦτα δεῖ συνιδόντας ἅπαντας βοηθεῖν
καὶ ἀπωθεῖν ἐκεῖσε τὸν πόλεμον, τοὺς μὲν εὐπόρους,
5 ἵν᾽ ὑπὲρ τῶν πολλῶν ὧν καλῶς ποιοῦντες ἔχουσι
μικρὰ ἀναλίσκοντες τὰ λοιπὰ καρπῶνται ἀδεῶς, τοὺς
δ᾽ ἐν ἡλικίᾳ, ἵνα τὴν τοῦ πολεμεῖν ἐμπειρίαν ἐν τῇ
Φιλίππου χώρᾳ κτησάμενοι φοβεροὶ φύλακες τῆς
οἰκείας ἀκεραίου γένωνται, τοὺς δὲ λέγοντας, ἵν᾽ αἱ
10 τῶν πεπολιτευμένων αὐτοῖς εὔθυναι ῥᾴδιαι γένωνται,
ὡς ὁποῖ᾽ ἅττ᾽ ἂν ὑμᾶς περιστῇ τὰ πράγματα, τοιοῦτοι κριταὶ καὶ τῶν πεπραγμένων αὐτοῖς ἔσεσθε.
χρηστὰ δ᾽ εἴη παντὸς εἵνεκα.

ΟΛΥΝΘΙΑΚΟΣ Β.

Ἐπὶ πολλῶν μὲν ἄν τις ἰδεῖν, ὦ ἄνδρες Ἀθηναῖοι, 1
δοκεῖ μοι τὴν παρὰ τῶν θεῶν εὔνοιαν φανερὰν γιγνομένην τῇ πόλει, οὐχ ἥκιστα δὲ ἐν τοῖς παροῦσι
πράγμασι· τὸ γὰρ τοὺς πολεμήσοντας Φιλίππῳ
γεγενῆσθαι καὶ χώραν ὅμορον καὶ δύναμίν τινα κεκ- 5
τημένους, καὶ τὸ μέγιστον ἁπάντων, τὴν ὑπὲρ τοῦ
πολέμου γνώμην τοιαύτην ἔχοντας ὥστε τὰς πρὸς
ἐκεῖνον διαλλαγὰς πρῶτον μὲν ἀπίστους, εἶτα ἑαυτῶν
πατρίδος νομίζειν ἀνάστασιν, δαιμονίᾳ τινὶ καὶ θείᾳ
παντάπασιν ἔοικεν εὐεργεσίᾳ. ↓ δεῖ τοίνυν, ὦ ἄνδρες 2
Ἀθηναῖοι, τοῦτ' ἤδη σκοπεῖν αὐτούς, ὅπως μὴ χεί- 11
ρους περὶ ἡμᾶς αὐτοὺς εἶναι δόξομεν τῶν ὑπαρχόντων, ὡς ἔστι τῶν αἰσχρῶν, μᾶλλον δὲ τῶν αἰσχί-
στων, μὴ μόνον πόλεων καὶ τόπων ὧν ἦμέν ποτε
κύριοι φαίνεσθαι προϊεμένους, ἀλλὰ καὶ τῶν ὑπὸ 15
τῆς τύχης παρασκευασθέντων συμμάχων καὶ καιρῶν.

Τὸ μὲν οὖν, ὦ ἄνδρες Ἀθηναῖοι, τὴν Φιλίππου 3
ῥώμην διεξιέναι καὶ διὰ τούτων τῶν λόγων προτρέ-
πειν τὰ δέοντα ποιεῖν ὑμᾶς οὐχὶ καλῶς ἔχειν ἡγοῦμαι. διὰ τί; ὅτι μοι δοκεῖ πάνθ', ὅσ' ἂν εἴποι τις 20
ὑπὲρ τούτων, ἐκείνῳ μὲν ἔχειν φιλοτιμίαν, ἡμῖν δ'
οὐχὶ καλῶς πεπρᾶχθαι. ὁ μὲν γὰρ ὅσῳ πλείονα

ὑπὲρ τὴν ἀξίαν πεποίηκε τὴν αὐτοῦ, τοσούτῳ θαυ-
μαστότερος παρὰ πᾶσι νομίζεται· ὑμεῖς δὲ ὅσῳ
χεῖρον ἢ προσῆκε κέχρησθε τοῖς πράγμασι, τοσούτῳ
4 πλείονα αἰσχύνην ὠφλήκατε. ταῦτα μὲν οὖν παρα-
5 λείψω. καὶ γὰρ εἰ μετ' ἀληθείας τις, ὦ ἄνδρες
Ἀθηναῖοι, σκοποῖτο, ἐνθένδ' ἂν αὐτὸν ἴδοι μέγαν
γεγενημένον, οὐχὶ παρ' αὐτοῦ. ὧν οὖν ἐκεῖνος μὲν
ὀφείλει τοῖς ὑπὲρ αὐτοῦ πεπολιτευμένοις χάριν, ὑμῖν
δὲ δίκην προσήκει λαβεῖν, τούτων οὐχὶ νῦν ὁρῶ τὸν
10 καιρὸν τοῦ λέγειν. ἃ δὲ καὶ χωρὶς τούτων ἔνι, καὶ
βέλτιόν ἐστιν ἀκηκοέναι πάντας ὑμᾶς, καὶ μεγάλα,
ὦ ἄνδρες Ἀθηναῖοι, κατ' ἐκείνου φαίνοιτ' ἂν ὀνείδη
βουλομένοις ὀρθῶς δοκιμάζειν, ταῦτ' εἰπεῖν πειράσομαι.

5   Τὸ μὲν οὖν ἐπίορκον καὶ ἄπιστον καλεῖν ἄνευ τοῦ
16 τὰ πεπραγμένα δεικνύναι λοιδορίαν εἶναί τις ἂν
φήσειε κενὴν δικαίως· τὸ δὲ πάνθ', ὅσα πώποτ'
ἔπραξε, διεξιόντα ἐφ' ἅπασι τούτοις ἐλέγχειν καὶ
βραχέος λόγου συμβαίνει δεῖσθαι, καὶ δυοῖν ἕνεκα
20 ἡγοῦμαι συμφέρειν εἰρῆσθαι, τοῦ τ' ἐκεῖνον, ὅπερ
καὶ ἀληθὲς ὑπάρχει, φαῦλον φαίνεσθαι, καὶ τοῦ
τοὺς ὑπερεκπεπληγμένους ὡς ἄμαχόν τινα τὸν Φίλιππον ἰδεῖν ὅτι πάντα διεξελήλυθεν οἷς πρότερον
παρακρουόμενος μέγας ηὐξήθη, καὶ πρὸς αὐτὴν ἥκει
6 τὴν τελευτὴν τὰ πράγματ' αὐτοῦ. ἐγὼ γάρ, ὦ ἄν-
26 δρες Ἀθηναῖοι, σφόδρ' ἂν ἡγούμην καὶ αὐτὸς φοβερὸν τὸν Φίλιππον καὶ θαυμαστόν, εἰ τὰ δίκαια

πράττοντα ἑώρων αὐτὸν ηὐξημένον· νῦν δὲ θεωρῶν
καὶ σκοπῶν εὑρίσκω τὴν μὲν ἡμετέραν εὐήθειαν τὸ
κατ᾽ ἀρχάς, ὅτε ᾽Ολυνθίους ἀπήλαυνόν τινες ἐνθένδε
βουλομένους ἡμῖν διαλεχθῆναι, τῷ τὴν Ἀμφίπολιν
φάσκειν παραδώσειν καὶ τὸ θρυλούμενόν ποτε ἀπόρ-   5
ρητον ἐκεῖνο κατασκευάσαι, τούτῳ προσαγαγόμενον,
τὴν δ᾽ Ὀλυνθίων φιλίαν μετὰ ταῦτα τῷ Ποτίδαιαν   7
οὖσαν ὑμετέραν ἐξελεῖν καὶ τοὺς μὲν πρότερον συμμάχους ὑμᾶς ἀδικῆσαι, παραδοῦναι δὲ ἐκείνοις,
Θετταλοὺς δὲ νῦν τὰ τελευταῖα, τῷ Μαγνησίαν   10
παραδώσειν ὑποσχέσθαι καὶ τὸν Φωκικὸν πόλεμον
πολεμήσειν ὑπὲρ αὐτῶν ἀναδέξασθαι. ὅλως δὲ
οὐδεὶς ἔστιν ὅντιν᾽ οὐ πεφενάκικεν ἐκεῖνος τῶν αὐτῷ
χρησαμένων· τὴν γὰρ ἑκάστων ἄνοιαν ἀεὶ τῶν ἀγ-
νοούντων αὐτὸν ἐξαπατῶν καὶ προσλαμβάνων οὕτως   15
ηὐξήθη. ὥσπερ οὖν διὰ τούτων ἤρθη μέγας, ἡνίκα   8
ἕκαστοι συμφέρον αὐτὸν ἑαυτοῖς ᾤοντό τι πράξειν,
οὕτως ὀφείλει διὰ τῶν αὐτῶν τούτων καὶ καθαιρεθῆναι πάλιν, ἐπειδὴ πάνθ᾽ ἕνεκα ἑαυτοῦ ποιῶν ἐξελή-
λεγκται. καιροῦ μὲν δή, ὦ ἄνδρες Ἀθηναῖοι, πρὸς   20
τοῦτο πάρεστι Φιλίππῳ τὰ πράγματα· ἢ παρελθών
τις ἐμοί, μᾶλλον δὲ ὑμῖν δειξάτω ὡς οὐκ ἀληθῆ
ταῦτ᾽ ἐγὼ λέγω, ἢ ὡς οἱ τὰ πρῶτα ἐξηπατημένοι
τὰ λοιπὰ πιστεύσουσιν, ἢ ὡς οἱ παρὰ τὴν αὑτῶν
ἀξίαν δεδουλωμένοι Θετταλοὶ νῦν οὐκ ἂν ἐλεύθεροι   25
γένοιντο ἄσμενοι.

Καὶ μὴν εἴ τις ὑμῶν ταῦτα μὲν οὕτως ἔχειν   9

ἡγεῖται, οἴεται δὲ βίᾳ καθέξειν αὐτὸν τὰ πράγματα
τῷ τὰ χωρία καὶ λιμένας καὶ τὰ τοιαῦτα προειλη-
φέναι, οὐκ ὀρθῶς οἴεται. ὅταν μὲν γὰρ ὑπ' εὐνοίας
τὰ πράγματα συστῇ καὶ πᾶσι ταὐτὰ συμφέρῃ τοῖς
5 μετέχουσι τοῦ πολέμου, καὶ συμπονεῖν καὶ φέρειν
τὰς συμφορὰς καὶ μένειν ἐθέλουσιν ἄνθρωποι· ὅταν
δ' ἐκ πλεονεξίας καὶ πονηρίας τις ὥσπερ οὗτος
ἰσχύσῃ, ἡ πρώτη πρόφασις καὶ μικρὸν πταῖσμα
10 ἅπαντα ἀνεχαίτισε καὶ διέλυσεν. οὐ γὰρ ἔστιν,
10 οὐκ ἔστιν, ὦ ἄνδρες Ἀθηναῖοι, ἀδικοῦντα καὶ ἐπιορ-
κοῦντα καὶ ψευδόμενον δύναμιν βεβαίαν κτήσασθαι,
ἀλλὰ τὰ τοιαῦτα εἰς μὲν ἅπαξ καὶ βραχὺν χρόνον
ἀντέχει, καὶ σφόδρα γε ἤνθησεν ἐπὶ ταῖς ἐλπίσιν,
ἂν τύχῃ, τῷ χρόνῳ δὲ φωρᾶται καὶ περὶ αὑτὰ κα-
15 ταρρεῖ. ὥσπερ γὰρ οἰκίας, οἶμαι, καὶ πλοίου καὶ
τῶν ἄλλων τῶν τοιούτων τὰ κάτωθεν ἰσχυρότατα
εἶναι δεῖ, οὕτω καὶ τῶν πράξεων τὰς ἀρχὰς καὶ
τὰς ὑποθέσεις ἀληθεῖς καὶ δικαίας εἶναι προσήκει. τοῦτο δὲ οὐκ ἔνι νῦν ἐν τοῖς πεπραγμένοις
20 Φιλίππῳ.

11   Φημὶ δὴ δεῖν ὑμᾶς τοῖς μὲν Ὀλυνθίοις βοηθεῖν,
καὶ ὅπως τις λέγει κάλλιστα καὶ τάχιστα, οὕτως
ἀρέσκει μοι· πρὸς δὲ Θετταλοὺς πρεσβείαν πέμπειν, ἢ τοὺς μὲν διδάξει ταῦτα, τοὺς δὲ παροξυνεῖ·
25 καὶ γὰρ νῦν εἰσιν ἐψηφισμένοι Παγασὰς ἀπαιτεῖν
12 καὶ περὶ Μαγνησίας λόγους ποιεῖσθαι. σκοπεῖσθε
μέντοι τοῦτο, ὦ ἄνδρες Ἀθηναῖοι, ὅπως μὴ λόγους

ὦ ἄνδρες Ἀθηναῖοι, τοῖς αὐτοῖς Φίλιππόν τε χαίρειν
καὶ τοὺς ἀρχομένους, ἀλλ᾽ ὁ μὲν δόξης ἐπιθυμεῖ καὶ
τοῦτο ἐζήλωκε, καὶ προῄρηται πράττων καὶ κινδυ-
νεύων, ἂν συμβῇ τι, παθεῖν, τὴν τοῦ διαπράξασθαι
5 ταῦτα ἃ μηδεὶς πώποτε ἄλλος Μακεδόνων βασιλεὺς
16 δόξαν ἀντὶ τοῦ ζῆν ἀσφαλῶς ᾑρημένος τοῖς δὲ τῆς
μὲν φιλοτιμίας τῆς ἀπὸ τούτων οὐ μέτεστι, κοπτόμενοι δὲ ἀεὶ ταῖς στρατείαις ταύταις ταῖς ἄνω κάτω
λυποῦνται καὶ συνεχῶς ταλαιπωροῦσιν οὔτ᾽ ἐπὶ τοῖς
10 ἔργοις οὔτ᾽ ἐπὶ τοῖς αὐτῶν ἰδίοις ἐώμενοι διατρίβειν,
οὔθ᾽ ὅσ᾽ ἂν πορίσωσιν οὕτως ὅπως ἂν δύνωνται, ταῦτ᾽
ἔχοντες διαθέσθαι κεκλειμένων τῶν ἐμπορίων τῶν ἐν
17 τῇ χώρᾳ διὰ τὸν πόλεμον. οἱ μὲν οὖν πολλοὶ Μακεδόνων πῶς ἔχουσι Φιλίππῳ, ἐκ τούτων ἄν τις σκέ-
15 ψαιτο οὐ χαλεπῶς· οἱ δὲ δὴ περὶ αὐτὸν ὄντες ξένοι
καὶ πεζέταιροι δόξαν μὲν ἔχουσιν ὡς εἰσὶ θαυμαστοὶ
καὶ συγκεκροτημένοι τὰ τοῦ πολέμου, ὡς δ᾽ ἐγὼ
τῶν ἐν αὐτῇ τῇ χώρᾳ γεγενημένων τινὸς ἤκουον, ἀν-
δρὸς οὐδαμῶς οἵου τε ψεύδεσθαι, οὐδένων εἰσὶ βελ-
18 τίους. εἰ μὲν γάρ τις ἀνήρ ἐστιν ἐν αὐτοῖς οἷος
21 ἔμπειρος πολέμου καὶ ἀγώνων, τούτους μὲν φιλοτιμίᾳ πάντας ἀπωθεῖν αὐτὸν ἔφη, βουλόμενον πάντα
αὐτοῦ δοκεῖν εἶναι τὰ ἔργα (πρὸς γὰρ αὖ τοῖς ἄλλοις καὶ τὴν φιλοτιμίαν ἀνυπέρβλητον εἶναι)· εἰ
25 δέ τις σώφρων ἢ δίκαιος ἄλλως, τὴν καθ᾽ ἡμέραν
ἀκρασίαν τοῦ βίου καὶ μέθην καὶ κορδακισμοὺς οὐ
δυνάμενος φέρειν, παρεῶσθαι καὶ ἐν οὐδενὸς εἶναι

μέρει τὸν τοιοῦτον. λοιποὺς δὴ περὶ αὐτὸν εἶναι 19
λῃστὰς καὶ κόλακας καὶ τοιούτους ἀνθρώπους οἵους
μεθυσθέντας ὀρχεῖσθαι τοιαῦτα οἷα ἐγὼ νῦν ὀκνῶ
πρὸς ὑμᾶς ὀνομάσαι. δῆλον δ᾽ ὅτι ταῦτ᾽ ἐστὶν
ἀληθῆ· καὶ γὰρ οὓς ἐνθένδε πάντες ἀπήλαυνον ὡς 5
πολὺ τῶν θαυματοποιῶν ἀσελγεστέρους ὄντας, Καλ-
λίαν ἐκεῖνον τὸν δημόσιον καὶ τοιούτους ἀνθρώπους,
μίμους γελοίων καὶ ποιητὰς αἰσχρῶν ᾀσμάτων ὧν
εἰς τοὺς συνόντας ποιοῦσιν ἕνεκα τοῦ γελασθῆναι,
τούτους ἀγαπᾷ καὶ περὶ αὐτὸν ἔχει. καίτοι ταῦτα, 20
εἰ καὶ μικρά τις ἡγεῖται, μεγάλα, ὦ ἄνδρες Ἀθη- 11
ναῖοι, δείγματα τῆς ἐκείνου γνώμης καὶ κακοδαιμο-
νίας ἐστὶ τοῖς εὖ φρονοῦσιν. ἀλλ᾽, οἶμαι, νῦν μὲν
ἐπισκοτεῖ τούτοις τὸ κατορθοῦν· αἱ γὰρ εὐπραξίαι
δειναὶ συγκρύψαι τὰ τοιαῦτα ὀνείδη· εἰ δέ τι 15
πταίσει, τότ᾽ ἀκριβῶς αὐτοῦ ταῦτ᾽ ἐξετασθήσεται.
δοκεῖ δ᾽ ἔμοιγε, ὦ ἄνδρες Ἀθηναῖοι, δείξειν οὐκ εἰς
μακράν, ἂν οἵ τε θεοὶ θέλωσι καὶ ὑμεῖς βούλησθε.
ὥσπερ γὰρ ἐν τοῖς σώμασιν, τέως μὲν ἂν ἐρρωμέ- 21
νος ᾖ τις, οὐδὲν ἐπαισθάνεται, ἐπὰν δὲ ἀρρώστημά 20
τι συμβῇ, πάντα κινεῖται, κἂν ῥῆγμα κἂν στρέμμα
κἂν ἄλλο τι τῶν ὑπαρχόντων σαθρὸν ᾖ, οὕτω καὶ
τῶν πόλεων καὶ τῶν τυράννων, ἕως μὲν ἂν ἔξω πο-
λεμῶσιν, ἀφανῆ τὰ κακὰ τοῖς πολλοῖς ἐστίν, ἐπειδὰν δὲ ὅμορος πόλεμος συμπλακῇ, πάντα ἐποίησεν 25
ἔκδηλα.

Εἰ δέ τις ὑμῶν, ὦ ἄνδρες Ἀθηναῖοι, τὸν Φίλιπ- 22

B

πον εὐτυχοῦντα ὁρῶν ταύτῃ φοβερὸν προσπολεμῆ-
σαι νομίζει, σώφρονος μὲν ἀνθρώπου λογισμῷ
χρῆται· μεγάλη γὰρ ῥοπή, μᾶλλον δὲ τὸ ὅλον ἡ
τύχη παρὰ πάντ᾽ ἐστὶ τὰ τῶν ἀνθρώπων πράγ-
5 ματα ου μὴν ἀλλ᾽ ἔγωγε, εἴ τις αἵρεσίν μοι δοίη,
τὴν τῆς ἡμετέρας πόλεως τύχην ἂν ἑλοίμην, ἐθε-
λόντων ἃ προσήκει ποιεῖν ὑμῶν αὐτῶν καὶ κατὰ
μικρόν, ἢ τὴν ἐκείνου· πολὺ γὰρ πλείους ἀφορμὰς
εἰς τὸ τὴν παρὰ τῶν θεῶν εὔνοιαν ἔχειν ὁρῶ ἡμῖν
23 ἐνούσας ἢ ἐκείνῳ. ἀλλ᾽ οἶμαι, καθήμεθα οὐδὲν
11 ποιοῦντες· οὐκ ἔνι δ᾽ αὐτὸν ἀργοῦντα οὐδὲ τοῖς
φίλοις ἐπιτάττειν ὑπὲρ αὐτοῦ τι ποιεῖν, μή τί γε
δὴ τοῖς θεοῖς. οὐ δὴ θαυμαστόν ἐστιν εἰ στρατευό-
μενος καὶ πονῶν ἐκεῖνος αὐτὸς καὶ παρὼν ἐφ᾽ ἅπασι
15 καὶ μηδένα καιρὸν μηδ᾽ ὥραν παραλείπων ἡμῶν
μελλόντων καὶ ψηφιζομένων καὶ πυνθανομένων
περιγίγνεται. οὐδὲ θαυμάζω τοῦτ᾽ ἐγώ· τοὐναν-
τίον γὰρ ἂν ἦν θαυμαστόν, εἰ μηδὲν ποιοῦντες ἡμεῖς
ὧν τοῖς πολεμοῦσι προσήκει τοῦ πάντα ποιοῦντος
24 περιῆμεν. ἀλλ᾽ ἐκεῖνο θαυμάζω, εἰ Λακεδαιμονίοις
21 μέν ποτε, ὦ ἄνδρες Ἀθηναῖοι, ὑπὲρ τῶν Ἑλληνικῶν
δικαίων ἀντήρατε, καὶ πολλὰ ἰδίᾳ πλεονεκτῆσαι
πολλάκις ὑμῖν ἐξὸν οὐκ ἠθελήσατε, ἀλλ᾽ ἵν᾽ οἱ ἄλλοι
τύχωσι τῶν δικαίων, τὰ ὑμέτερ᾽ αὐτῶν ἀνηλίσκετε
25 εἰσφέροντες καὶ προεκινδυνεύετε στρατευόμενοι, νυνὶ
δ᾽ ὀκνεῖτε ἐξιέναι καὶ μέλλετε εἰσφέρειν ὑπὲρ τῶν
ὑμετέρων αὐτῶν κτημάτων, καὶ τοὺς μὲν ἄλλους

σεσώκατε πολλάκις πάντας καὶ καθ᾽ ἕνα αὐτῶν
ἕκαστον ἐν μέρει, τὰ δ᾽ ὑμέτερ᾽ αὐτῶν ἀπολωλεκό-
τες κάθησθε. ταῦτα θαυμάζω, καὶ ἔτι πρὸς τού- 25
τοις εἰ μηδὲ εἷς ὑμῶν, ὦ ἄνδρες Ἀθηναῖοι, δύναται
λογίσασθαι πόσον πολεμεῖτε χρόνον Φιλίππῳ, καὶ 5
τί ποιούντων ὑμῶν ὁ χρόνος διελήλυθεν οὗτος. ἴστε
γὰρ δήπου τοῦθ᾽, ὅτι μελλόντων αὐτῶν, ἑτέρους
τινὰς ἐλπιζόντων πράξειν, αἰτιωμένων ἀλλήλους,
κρινόντων, πάλιν ἐλπιζόντων, σχεδὸν ταυτὰ ἅπερ
νυνὶ ποιούντων ἅπας ὁ χρόνος διελήλυθεν. εἶθ᾽ 26
οὕτως ἀγνωμόνως ἔχετε, ὦ ἄνδρες Ἀθηναῖοι, ὥστε 11
δι᾽ ὧν ἐκ χρηστῶν φαῦλα τὰ πράγματα τῆς πόλεως
γέγονε, διὰ τούτων ἐλπίζετε τῶν αὐτῶν πράξεων ἐκ
φαύλων αὐτὰ χρηστὰ γενήσεσθαι; ἀλλ᾽ οὔτ᾽ εὔλο-
γον οὔτ᾽ ἔχον ἐστὶ φύσιν τοῦτό γε· πολὺ γὰρ ῥᾷον 15
ἔχοντας φυλάττειν ἢ κτήσασθαι πάντα πέφυκεν.
νυνὶ δὲ ὅ τι μὲν φυλάξομεν, οὐδέν ἐστιν ὑπὸ τοῦ
πολέμου λοιπὸν τῶν πρότερον, κτήσασθαι δὲ δεῖ.
αὐτῶν οὖν ἡμῶν ἔργον τοῦτ᾽ ἤδη. φημὶ δὴ δεῖν εἰσφέ- 27
ρειν χρήματα, αὐτοὺς ἐξιέναι προθύμως, μηδέν᾽ αἰτιᾶ- 20
σθαι πρὶν ἂν τῶν πραγμάτων κρατήσητε, τηνικαῦτα
δὲ ἀπ᾽ αὐτῶν τῶν ἔργων κρίναντας τοὺς μὲν ἀξίους
ἐπαίνου τιμᾶν, τοὺς δ᾽ ἀδικοῦντας κολάζειν, τὰς προφάσεις δ᾽ ἀφελεῖν καὶ τὰ καθ᾽ ὑμᾶς ἐλλείμματα·
οὐ γὰρ ἔστι πικρῶς ἐξετάσαι τί πέπρακται τοῖς 25
ἄλλοις, ἂν μὴ παρ᾽ ὑμῶν αὐτῶν πρῶτον ὑπάρξῃ τὰ
δέοντα. τίνος γὰρ ἕνεκα, ὦ ἄνδρες Ἀθηναῖοι, νομί- 28

νον, ἄλλο δὲ μηδ᾽ ὁτιοῦν συμπονεῖν, οὐχὶ γενήσεται
τῶν δεόντων ὑμῖν οὐδὲν ἐν καιρῷ τὸ γὰρ ἠδικημένον
ἀεὶ μέρος ἐλλείψει, εἶθ᾽ ὑμῖν τούτους κολάζειν ἀντὶ
τῶν ἐχθρῶν περιέσται. λέγω δὴ κεφάλαιον, πάντας 31
εἰσφέρειν ἀφ᾽ ὅσων ἕκαστος ἔχει, τὸ ἴσον· πάντας 5
ἐξιέναι κατὰ μέρος, ἕως ἂν ἅπαντες στρατεύσησθε·
πᾶσι τοῖς παριοῦσι λόγον διδόναι, καὶ τὰ βέλτιστα
ὧν ἂν ἀκούσητε αἱρεῖσθαι, μὴ ἃ ἂν ὁ δεῖνα ἢ ὁ
δεῖνα εἴπῃ. κἂν ταῦτα ποιῆτε, οὐ τὸν εἰπόντα
μόνον παραχρῆμα ἐπαινέσεσθε, ἀλλὰ καὶ ὑμᾶς 10
αὐτοὺς ὕστερον, βέλτιον τῶν ὅλων πραγμάτων ὑμῖν
ἐχόντων.

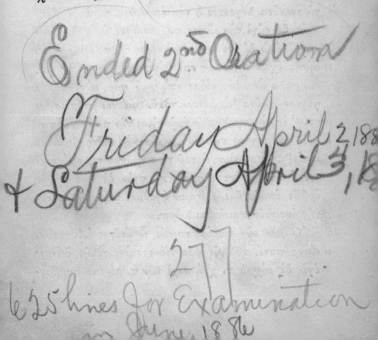

Ended 2nd Oration

Friday April 2 188

& Saturday April 3, 18

27

625 lines for Examination
in June 188

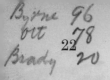

ΟΛΥΝΘΙΑΚΟΣ Γ.

1   Οὐχὶ ταὐτὰ παρίσταταί μοι γιγνώσκειν, ὦ ἄνδρες Ἀθηναῖοι, ὅταν τε εἰς τὰ πράγματα ἀποβλέψω
καὶ ὅταν πρὸς τοὺς λόγους οὓς ἀκούω· τοὺς μὲν
γὰρ λόγους περὶ τοῦ τιμωρήσασθαι Φίλιππον ὁρῶ
5 γιγνομένους, τὰ δὲ πράγματα εἰς τοῦτο προήκοντα
ὥστε ὅπως μὴ πεισόμεθα αὐτοὶ πρότερον κακῶς
σκέψασθαι δέον. οὐδὲν οὖν ἄλλο μοι δοκοῦσιν οἱ
τὰ τοιαῦτα λέγοντες ἢ τὴν ὑπόθεσιν, περὶ ἧς βουλεύεσθε, οὐχὶ τὴν οὖσαν παριστάντες ὑμῖν ἁμαρτά-
2 νειν.   ἐγὼ δ' ὅτι μέν ποτ' ἐξῆν τῇ πόλει καὶ τὰ
11 αὑτῆς ἔχειν ἀσφαλῶς καὶ Φίλιππον τιμωρήσασθαι,
καὶ μάλα ἀκριβῶς οἶδα· ἐπ' ἐμοῦ γάρ, οὐχὶ πάλαι
γέγονε ταῦτα ἀμφότερα· νῦν μέντοι πέπεισμαι
τοῦθ' ἱκανὸν προλαβεῖν ἡμῖν εἶναι τὴν πρώτην, ὅπως
15 τοὺς συμμάχους σώσομεν.   ἐὰν γὰρ τοῦτο βεβαίως
ὑπάρξῃ, τότε καὶ περὶ τοῦ τίνα τρόπον τιμωρήσεταί
τις ἐκεῖνον ἐξέσται σκοπεῖν· πρὶν δὲ τὴν ἀρχὴν
ὀρθῶς ὑποθέσθαι, μάταιον ἡγοῦμαι περὶ τῆς τελευ-
τῆς ὁντινοῦν ποιεῖσθαι λόγον.

3   Ὁ μὲν οὖν παρὼν καιρός, ὦ ἄνδρες Ἀθηναῖοι,
21 εἴπερ ποτέ, πολλῆς φροντίδος καὶ βουλῆς δεῖται·
ἐγὼ δὲ οὐχ ὅ τι χρὴ περὶ τῶν παρόντων συμβου-

ἐκεῖσε ἐβοηθήσαμεν, ὥσπερ ἐψηφισάμεθα, προθύμως, οὐκ ἂν ἠνώχλει νῦν ἡμῖν ὁ Φίλιππος σωθείς.

6   Τὰ μὲν δὴ τότε πραχθέντα οὐκ ἂν ἄλλως ἔχοι·
νῦν δ' ἑτέρου πολέμου καιρὸς ἥκει τις, δι' ὃν καὶ
5 περὶ τούτων ἐμνήσθην, ἵνα μὴ ταὐτὰ πάθητε. τί
δὴ χρησόμεθα, ὦ ἄνδρες Ἀθηναῖοι, τούτῳ; εἰ γὰρ
μὴ βοηθήσετε παντὶ σθένει κατὰ τὸ δυνατόν, θεάσασθε ὃν τρόπον ὑμεῖς ἐστρατηγηκότες πάντα
7 ἔσεσθε ὑπὲρ Φιλίππου. ὑπῆρχον Ὀλύνθιοι δύνα-
10 μίν τινα κεκτημένοι, καὶ διέκειθ' οὕτω τὰ πράγματα·
οὔτε Φίλιππος ἐθάρρει τούτους οὔθ' οὗτοι Φίλιππον.
ἐπράξαμεν ἡμεῖς κἀκεῖνοι πρὸς ἡμᾶς εἰρήνην· ἦν
τοῦτο ὥσπερ ἐμπόδισμά τι τῷ Φιλίππῳ καὶ δυσχερές, πόλιν μεγάλην ἐφορμεῖν τοῖς ἑαυτοῦ καιροῖς
15 διηλλαγμένην πρὸς ἡμᾶς. ἐκπολεμῶσαι δεῖν ᾠόμεθα
τοὺς ἀνθρώπους ἐκ παντὸς τρόπου· καὶ ὃ πάντες
8 ἐθρύλουν, τοῦτο πέπρακται νυνὶ ὁπωσδήποτε. τί
οὖν ὑπόλοιπον, ὦ ἄνδρες Ἀθηναῖοι, πλὴν βοηθεῖν
ἐρρωμένως καὶ προθύμως; ἐγὼ μὲν οὐχ ὁρῶ· χωρὶς
20 γὰρ τῆς περιστάσης ἂν ἡμᾶς αἰσχύνης εἰ καθυφεί-
μεθά τι τῶν πραγμάτων, οὐδὲ τὸν φόβον, ὦ ἄνδρες
Ἀθηναῖοι, μικρὸν ὁρῶ τὸν τῶν μετὰ ταῦτα, ἐχόντων
μὲν ὡς ἔχουσι Θηβαίων ἡμῖν, ἀπειρηκότων δὲ χρή-
μασι Φωκέων, μηδενὸς δ' ἐμποδὼν ὄντος Φιλίππῳ
25 τὰ παρόντα καταστρεψαμένῳ πρὸς ταῦτα ἐπικλῖ-
9 ναι τὰ πράγματα. ἀλλὰ μὴν εἴ τις ὑμῶν εἰς τοῦτο
ἀναβάλλεται ποιήσειν τὰ δέοντα, ἰδεῖν ἐγγύθεν βού-

λεται τὰ δεινά, ἐξὸν ἀκούειν ἄλλοθι γιγνόμενα, καὶ
βοηθοὺς ἑαυτῷ ζητεῖν, ἐξὸν νῦν ἑτέροις αὐτὸν βοη-
θεῖν· ὅτι γὰρ εἰς τοῦτο περιστήσεται τὰ πράγματα
ἐὰν τὰ παρόντα προώμεθα, σχεδὸν ἴσμεν ἅπαντες
δήπου. 5

Ἀλλ' ὅτι μὲν δὴ δεῖ βοηθεῖν, εἴποι τις ἄν, πάν- 10
τες ἐγνώκαμεν, καὶ βοηθήσομεν· τὸ δὲ ὅπως, τοῦτο
λέγε. μὴ τοίνυν, ὦ ἄνδρες Ἀθηναῖοι, θαυμάσητε
ἂν παράδοξον εἴπω τι τοῖς πολλοῖς. νομοθέτας
καθίσατε. ἐν δὲ τούτοις τοῖς νομοθέταις μὴ θῆσθε 10
νόμον μηδένα (εἰσὶ γὰρ ἱκανοὶ ὑμῖν), ἀλλὰ τοὺς εἰς
τὸ παρὸν βλάπτοντας ὑμᾶς λύσατε. λέγω δὲ τοὺς 11
περὶ τῶν θεωρικῶν, σαφῶς οὑτωσί, καὶ τοὺς περὶ
τῶν στρατευομένων ἐνίους, ὧν οἱ μὲν τὰ στρατιω-
τικὰ τοῖς οἴκοι μένουσι διανέμουσι θεωρικά, οἱ δὲ 15
τοὺς ἀτακτοῦντας ἀθώους καθιστᾶσιν, εἶτα καὶ τοὺς
τὰ δέοντα ποιεῖν βουλομένους ἀθυμοτέρους ποιοῦσιν. ἐπειδὰν δὲ ταῦτα λύσητε καὶ τὴν τοῦ τὰ βέλτιστα λέγειν ὁδὸν παράσχητε ἀσφαλῆ, τηνικαῦτα
τὸν γράφοντα ἃ πάντες ἴστε ὅτι συμφέρει ζητεῖτε.
πρὶν δὲ ταῦτα πρᾶξαι, μὴ σκοπεῖτε τίς εἰπὼν τὰ 12
βέλτιστα ὑπὲρ ὑμῶν ὑφ' ὑμῶν ἀπολέσθαι βουλήσε-
ται· οὐ γὰρ εὑρήσετε, ἄλλως τε καὶ τούτου μόνου
περιγίγνεσθαι μέλλοντος, παθεῖν ἀδίκως τι κακὸν
τὸν ταῦτ' εἰπόντα καὶ γράψαντα, μηδὲν δὲ ὠφελῆ- 25
σαι τὰ πράγματα, ἀλλὰ καὶ εἰς τὸ λοιπὸν μᾶλλον
ἔτι ἢ νῦν τὸ τὰ βέλτιστα λέγειν φοβερώτερον

2

ποιῆσαι. καὶ λύειν γε, ὦ ἄνδρες Ἀθηναῖοι, τοὺς
νόμους δεῖ τούτους τοὺς αὐτοὺς ἀξιοῦν οἵπερ καὶ
13 τεθείκασιν· οὐ γάρ ἐστι δίκαιον τὴν μὲν χάριν, ἢ
πᾶσαν ἔβλαψε τὴν πόλιν, τοῖς τότε θεῖσιν ὑπάρ-
5 χειν, τὴν δ' ἀπέχθειαν, δι' ἧς ἂν ἅπαντες ἄμεινον
πράξαιμεν, τῷ νῦν τὰ βέλτιστα εἰπόντι ζημίαν γενέσθαι. πρὶν δὲ ταῦτα εὐτρεπίσαι, μηδαμῶς, ὦ
ἄνδρες Ἀθηναῖοι, μηδένα ἀξιοῦτε τηλικοῦτον εἶναι
παρ' ὑμῖν ὥστε τοὺς νόμους τούτους παραβάντα μὴ
10 δοῦναι δίκην, μηδ' οὕτως ἀνόητον ὥστε εἰς προὖπτον
κακὸν αὑτὸν ἐμβαλεῖν.

14 Οὐ μὴν οὐδ' ἐκεῖνό γ' ὑμᾶς ἀγνοεῖν δεῖ, ὦ ἄνδρες
Ἀθηναῖοι, ὅτι ψήφισμα οὐδενὸς ἄξιόν ἐστιν, ἂν μὴ
προσγένηται τὸ ποιεῖν ἐθέλειν τά γε δόξαντα προ-
15 θύμως ὑμᾶς. εἰ γὰρ αὐτάρκη τὰ ψηφίσματα ἦν ἢ
ὑμᾶς ἀναγκάζειν ἃ προσήκει πράττειν ἢ περὶ ὧν ἂν
γραφῇ διαπράξασθαι, οὔτ' ἂν ὑμεῖς πολλὰ ψηφιζό-
μενοι μικρά, μᾶλλον δ' οὐδὲν ἐπράττετε τούτων,
οὔτε Φίλιππος τοσοῦτον ὑβρίκει χρόνον· πάλαι γὰρ
15 ἂν ἕνεκά γε ψηφισμάτων ἐδεδώκει δίκην. ἀλλ' οὐχ
21 οὕτω ταῦτ' ἔχει· τὸ γὰρ πράττειν τοῦ λέγειν καὶ
χειροτονεῖν ὕστερον ὂν τῇ τάξει, πρότερον τῇ δυνά-
μει καὶ κρεῖττον ἐστίν. τοῦτ' οὖν δεῖ προσεῖναι,
τὰ δ' ἄλλα ὑπάρχει· καὶ γὰρ εἰπεῖν τὰ δέοντα
25 παρ' ὑμῖν εἰσιν, ὦ ἄνδρες Ἀθηναῖοι, δυνάμενοι, καὶ
γνῶναι πάντων ὑμεῖς ὀξύτατοι τὰ ῥηθέντα, καὶ
16 πρᾶξαι δὲ δυνήσεσθε νῦν, ἐὰν ὀρθῶς ποιῆτε. τίνα

γὰρ χρόνον ἢ τίνα καιρὸν, ὦ ἄνδρες Ἀθηναῖοι, τοῦ
παρόντος βελτίω ζητεῖτε ; ἢ πότε ἃ δεῖ πράξετε, εἰ
μὴ νῦν ; οὐχ ἅπαντα μὲν ἡμῶν προείληφε τὰ χωρία
ἄνθρωπος, εἰ δὲ καὶ ταύτης κύριος τῆς χώρας γενήσεται, πάντων αἴσχιστα πεισόμεθα ; οὐχ οὕς, εἰ 5
πολεμήσαιεν, ἑτοίμως σώσειν ὑπισχνούμεθα, οὗτοι
νῦν πολεμοῦνται ; οὐκ ἐχθρός ; οὐκ ἔχων τὰ ἡμέτερα ; οὐ βάρβαρος ; οὐχ ὅ τι ἂν εἴποι τις ; ἀλλὰ 17
πρὸς θεῶν πάντα ἐάσαντες καὶ μόνον οὐχὶ συγκα-
τασκευάσαντες αὐτῷ τότε τοὺς αἰτίους, οἵτινές εἰσι, 10
τούτων ζητήσομεν ; οὐ γὰρ αὐτοί γ' αἴτιοι φήσομεν
εἶναι, σαφῶς οἶδα τοῦτ' ἐγώ. ↲ οὐδὲ γὰρ ἐν τοῖς τοῦ
πολέμου κινδύνοις τῶν φυγόντων οὐδεὶς ἑαυτοῦ
κατηγορεῖ, ἀλλὰ τοῦ στρατηγοῦ καὶ τῶν πλησίον
καὶ πάντων μᾶλλον, ἥττηνται δ' ὅμως διὰ πάντας 15
τοὺς φυγόντας δήπου· μένειν γὰρ ἐξῆν τῷ κατηγο-
ροῦντι τῶν ἄλλων, εἰ δὲ τοῦτ' ἐποίει ἕκαστος,
ἐνίκων ἄν. καὶ νῦν οὐ λέγει τις τὰ βέλτιστα· 18
ἀναστὰς ἄλλος εἰπάτω, μὴ τοῦτον αἰτιάσθω. ἕτερος λέγει τις βελτίω· ταῦτα ποιεῖτε ἀγαθῇ τύχῃ. 20
ἀλλ' οὐχ ἡδέα ταῦτα· οὐκέτι τοῦθ' ὁ λέγων ἀδικεῖ,
πλὴν εἰ δέον εὔξασθαι παραλείπει. εὔξασθαι μὲν
γάρ, ὦ ἄνδρες Ἀθηναῖοι, ῥᾴδιον, εἰς ταὐτὸ πάνθ'
ὅσα βούλεταί τις ἀθροίσαντα ἐν ὀλίγῳ· ἑλέσθαι δέ,
ὅταν περὶ πραγμάτων προτεθῇ σκοπεῖν, οὐκέθ' 25
ὁμοίως εὔπορον, ἀλλὰ δεῖ τὰ βέλτιστα ἀντὶ τῶν
ἡδέων, ἂν μὴ συναμφότερα ἐξῇ, λαμβάνειν. εἰ δέ 19

τις ἡμῖν ἔχει καὶ τὰ θεωρικὰ ἐᾶν καὶ πόρους ἑτέρους
λέγειν στρατιωτικούς, οὐχ οὗτος κρείττων; εἴποι
τις ἄν. φήμ' ἔγωγε, εἴπερ ἔστιν, ὦ ἄνδρες Ἀθηναῖοι·
ἀλλὰ θαυμάζω εἴ τῳ ποτε ἀνθρώπων ἢ γέγονεν ἢ
5 γενήσεται, ἂν τὰ παρόντα ἀναλώσῃ πρὸς ἃ μὴ δεῖ,
τῶν ἀπόντων εὐπορῆσαι πρὸς ἃ δεῖ. ἀλλ' οἶμαι,
μέγα τοῖς τοιούτοις ὑπάρχει λόγοις ἡ παρ' ἑκάστου
βούλησις, διόπερ ῥᾷστον ἁπάντων ἐστὶν αὑτὸν
ἐξαπατῆσαι· ὃ γὰρ βούλεται, τοῦθ' ἕκαστος καὶ
10 οἴεται, τὰ δὲ πράγματα πολλάκις οὐχ οὕτω πέφυκεν.
20 ὁρᾶτε οὖν, ὦ ἄνδρες Ἀθηναῖοι, ταῦθ' οὕτως, ὅπως
καὶ τὰ πράγματα ἐνδέχεται, καὶ δυνήσεσθε ἐξιέναι
καὶ μισθὸν ἕξετε. οὔ τοι σωφρόνων οὐδὲ γενναίων
ἐστὶν ἀνθρώπων, ἐλλείποντάς τι δι' ἔνδειαν χρημά-
15 των τῶν τοῦ πολέμου εὐχερῶς τὰ τοιαῦτα ὀνείδη
φέρειν, οὐδ' ἐπὶ μὲν Κορινθίους καὶ Μεγαρέας ἁρπά-
σαντας τὰ ὅπλα πορεύεσθαι, Φίλιππον δ' ἐᾶν πόλεις Ἑλληνίδας ἀνδραποδίζεσθαι δι' ἀπορίαν ἐφο-
δίων τοῖς στρατευομένοις.

21 Καὶ ταῦτ' οὐχ ἵν' ἀπέχθωμαί τισιν ὑμῶν τὴν
21 ἄλλως προῄρημαι λέγειν· οὐ γὰρ οὕτως ἄφρων οὐδ'
ἀτυχής εἰμι ἐγὼ ὥστε ἀπεχθάνεσθαι βούλεσθαι
μηδὲν ὠφελεῖν νομίζων· ἀλλὰ δικαίου πολίτου
κρίνω τὴν τῶν πραγμάτων σωτηρίαν ἀντὶ τῆς ἐν
25 τῷ λέγειν χάριτος αἱρεῖσθαι. καὶ γὰρ τοὺς ἐπὶ
τῶν προγόνων ἡμῶν λέγοντας ἀκούω, ὥσπερ ἴσως
καὶ ὑμεῖς, οὓς ἐπαινοῦσι μὲν οἱ παριόντες ἅπαντες

μιμοῦνται δ' οὐ πάνυ, τούτῳ τῷ ἔθει καὶ τῷ τρόπῳ
τῆς πολιτείας χρῆσθαι, τὸν Ἀριστείδην ἐκεῖνον,
τὸν Νικίαν, τὸν ὁμώνυμον ἐμαυτῷ, τὸν Περι-
κλέα. ἐξ οὗ δ' οἱ διερωτῶντες ὑμᾶς οὗτοι πεφή- 22
νασι ῥήτορες "τί βούλεσθε; τί γράψω; τί ὑμῖν 5
χαρίσωμαι;" προπέποται τῆς παραυτίκα χάριτος
τὰ τῆς πόλεως πράγματα καὶ τοιαυτὶ συμβαίνει,
καὶ τὰ μὲν τούτων πάντα καλῶς ἔχει, τὰ δ'
ὑμέτερα αἰσχρῶς. καίτοι σκέψασθε, ὦ ἄνδρες 23
Ἀθηναῖοι, ἅ τις ἂν κεφάλαια εἰπεῖν ἔχοι τῶν τ' ἐπὶ 10
τῶν προγόνων ἔργων καὶ τῶν ἐφ' ὑμῶν. ἔσται δὲ
βραχὺς καὶ γνώριμος ὑμῖν ὁ λόγος· οὐ γὰρ ἀλλο-
τρίοις ὑμῖν χρωμένοις παραδείγμασιν ἀλλ' οἰκείοις,
ὦ ἄνδρες Ἀθηναῖοι, εὐδαίμοσιν ἔξεστι γενέσθαι.
ἐκεῖνοι τοίνυν, οἷς οὐκ ἐχαρίζονθ' οἱ λέγοντες οὐδ' 24
ἐφίλουν αὐτοὺς ὥσπερ ὑμᾶς οὗτοι νῦν, πέντε μὲν 16
καὶ τετταράκοντα ἔτη τῶν Ἑλλήνων ἦρξαν ἑκόντων, πλείω δ' ἢ μύρια τάλαντα εἰς τὴν ἀκρόπολιν
ἀνήγαγον, ὑπήκουε δὲ ὁ ταύτην τὴν χώραν ἔχων
αὐτοῖς βασιλεὺς ὥσπερ ἐστὶ προσῆκον βάρβαρον 20
Ἕλλησι, πολλὰ δὲ καὶ καλὰ καὶ πεζῇ καὶ ναυμα-
χοῦντες ἔστησαν τρόπαια αὐτοὶ στρατευόμενοι, μό-
νοι δὲ ἀνθρώπων κρείττω τὴν ἐπὶ τοῖς ἔργοις δόξαν
τῶν φθονούντων κατέλιπον. ἐπὶ μὲν δὴ τῶν Ἑλ- 25
ληνικῶν ἦσαν τοιοῦτοι· ἐν δὲ τοῖς κατὰ τὴν πόλιν 25
αὐτὴν θεάσασθε ὁποῖοι, ἔν τε τοῖς κοινοῖς καὶ ἐν
τοῖς ἰδίοις. δημοσίᾳ μὲν τοίνυν οἰκοδομήματα καὶ

κάλλη τοιαῦτα καὶ τοσαῦτα κατεσκεύασαν ἡμῖν
ἱερῶν καὶ τῶν ἐν τούτοις ἀναθημάτων ὥστε μηδενὶ
26 τῶν ἐπιγιγνομένων ὑπερβολὴν λελεῖφθαι. ἰδίᾳ δ᾽
οὕτω σώφρονες ἦσαν καὶ σφόδρα ἐν τῷ τῆς πολι-
5 τείας ἤθει μένοντες ὥστε τὴν Ἀριστείδου καὶ τὴν
Μιλτιάδου καὶ τῶν τότε λαμπρῶν οἰκίαν εἴ τις ἄρα
οἶδεν ὑμῶν ὁποία ποτ᾽ ἐστίν, ὁρᾷ τῆς τοῦ γείτονος
οὐδὲν σεμνοτέραν οὖσαν· οὐ γὰρ εἰς περιουσίαν
ἐπράττετο αὐτοῖς τὰ τῆς πόλεως, ἀλλὰ τὸ κοινὸν
10 αὔξειν ἕκαστος ᾤετο δεῖν. ἐκ δὲ τοῦ τὰ μὲν Ἑλλη-
νικὰ πιστῶς, τὰ δὲ πρὸς τοὺς θεοὺς εὐσεβῶς, τὰ δ᾽
ἐν αὑτοῖς ἴσως διοικεῖν μεγάλην εἰκότως ἐκτήσαντο
27 εὐδαιμονίαν. τότε μὲν δὴ τοῦτον τὸν τρόπον εἶχε
τὰ πράγματα ἐκείνοις, χρωμένοις οἷς εἶπον προστά-
15 ταις· νυνὶ δὲ πῶς ὑμῖν ὑπὸ τῶν χρηστῶν τῶν νῦν
τὰ πράγματα ἔχει; ἆρά γε ὁμοίως καὶ παρα-
πλησίως; τὰ μὲν ἄλλα σιωπῶ, πόλλ᾽ ἂν ἔχων
εἰπεῖν· ἀλλ᾽ ὅσης ἅπαντες ὁρᾶτε ἐρημίας ἐπειλημ-
μένοι, καὶ Λακεδαιμονίων μὲν ἀπολωλότων, Θη-
20 βαίων δ᾽ ἀσχόλων ὄντων, τῶν δ᾽ ἄλλων οὐδενὸς
ὄντος ἀξιόχρεω περὶ τῶν πρωτείων ἡμῖν ἀντιτάξα-
σθαι, ἐξὸν δ᾽ ἡμῖν καὶ τὰ ἡμέτερ᾽ αὐτῶν ἀσφαλῶς
28 ἔχειν καὶ τὰ τῶν ἄλλων δίκαια βραβεύειν, ἀπεστερήμεθα μὲν χώρας οἰκείας, πλείω δ᾽ ἢ χίλια καὶ
25 πεντακόσια τάλαντα ἀνηλώκαμεν εἰς οὐδὲν δέον,
οὓς δ᾽ ἐν τῷ πολέμῳ συμμάχους ἐκτησάμεθα, εἰρήνης οὔσης ἀπολωλέκασιν οὗτοι, ἐχθρὸν δ᾽ ἐφ᾽ ἡμᾶς

32 καὶ τιθασεύουσι χειροήθεις αὑτοῖς ποιοῦντες. ✓ ἔστι
δ᾽ οὐδέποτ᾽, οἶμαι, μέγα καὶ νεανικὸν φρόνημα
λαβεῖν μικρὰ καὶ φαῦλα πράττοντας· ὁποῖ᾽ ἄττα
γὰρ ἂν τὰ ἐπιτηδεύματα τῶν ἀνθρώπων ᾖ, τοιοῦτον
5 ἀνάγκη καὶ τὸ φρόνημα ἔχειν. ταῦτα μὰ τὴν Δή-
μητρα οὐκ ἂν θαυμάσαιμι, εἰ μείζων εἰπόντι ἐμοὶ
γένοιτο παρ᾽ ὑμῶν βλάβη τῶν πεποιηκότων αὐτὰ
γενέσθαι· οὐδὲ γὰρ παρρησία περὶ πάντων ἀεὶ παρ᾽
ὑμῖν ἐστιν, ἀλλ᾽ ἔγωγε ὅτι καὶ νῦν γέγονε θαυμάζω.
33 Ἐὰν οὖν ἀλλὰ νῦν γ᾽ ἔτι ἀπαλλαγέντες τούτων
11 τῶν ἐθῶν ἐθελήσητε στρατεύεσθαί τε καὶ πράττειν
ἀξίως ὑμῶν αὐτῶν, καὶ ταῖς περιουσίαις ταῖς οἴκοι
ταύταις ἀφορμαῖς ἐπὶ τὰ ἔξω τῶν ἀγαθῶν χρήσῃ-
σθε, ἴσως ἄν, ἴσως, ὦ ἄνδρες Ἀθηναῖοι, τέλειόν
15 τι καὶ μέγα κτήσαισθε ἀγαθόν, καὶ τῶν τοιούτων
λημμάτων ἀπαλλαγείητε, ἃ τοῖς ἀσθενοῦσι παρὰ
τῶν ἰατρῶν σιτίοις διδομένοις ἔοικε. καὶ γὰρ οὔτ᾽
ἰσχὺν ἐκεῖνα ἐντίθησιν οὔτ᾽ ἀποθνήσκειν ἐᾷ· καὶ
ταῦτα, ἃ νέμεσθε νῦν ὑμεῖς, οὔτε τοσαῦτά ἐστιν
20 ὥστε ὠφέλειαν ἔχειν τινὰ διαρκῆ, οὔτ᾽ ἀπογνόν-
τας ἄλλο τι πράττειν ἐᾷ, ἀλλ᾽ ἔστι ταῦτα τὴν
34 ἑκάστου ῥᾳθυμίαν ὑμῶν ἐπαυξάνοντα. οὐκοῦν σὺ
μισθοφορὰν λέγεις; φήσει τις. καὶ παραχρῆμά
γε τὴν αὐτὴν σύνταξιν ἁπάντων, ὦ ἄνδρες Ἀθη-
25 ναῖοι, ἵνα τῶν κοινῶν ἕκαστος τὸ μέρος λαμβάνων, ὅτου δέοιτο ἡ πόλις, τοῦθ᾽ ὑπάρχοι. ✓ ἔξεστιν ἄγειν ἡσυχίαν· οἴκοι μένων βελτίων, τοῦ δι᾽

ἔνδειαν ἀνάγκη τι ποιεῖν αἰσχρὸν ἀπηλλαγμένος.
συμβαίνει τι τοιοῦτον οἷον καὶ τὰ νῦν· στρατιώτης
αὐτὸς ὑπάρχων ἀπὸ τῶν αὐτῶν τούτων λημμάτων,
ὥσπερ ἐστὶ δίκαιον ὑπὲρ τῆς πατρίδος. ἔστι τις
ἔξω τῆς ἡλικίας ἡμῶν· ὅσα οὗτος ἀτάκτως νῦν λαμ- 5
βάνων οὐκ ὠφελεῖ, ταῦτ' ἐν ἴσῃ τάξει λαμβάνων,
πάντ' ἐφορῶν καὶ διοικῶν ἃ χρὴ πράττεσθαι. ὅλως 35
δὲ οὔτ' ἀφελὼν οὔτε προσθείς, πλὴν μικρὸν τὴν
ἀταξίαν ἀνελὼν εἰς τάξιν ἤγαγον τὴν πόλιν, τὴν
αὐτὴν τοῦ λαβεῖν, τοῦ στρατεύεσθαι, τοῦ δικάζειν, 10
τοῦ ποιεῖν τοῦθ' ὅ τι καθ' ἡλικίαν ἕκαστος ἔχοι καὶ
ὅτου καιρὸς εἴη, τάξιν ποιήσας. οὐκ ἔστιν ὅπου
μηδὲν ποιοῦσιν ἐγὼ τὰ τῶν ποιησόντων εἶπον ὡς
δεῖ νέμειν, οὐδ' αὐτοὺς μὲν ἀργεῖν καὶ σχολάζειν
καὶ ἀπορεῖν, ὅτι δὲ οἱ τοῦ δεῖνος νικῶσι ξένοι, ταῦτα 15
πυνθάνεσθαι· ταῦτα γὰρ νυνὶ γίγνεται. καὶ οὐχὶ 36
μέμφομαι τὸν ποιοῦντά τι τῶν δεόντων ὑπὲρ ὑμῶν,
ἀλλὰ καὶ ὑμᾶς ὑπὲρ ὑμῶν αὐτῶν ἀξιῶ πράττειν
ταῦτα ἐφ' οἷς ἑτέρους τιμᾶτε, καὶ μὴ παραχωρεῖν,
ὦ ἄνδρες Ἀθηναῖοι, τῆς τάξεως, ἣν ὑμῖν οἱ πρόγο- 20
νοι τῆς ἀρετῆς μετὰ πολλῶν καὶ καλῶν κινδύνων
κτησάμενοι κατέλιπον.

Σχεδὸν εἴρηκα ἃ νομίζω συμφέρειν· ὑμεῖς δ'
ἕλοισθε ὅ τι καὶ τῇ πόλει καὶ ἅπασι συνοίσειν ὑμῖν
μέλλει. 25

NOTES.

NOTES.

1. Page 1, line 1. πολλῶν, emphatic in position, is further emphasized by separation from χρημάτων and association with ἄν. C. 621. It is not necessary to suppose, with the Scholiast, that in χρημάτων there is a distinct allusion to the theoric fund; for the same phraseology is used not unfrequently by Greek authors (cf. Andoc. 2, 21; Thuc. 1, 33; Isoc. 13, 11), and a similar expression is common in English; but the fact that he would fain persuade them in this oration to relinquish that fund for the military service, at least, gives additional fitness and force to this introduction. Thucydides and Isocrates use πρό instead of ἀντί in the parallel passages just cited. — ὦ ἄνδρες Ἀθηναῖοι, the usual address of Demosthenes, who never omits the respectful ἄνδρες, *gentlemen*, although he sometimes, in reproof, leaves out the ὦ. — 2. νομίζω, *I am persuaded*, I consider it as an established fact, or characteristic. — 3. περὶ ὧν = περὶ τούτων περὶ ὧν, *touching these things about which you are deliberating.* — ὅτε, lit. *when, while* = quandoquidem; less causal than ἐπεί, less contingent than εἰ, and more complimentary than either. — 4. ἐθέλειν, *to be willing*: βουλομένων, *wishing, intending*, cf. Ol. 2, 23: ἂν οἵ τε θεοὶ θέλωσι καὶ ὑμεῖς βούλησθε, *if the gods will and you wish*, that is, *choose*, or *resolve.* βούλεσθαι implies choice after deliberation (cf. βουλή), hence said only of rational beings; ἐθέλειν, a natural instinct or inclination, hence sometimes used of animals and the inanimate creation. So Pillon, Greek Synonymes, after the old grammarians, though contrary to Buttmann. See in Yonge's Eng. Gr. Lex., Drisler's ed., 129, where this passage is quoted in proof. Compare also de Contr. 3: μὴ μόνον ταῦτ᾽ ἀκούειν ἐθέλοντα, ἀλλὰ καὶ πράττειν βουλόμενον, *not only willing to hear, but also choosing*, or *resolving to act.* — 6. ἐσκεμμένος, *with*

previous preparation, ant. to ἐκ τοῦ παραχρῆμα, *extempore*. The former was Demosthenes's usual way of speaking (Plut. Dem. 8), and he doubtless means or includes himself in ἥκει τις ; hence the ind. denoting a matter of fact. Demades, who spoke against Demosthenes in the matter of Olynthus, was a ready extemporizer, and a popular demagogue. Hence our orator might well ask a hearing for his *well-considered advice*, not less than the unpremeditated harangues of others. See Rehdantz in loc. — 7. ἀκούσαντες, not as Schäfer, the protasis of ἂν λάβοιτε, but as Heslop, the complement or preliminary of that verb. The condition is implied in γάρ and expressed in ἐθέλειν ἀκούειν : *for* (if you are willing to hear) *not only in case some one has come prepared with some useful advice would you listen and adopt it.* — τύχης, pred. gen., εἶναι being understood. The genitive denotes property or characteristic : *I conceive it to belong to your fortune.* C. 440, b ; Cu. 417 ; G. 169, 1 ; H. 568.* The fortunateness (felicitas) of Athens implies the favor of the gods, and is a compliment frequently paid to the Athenians by Demosthenes. Ol. 2, 22 ; Phil. 2, 12, et al. — 9. ἐξ ἁπάντων, *out of all*, sc. both the prepared and the unpremeditated. This exordium is justly admired for its brevity, simplicity, and appropriateness. It is at once complimentary, manly, and patriotic, and happily unites self-respect with respect for the hearers.

2. 11. οὖν, not inferential, simply marks the transition from the exordium to the subject-matter of the oration. — 12. μόνον οὐχί, only not = all but, *almost*. — φωνὴν ἀφιείς, *with audible voice.* — ὅτι...φροντίζετε, *that you must take those affairs in hand in person, if you care for their safety.* Notice the emphatic separation of ἐκείνων, *those* affairs of Olynthus, from πραγμάτων, and of αὐτοῖς, *in person*, not by mercenaries, from ὑμῖν. One MS. and a few editors read αὐτῶν = *your own* safety. But the best have αὐτῶν referring to πραγμάτων. Cf. Ol. 3, 24 : τὴν τῶν πραγμάτων σωτηρίαν. — 14. ἡμεῖς ...αὐτα, *but we seem to be conducting ourselves I know not how in regard to them.* ἡμεῖς instead of ὑμεῖς for politeness ; for the same reason οὐκ οἶδ, κ. τ. λ., instead of πάνυ ὀλιγώρως ἔχειν, which Lucian puts in its place in his burlesque of this exordium. Jov. Trag. 15. — 15. δή, est colligentis : est *igitur*. Franke. The γέ limits the clause, and not merely the pronoun. τά γ᾽ ἐμοὶ δοκοῦντα is strictly,

---

* The references are to the grammars of Crosby, Rev. Ed., 1871 ; Curtius, Harper's ed., 1872 ; Goodwin, 1870 ; Hadley, 1860.

= around ; ὑπέρ = over. Hence ὑπέρ usually expresses a nearer relation and interest. ὑπέρ is to be supplied with ἀναστάσεως, κ. τ. λ., in a somewhat different sense = to *ward off*, or *prevent*. Dem. and other orators often use ὑπέρ where the historians used περί. — 18. ἅ... τούς, double acc. C. 480, b ; Cu. 402 ; G. 165 ; H. 555. — 19. Ἀμφιπολιτῶν, part. gen. after τούς. For the situation of Amphipolis and its importance to the Athenians, see Smith's Dic. of Geog. For the history of its capture by Philip, see Thirlwall, 5, 196 ; Grote, 11, 330. For Pydna, Thirl. 5, 197 ; Grote, 11, 333. According to the Scholiast, Philip banished the betrayers of Amphipolis, and put to death those of Pydna. While he was engaged in the siege of Amphipolis, Philip quieted the Athenians with the assurance that he intended to restore it to them in exchange for Pydna ; but when he had taken it, he seized Pydna also, and kept both under the pretext that inasmuch as they had not given him Pydna, he was not bound to restore Amphipolis to them, — an act of duplicity quite characteristic of Philip. — 21. καὶ ὅλως, κ. τ. λ., *and generally, I think, a despotism is an object of mistrust to free states.* The article with each of these nouns generalizes it, that is, defines despotisms and free states as a *genus* or class. C. 522 ; Cu. 375 ; H. 529. The neuter predicate corresponds with this and emphasizes it. C. 507 ; Cu. 366 ; H. 522. Demosthenes often repeats this maxim in sentiment and spirit ; compare especially Phil. 2, 21–23, where he says that too close alliances with despots are dangerous to free states, and warns the Messenians to cherish mistrust (ἀπιστία) as their only safeguard. — 22. ἄλλως τε κἂν = *especially if*. See Lexicon and Grammar for explanation of this meaning. — 6. 23. ἐγνωκότας = *convinced of.* — ἃ προσήκει, sc. gloriam majorum, Graeciae principatum, oppressis opitulandi consuetudinem, injurias Philippi, periculi magnitudinem. Wolf. — 24. ἐθελῆσαι, taken absolutely = *be ready for action.* Westermann makes the following infin. depend on it. But cf. Thuc. 5, 9. — 25. παροξυνθῆναι, *be provoked to indignation.* — 27. αὐτούς, see note on αὐτοῖς, 2, above. — P. 3, l. 1. λόγος = *argument,* or *plea ;* σκῆψις = *pretext,* or *excuse.* — ἔθ' with a negative = *no longer.* — ὑπολείπεται = left *remaining,* lit. left *under,* as a support. — 7. 2. ἐθρυλεῖτε ὥς, al. ἐθρύλουν τέως, but ἐθρυλεῖτε is the reading of the most and best MSS., and τέως is not only a mere conjecture, but very improbable as *here* used. Render : *what you were all talking,* viz. *that,* etc. — 3. ἐκπολεμῶσαι, *to stir up to war.*

good-will. — 9. ἀπολωλεκέναι, sc. ἡμᾶς. — κατὰ τὸν πόλεμον, *in the course of the war*, sc. about Amphipolis. — 10. ἀμελείας, gen. of property, after θείη = *set to the account of*, or reckon as belonging to. — μήτε πάλαι, *not long ago*, but recently, so that there is still hope of recovery. — μήτε...τε, like Lat. neque...et. — 13. παρ᾽ ἐκείνων, *from them*, lit. *from near them*, from their presence ; render, *as a blessing proceeding from their good-will.* — 11. 14. παρόμοιόν ἐστιν ὅπερ, *it is much like what takes place.* παρα- adds emphasis, lit. when laid alongside, it is a *parallel* case. — 17. λάθῃ, render by an adverb *unconsciously*, i. e. gradually and before he is aware. — συνανάλωσε καί, *he loses with it also*, gnomic aorist parallel with the present ἔχει in the antithesis, but emphasizing the proverbial .character of the saying. C. 606 ; Cu. 494 ; G. 205 ; H. 707. — 18. καὶ περὶ ...οὕτως, *so also in regard to public affairs.* — οὐδ᾽ εἰ...μνημονεύουσι = καὶ εἰ...οὐ μνημονεύουσι. Rehdantz. Well rendered by Heslop, *forget too any good thing that has come to them from the gods.* — 20. πρός, in reference to = *by ; for every previous event is judged by the final result.* — 22. καὶ σφόδρα is emphatic, and emphasizes not only δεῖ, but φροντίσαι. Well rendered by Whiston : *wherefore must we, and that vigorously, turn our thoughts to the future* ; lit. what remains, sc. the succor of Olynthus. — 23. ταῦτ᾽ ἐπανορθωσάμενοι, *by amending this*, sc. the future. This lofty political ethics, enforced by the logic of common-sense, and illustrated from the common affairs of life, is characteristic of our orator. — 12. 25. καὶ τούτους, *these men also*, sc. the Olynthians, as well as the Amphipolitans and others mentioned in §§ 8, 9. — 26. εἶτ᾽ = *and then*, or *and in consequence.* — 27. τί...ἔσται, *what will there be that any longer prevents.* — P. 5, l. 1. ὅποι βούλεται, e. g. to Athens. Cf. §§ 15 and 25 below. — 3. δι᾽ ὅν, *through which.* — 4. τὸ πρῶτον, κ. τ. λ. Observe the order of the captures, cf. note 9, and the rapidity of them *pictured* by the rapid succession of clauses. — 6. ἐπέβη, B. C. 353 – 2, Grote, 11, 408 ; Thirlwall, 2, 97, Am. ed. — 7. εὐτρεπίσας, *having made ready.* — πάνθ᾽ ὅν...τρόπον, *in short, the whole country at his pleasure.* Heslop. — 8. ᾤχετ᾽ εἰς, *he was off into.* — ἐκβαλών, *after expelling some*, e. g. Cersobleptes. — 9. καταστήσας, e. g. Amadocus and Berisades, B. C. 352. — ἠσθένησε, *he fell sick.* — 12 – 14. τὰς...στρατείας, *his expeditions against the Illyrians and Paeonians* (B. C. 359 – 8, near the beginning of his reign) *and against Arymbas* (king of the Molossians in Epirus, B. C. 351, succeeded by Alexander, his nephew, and brother of Olympias, Philip's wife), *and whithersoever one might speak of* = *and ever so many others one might mention.*

14. 14. **Τί οὖν τις ἂν εἴποι**, *Why, then, some one may say, do you speak these things to us now ?* In order to prevent τίς from standing first in its clause, the best editors omit the comma after οὖν, supposing the whole to be spoken as one clause in the Greek, although in English we must make two. — 16. **καὶ τὸ προΐεσθαι**, *both how hurtful it is to be throwing away one after another continually some of our interests, and the restless activity which Philip practises and lives with,* i. e. in which he finds his business and has his being. — 18. **ὑφ' ἧς**, *under the influence of which.* — 21. **ἐγνωκὼς ἔσται**, *shall have resolved.* — **ἀντιληπτέον ἐρρωμένως**, *must take hold vigorously.* — 22. **εἰς... τελευτῆσαι**, *to what end, pray, is it to be expected that these things will come ?* — **ποτ'** = tandem. — 15. 24. **ἐκεῖθεν** for ἐκεῖ. C. 704. — 27. **τὸν αὐτὸν τρόπον** is an emphatic anticipation of οὕτω, and **ὥσπερ** is correlative to both. — **ῥᾳδίως**, *thoughtlessly.* — P. 6, l. 1. **ἐπὶ τοῖς μεγάλοις τόκοις**, *at the high rates of interest* exacted of such borrowers, — sometimes as high as 3 per cent a month, 36 per cent a year. Boeckh. Pub. Econ. I. chap. 22. — 2. **καὶ**, emphatic = *even.* — **ἀπέστησαν**, gnomic aorist. Render, *I fear lest just as those who borrow money thoughtlessly at such high rates of interest, after having luxuriated in plenty for a short time, afterwards lose even their original estates, so also we shall be found to have enjoyed our ease at a great cost.* — 4. **πολλά...ὧν**, *many of the disagreeable things.* Heslop. ὧν, partitive gen. — **ποιεῖν** depends on εἰς ἀνάγκην ἔλθωμεν = ἀναγκασθῶμεν, with the additional idea of *becoming* necessitated, emphatic for ἀναγκασθῶμεν. Here again political warning is enforced by familiar illustrations from common life.

16. 9. **παντός**, gen. of property or characteristic, *is anybody's work.* Whiston. — **ὑπέρ**, see note § 5. — 13. **ἐν ὀργῇ ποιεῖσθε**, *visit with your displeasure.* — 14. **μήν** = *yet* in antithesis to μέν. — 15. **ὑποστείλασθαι**, *to suppress* my sentiments, lit. *to furl* or *take down sails.* — 17. 17. **τοῖς πράγμασιν**, *the interests at stake,* dat. after βοηθητητέον. So Heslop. Whiston says: *in the case.* But the former is preferable. — **τὰς πόλεις**, sc. in Chalcidice, Olynthus and its allies. — 22. **μάταιος...γένηται**, *be rendered fruitless.* — 18. **εἴτε γὰρ...εἴτε**, *for if, on the one hand, in case you ravage his country, he shall suffer this and reduce Olynthus, he will then easily come to the relief of his own territory ; or if, on the other hand, in case you only send aid to Olynthus, he, seeing things at home in no danger, shall press the siege,*

*and keep close watch of things there, he will overcome the besieged by the
lapse of time.* — 24. **παραστήσεται,** *bring over,* i. e. *reduce.* See Lex.
L. & S. sub v. C. II. — 27. **τοῖς πράγμασι,** which Heslop translates
his opportunity and Whiston *the situation,* I have ventured to render
things there. The commentators remark the emphasis of meaning in
the two kindred words προσκαθεδεῖται and προσεδρεύσει. Demosthenes is fond of such *pairs* of words. See examples in my note on
Dem. de Cor. § 4, l. 14. — P. 7, l. 1. **τῷ χρόνω.** Observe the article,
not merely *in time,* but *by means of the lapse of time. Mora obsidio-
nis* is Wolf's version. — **δή** = *then,* in conclusion.

19. 3. **περὶ χρημάτων πόρου,** *in regard to ways and means.* —
ἔστιν...ἔστιν, *you have money, gentlemen of Athens, you have money
to an amount which no people in the world has for military purposes.*
Such emphatic repetitions are frequent in Demosthenes. — **οὕτως ὡς
βούλεσθε,** *in such ways as you please,* i. e. for your pleasures, sc.
theatricals and festivals. — 8. **ἀποδώσετε,** *restore* to its original military use, from which it had been perverted. — 8, 9. **οὐδενὸς...πόρου,**
*there is no need of additional means...or rather there is an entire want
of all such means.* Observe the article with the second πόρου. —
10. **σὺ γράφεις,** *do you move.* Such a motion would have exposed
him to impeachment according to the law of Eubulus. Thirl. 5, 300 ;
Grote, 11, 466. — **20.** 12. **εἶναι σρατιωτικά,** *and this* (theoric fund)
ought to be a war fund. The force of δεῖν extends through the member, what Demosthenes thinks *ought* to be done being set in emphatic contrast with what the people actually *do.* Dindorf omits the
whole clause ; Bekker brackets ταῦτ', and Heslop omits it. But the
words are in all the MSS., and are retained by Whiston. — 13. **τὴν
αὐτήν,** that is, the same persons who receive the money should do
military duty. Then they could have the money, and at the same
time the state have soldiers. — **ὑμεῖς δέ,** *but you receive it thus somehow without service* — for your festivals. — **οὕτω...πραγμάτων** here =
οὕτως...βούλεσθε above. — 16. **εἰσφέρειν,** make extraordinary contributions. The εἰσφορά was a special war tax. See Smith's Dic. Antiq.
sub v. — 17. **δεῖ δὲ χρημάτων,** *but there is a necessity for money,* that
is, money must be had. — 19. **ἄλλους,** other than an extraordinary
contribution. ἄλλους ἄλλοι, *some one way of raising money, and some
another.* — **ἀντιλάβεσθε, κ. τ. λ.,** cf. note on ἀντιληπτέον, 14.

21. **οὔτε...ἔχει,** al. ἔχοι, but that is to be supplied. ἔχει goes with
εὐτρεπῶς as well as with ὡς κάλλιστ', *for neither are things at present*

in good trim as they appear to be, and as one might say that they are without careful examination, nor in the best state they might be for him. The οὐδ' in the last clause is not correlative with οὔτε at the beginning; it only adds a co-ordinate, but emphatic negative clause, C. 701, c; Cu. 625, obs.; H. 859, a; and the οὔτε finds its correlative in the οὔτ' ἂν ἐξήνεγκε : *nor would he ever have engaged in this war,* lit. carried it out. — 27. ὡς ἐπιών, elliptical for ὡς ἐπιὼν ἀναιρεῖται = primo statim impetu, *on the first advance.* — P. 8, l. 1. ἀναιρήσεσθαι, *to carry all before him.* — κᾆτα διέψευσται, *and therein he finds himself mistaken.* — 3. γεγονός denotes the cause of Philip's trouble, *by* or *because of its having turned out contrary to expectation.* — 22. 4. ταῦτα, sc. the character and conduct of the Thessalians. The neuter pronoun is used to comprehend *all that pertains* to the Thessalians. See Franke in loc. The Thessalians were proverbially fickle and faithless. Cf. contra Aristoc., where Demosthenes says, that while the Athenians never betrayed any of their friends, there was none of *theirs* that the *Thessalians* did *not* betray. See also the disorder and license imputed to the Thessalians by Socrates. Crit. Cap. XV. — 5. δήπου, *you know.* καί connects φύσει and ἀεί, *by nature and always.* κομιδῇ δέ instead of ἄπιστα δέ correlative to ἄπιστα μέν, hence the dative τούτῳ. — 8. κεκωλύκασι, by their remonstrances. Cf. Ol. 2, 11, where the fact seems to be stated with more exactness. Cf. Thirl. 5, 306 ; Grote, 11, 425. — ἤκουον as imperfect denotes a continued or repeated hearing. — 9. οὐδὲ...ἔτι, *no longer,* as they had permitted him to do since he ejected these tyrants. — 10. καρποῦσθαι, lit. to harvest, that is, *to collect the revenues of.* — 11. δέοι, opt. in or. obliqua, this being a part of what they said and he heard. — ἀπό, *from,* i. e. by means of. — λαμβάνειν, pres. inf., *to be receiving.* — 13. κομιδῇ = πάνυ, *altogether.* — τὰ τῆς τροφῆς, *the means of support for his mercenaries.* — 23. 15. ἁπλῶς...ἅπαντας, *and all these tribes generally.* — 17. ἄνθρωπος, *the man,* sc. Philip. — 18. ὑβριστής, *tyrannical.* — 19. ἴσως, *perhaps.* Attic urbanity. — τὸ γὰρ, κ. τ. λ. The idea is well expressed by Heslop : *for an undeserved career of success becomes a source of folly to persons of weak mind.* But there is a pith and point in the Greek, particularly in the antithesis between εὖ πράττειν, *doing well,* and κακῶς φρονεῖν, *thinking* or *planning ill,* that is inevitably lost in a translation. This gnome has been often quoted and much admired both for its form and its sentiment ; and the application of it in the next clause, διόπερ, κ. τ. λ.,

threatening ind. fut. — 27. 18. ἡλίκα...ἥ, *but how great the differences are between.* — 19. προσδεῖν. Observe the force of προσ-, the thing is so clear in itself as to require no argument *in addition.* — 21. ἔξω, *out of* the city. — 22. χρωμένους λαμβάνειν. Observe the present, *to be continually taking and using,* sc. during the month. τῶν is part. gen., *of the produce.* — 23. λέγω, *I mean.* — 25. τὸν πρὸ τοῦ πόλεμον, *the late war,* sc. the Amphipolitan, which lasted ten years and cost 1,500 talents. Ol. 3, 28. — ζημιώσεσθαι rem durantem indicat, ζημιωθῆναι (l. 24) rem unius momenti. Franke. The latter is the general statement, the former is more definite. For the fut. mid. instead of fut. pass. see Lex. C. 576 a ; Jelf 365, 6 a. — προσέσθ', *there is besides* (the loss of property) *the insult.* — P. 10, l. 1. οὐδεμιᾶς, κ. τ. λ., *greater* (i. e. worse) *than any loss, at least in the view of sensible men.* Litotes. C. 686 i ; H. 665.

28. 3. συνιδόντας, *taking, then, all these things into consideration together, we ought all of us.* — 5. καλῶς ποιοῦντες may be rendered *fortunately, happily,* with Heslop and Kennedy, or *rightly, deservedly,* with Franke and L. & S., which see. Rüdiger : deorum benignitate, by the blessing of the gods. — 6. τοὺς ἐν ἡλικίᾳ, *those of age,* sc. to serve in the army, viz. from eighteen to sixty. — 9. ἀκεραίου, proleptic = *kept inviolate.* — τοὺς δὲ λέγοντας, *and the orators* (politicians) *that it may be easy for them to render an account of their administration since you will judge of their measures according to the state of your affairs, whatever it may be.* — 10. εὔθυναι, primarily of money ; here of measures. — 13. παντός is masc., acc. to Franke, Westermann, and the scholiast = *for the sake of every* citizen, i. e. the rich, the poor, etc., as above enumerated. But the more and better authorities make it neuter = *on every account ; and may they* (sc. τὰ πράγματα) *be prosperous on every account.* This oration, like that on the Crown and many others, closes with a prayer or wish for the well-being of his country. To begin with a prayer, as in the Or. de Cor., is less frequent. — εἵνεκα, al. ἔνεκα, Dem. seems sometimes to use the Ionic form of this word, perhaps for the sake of the rhythm. This peroration, or rather conclusion, which consists only of one section, and that a single sentence, is as simple and concise as the introduction. It is free from rhetorical display, and savors even more of the statesman than of the orator.

ΟΛΥΝΘΙΑΚΟΣ Β.

THE second Olynthiac opens in language and manner very like the first ; and Dindorf suggests that Dionysius, who cites the Orations by their opening words, has thus, by a slip of the memory, been led to confound them, and cite the second as the first. (See Introduction.)

1. Page 11, line 1. πολλῶν, emphatic as at the beginning of Ol. 1, where see note. ἄν with ἰδεῖν marks the conclusion of a hypothetical sentence (C. 618 ; Cu. 575 ; G. 211 ; H. 783), of which, however, the condition is omitted : *could see*, sc. if he would. C. 636 ; Cu. 544 ; G. 226, 2 ; H. 752. The structure of the sentence and the sentiment are quite similar to Ol. I. 10, where see notes particularly on δοκεῖ and παρά. Dem. is never weary of insisting on this topic, — the favor and good-will of the gods towards Athens. Cf. I. 1, and note there. — 2. γιγνομένην, *being continually manifested.* — 3. ἐν, not merely for variety (after ἐπὶ πολλῶν), but more exact and emphatic = not *at* or *on*, but *in.* — 4. τὸ γὰρ, κ. τ. λ., *for the fact that there have arisen those who are ready to wage war with Philip possessing both* (καὶ) *a neighboring country and some power and* (*what is most important of all*) *having their convictions about the war such as to think reconciliations with him to be in the first place untrustworthy and in the next ruinous to their country,* — *this is like some providential and altogether divine benefaction.* So Whiston. παντάπασιν, however, limits ἔοικεν, *is altogether like.* τινα = *some considerable.* δύναμιν = military power, *force.* In the Or. cont. Lept. the army of Olynthus about this time is stated at more than 10,000 hoplites and 1000 horse. διαλλαγάς here seems to differ from καταλλαγάς, Ol. 1, 4 (as Professor Champlin suggests), only as implying a *mutual* reconciliation, while there the orator is speaking expressly of the reconciliation *which Philip would gladly make with the Olynthians.* — 2. 11. αὑτούς, *ourselves,* in distinction from the gods, who are ready to help if we will help ourselves. — ὅπως, *how.* — 12. τῶν ὑπαρχόντων, *than our opportunities.* — αἰσχρῶν is usually considered as neuter and part. gen.; it could be masc. and gen. of property or characteristic : *it is the*

frequently followed by ἐπί with dat. — 23. διεξελήλυθεν, run through
and so *exhausted all the arts of deception by which he formerly grew
to be great.* παρακρούεσθαι, lit. to cheat in weighing. πρότερον
limits both part. and verb. — 6. Observe the separation for emphasis
of καὶ αὐτός from ἐγώ and σφόδρα from φοβερόν. — P. 13, l. 1. πράττοντα, *by doing.* The ethics of Dem. are always high-toned. — θεωρῶν καὶ σκοπῶν, *observing and examining.* Observe the pair of words
of kindred meaning so frequent in Dem. — 2–10. τὴν μὲν ἡμετέραν...
τὴν δ' Ὀλυνθίων...Θετταλοὺς δέ, *that he gained over* (προσαγαγόμενον)
in the first place (μέν) *our simplicity...in the second place the friendship
of the Olynthians...and now the Thessalians.* The *means* by which
each was gained is expressed by three clauses, each beginning with
τῷ. — τὸ κατ' ἀρχάς, *at the outset.* — Ἀμφίπολιν, cf. note, I. 4; Thirl.
5, 192; Grote 11, 328. — 5. τὸ...ἀπόρρητον, *by getting up* (lit. con-
structing, τῷ...κατασκευάσαι) *that secret article once so famous.* "The
Pydnæans being averse to this scheme (of transfer), it was alleged
that secrecy was essential to success, and consequently it was determined that the arrangement should be discussed before the senate
exclusively, and not before the assembly of the people" (Whiston).
6. τούτῳ, *by this means,* resumes and emphasizes the *means* expressed
in the foregoing clause. — 7. 7. Ποτίδαιαν. Cf. Thirl. 5, 198; Grote,
11, 332. — 8. τοὺς μὲν...παραδοῦναι δέ, *and handing it over to them,
thus wronging you his former allies.* So we may express in idiomatic
English the force of μὲν...δέ. — 10. Μαγνησίαν...ὑποσχέσθαι. Cf.
Phil. II. 24: Μαγνησίαν ἐδίδου. The dismission of the Olynthian
ambassadors took place B. C. 358–7; the capture and transfer of
Potidæa, 356; and the engagements in regard to Magnesia and the
Phocian War (often called the Second Sacred War), 353. The fulfil-
ment of the promise in regard to Magnesia did not take place till
after the close of that war, which lasted ten years, 356–46. — ὅλως,
in fine. — 14. ἄνοιαν. Dem. attributes εὐήθεια to his own countrymen, but ἄνοια to foreigners. W. — ἀεί, *from time to time.* —
15. προσλαμβάνων, *taking advantage of.* See προσαγαγόμενον used
in essentially the same sense above, and observe the difference between the aor. part., which denotes a completed action, and the
imperf., which expresses a continued and repeated action. — οὕτως,
sc. by deceiving and taking advantage: emphatic resumption. —
8. 16. διὰ τούτων, *through the instrumentality of these persons*
(peoples). So Franke and Rehdantz. But editors generally: *by these*

arts. The language and the argument will admit of either. Dem. believed that Philip would be *pulled down* by the *very same persons* and *the very same means* by which he was *raised to greatness.* (Observe the exact antithesis between καθαιρεθῆναι and ἤρθη). But ἕκαστοι, which naturally refers to τούτων, and which *must* mean *persons,* is in favor of the former interpretation. — 20. καιροῦ...πράγματα, *to such a crisis, then, the affairs of Philip have come.* καιροῦ is gen. after τοῦτο. C. 416; Cu. 412; G. 168, N. 2; H. 559, c. — 21. ἤ = *or else.* — 22. ὡς...λέγω, *that these things which I say are not true.* — 25. δεδουλωμένοι here denotes political subjection, not literal subjugation. It is pronounced an exaggeration by Whiston and most of the commentators.

9. 22. Καὶ μήν, *And verily.* Whiston: And then indeed. — μὲν ...ἡγεῖται...οἴεται δέ, *while he believes...yet thinks.* ἡγεῖται implies reasons by which one is *led* to believe or admit, while οἴεται expresses a mere supposition. — P. 14, l. 2. τὰ χωρία καὶ λιμένας, the use of one art. for the two nouns links them more closely: *the fortresses and harbors.* — 3. ὑπ'...συστῇ. The passive sense leads to a passive construction: *when affairs* (powers) *are held together by good-will.* — 5. καὶ συμπονεῖν...ἄνθρωποι, *the men* (who are concerned) *are willing* (both, καί, unnecessary in English) *to toil together and to bear the calamities* (incident to the war) *and to persevere.* Schaefer and Voemel regard the force of σύν as extending to φέρειν = *bear together;* but this is not necessary. — 8. ἰσχύσῃ, *has become powerful,* cf. 1, 13, ἠσθένησε, fell sick. — 9. ἀνεχαίτισε, as well as πταῖσμα, refers primarily to a horse throwing his rider. It is gnomic aorist: *overthrows and scatters the whole.* —10. 10. οὐκ ἔστιν, *it is not possible,* IT IS NOT POSSIBLE. Cf. 1. 19. — ἀδικοῦντα, *by injustice,* the part. denoting means, and the pres. part. a continual course of injustice.—12. τὰ τοιαῦτα, such power as Philip's, and acquired by such means. — ἤνθησεν. Cf. Madv. Synt. 111 a: "The aor. is used of that which has often happened and consequently (in single instances) is wont to happen, in which use it is sometimes connected with the present." The figure contained in ἤνθησεν is kept up through the sentence. The whole passage may be rendered thus: *such powers hold out* (cf. ἀντέχῃ, 1. 25) *in a single instance and for a short time and flourish exceedingly mayhap in the hopes* (which they excite), *but in and by the lapse of time their weakness is discovered, and they fall beneath their own weight.* τῷ χρόνῳ

denotes means. Cf. 1, 18. περὶ αὐτά, lit. *about themselves*, like drooping flowers round the stem of the plant. — 16. τὰ κάτωθεν, strictly the parts from below upwards, and particularly *the lower parts.*

11. 22. ὅπως…οὕτως, that is, *the better and quicker the way any one proposes the more I shall be pleased.* — 23. πρὸς δέ, δέ should be rendered *and also*, to correspond with μέν. — ταῦτα is referred by Schaefer and Franke to the weakness and instability of Philip's power, as above described; but better, with Rehdantz, Westermann, Whiston, Heslop, and others, to refer it to the purpose of sending aid. Cf. 1, 2: ταῦτ᾽ ἐρεῖ, where the same twofold counsel is given. — 26. λογοὺς ποιεῖσθαι = *to remonstrate.* Cf. 1, 22, note on κεκωλύκασι. — 12. P. 15, line 3. ἅπας μὲν λόγος, *all words*, no matter whose, *but especially* (μάλιστα δέ) those that come from (παρά) Athens. τὰ πράγματα, the corresponding *actions*. — 6. δοκοῦμεν refers to the common opinion or *reputation* (δόξα) of the Athenians in this respect, viz. as excelling in speech. — 13. 8. μετάστασιν is properly the *changed state* resulting from μεταβολήν, which is the *act* or *process* of change. But Dem. uses the *pair* as usual for emphasis, which he further enforces by repeating and varying the adjective: *much, then, is the change and great the revolution you must show.* — 9. εἰσφέροντας agrees with ὑμᾶς implied in δεικτέον = δεικνύναι ὑμᾶς δεῖ. — 10. κἂν ἐθελήσητε, *if you are resolved* (aorist) *to carry these things through to their consummation* (πέρας, Lat. per) *as it becomes and behooves you to do.*

14. 16. Ὅλως. *On the whole.* — γάρ introduces the proof of the clause immediately preceding, viz. that his own kingdom and power are in a bad state. — 17. ἐν μὲν…μέρει, *as an auxiliary*, lit. in the role of an adjunct; opposed to αὐτὴ δέ, *but itself by itself.* Dem. was the first of the Athenian statesmen to discover and expose the ambitious designs of Philip. But *he* was slow to appreciate the new and strange power which Macedon was to derive from the personal influence and military genius of this one man. — οἷον, *as, for instance, it once joined you under Timotheus against the Olynthians.* In 364 B. C. the Athenians, under command of Timotheus, entered Thrace, and, aided by Perdiccas, king of Macedon, made a successful campaign, though they did not subdue the Olynthians. — 19. πάλιν αὖ, *again, on the other hand, against Potidæa for the Olynthians, this force consisting of both together* (Macedonians and Olynthians) *proved to be*

something considerable. This was in B. C. 357. See Grote 11, 334. πάλιν introduces a second instance, while αὖ marks the change of sides, *for* Olynthus instead of *against* it. — νυνί, *quite recently.* — 21. ἐπὶ...οἰκίαν, *against the reigning family,* sc. the despots of Pheræ, B. C. 352. — πάντ' is usually taken adverbially; *it helps altogether,* i. e. *essentially.* It can, however, be taken as subject of ὠφελεῖ, *all helps,* like our proverb, every little helps. So Whiston, and apparently Dindorf and Sauppe. — 15. 25. οἷς = *wherein.* — 26. ἐπισφαλεστέραν, sc. δύναμιν, *has rendered it still more insecure.* — P. 16, l. 3. τοῦτο ἐζήλωκε, *and has made this his passion.* Whiston. The change of tense and of gender both intensify the expression. — 4. ἄν...τι, *whatever may happen.* — 4–6. τὴν...δόξαν, the separation of the art. from the subs. is noticed by the commentators. Heslop refers to Phil. II. 29, where twenty-nine words intervene between the art. and its participle. — 5. μηδείς instead of οὐδείς, because it is subjective and represents Philip's view of the case. — 16. 7. φιλοτιμίας, see note, § 3. — κοπτόμενοι, *harassed,* lit. stricken, Eng. chop. — ἄνω κάτω. The omission of the connection *represents* the rapidity of Philip's movement, *up and down,* in which he resembled Napoleon. — 9. ταλαιπωροῦσιν, *toil and suffer.* — 9–11. οὔτ' ...οὔτ'...οὔθ', *neither being allowed to employ themselves on their occupations nor on their private concerns, nor being able to dispose of such things as they may perchance have earned in such ways as they can.* The οὔτ'...οὔτ' together correlate with οὔθ'...ἔργοις, which refers especially, but not exclusively, to agricultural works. — 12. κεκλειμένων, κ. τ. λ, gen. abs., giving the reason — *because* the markets are closed. — 17. 16. πεζέταιροι, foot attendants, that is, *body guards.* — δόξαν μέν, well rendered by Heslop, *have the reputation, it is true* (μέν), *of being admirable soldiers and thoroughly trained in matters pertaining to war.* — συγκεκροτημένοι, lit. welded together, see L. & S. — ἐγώ, emphatic. — 18. τῶν...γεγενημένων, *who have been in the very country* of Philip. — ἤκουον, *was hearing,* sc. recently. — 19. οὐδένων, *they are no better than others.* — 20. οἷος is not entirely pleonastic = *of a character experienced in war and campaigns.* — 21. τούτους, pl. referring to those implied in εἰ τίς = siquis, *whoever.* μέν resumptive of μέν in the previous clause. — φιλοτιμίᾳ is here used more nearly in its literal sense, love of honor, that is, *ambition,* or *jealousy.* — 24. εἶναι, sc. ἔφη; so in § 19 again. — 25. ἄλλως, *otherwise = generally; temperate or upright generally,* sc. in other virtues besides tem-

diseases of the body politic. ἔκδηλα is opposed to ἀφανῆ, and implies the bringing of these diseases *out* to the light of day. — ἐποίη-σεν, gnomic aorist.

22. P. 18, l. 2 – 5. σώφρονος μέν...οὐ μὴν ἀλλ', *he uses the reasoning of a wise man, I admit...nevertheless.* — 3. τὸ ὅλον, the whole, that is, it is *every thing.* Compare De Cor. 194, where he says, Fortune is mistress of all, κύριος τῶν πάντων. — παρά, *through the entire course of.* — 6. τύχην, cf. note, I. 1. — 8. ἀφορμάς, lit. starting points, here *grounds,* or *reasons: far more grounds for obtaining the good-will of the gods.* — 23. 10. οἶμαι, *methinks.* — 11. αὐτόν, *while he is doing nothing himself.* — 12. μή τί γε, *much less.* Cf. 717. — 14. αὐτός, *in person.* — 17. οὐδέ...ἐγώ, *and I do not wonder at this.* — 24. 20. εἰ = *that.* — 21 – 25. μέν ποτε...νυνὶ δέ, *although once...yet now.* — Λακ...ἀντήρατε, *you withstood the Lacedæmonians,* sc. in the Bœotian war, B. C. 378. — 23. ὑμῖν ἐξόν, *when it was in your power.* — οἱ ἄλλοι, *the other* Greeks = all the others. — 24. ἀνηλίσκετε. Observe the change from the aor. to the imperf.: *were continually spending.* — 27. τοὺς μὲν ἄλλους, *after often saving the rest of the Greeks collectively and every one of them individually in turn, you nevertheless sit still when you have lost your own,* i. e. Amphipolis, Pydna, Methone, and Potidæa. W. — καθ' is distributive, *one by one.* — P. 19, l. 5. πολεμεῖτε, *you have been and still are carrying on the war,* sc. ten years, reckoning from the capture of Amphipolis. — 6. τί ποιούντων, *what you have been doing while all this* (οὗτος is emphatic) *has passed away,* lit. *while you have been doing what, all this,* etc. — ἴστε γὰρ δήπου, *for you know surely.* — 7. αὐτῶν is opposed to ἑτέρους, *procrastinating yourselves, hoping that somebody else would act.* — 9. κρινόντων, *bringing one another to trial.* This spirited passage is made more lively and rapid by the omission of the connectives. — 26. 10. εἶθ'...γενήσεσθαι, *are you then so senseless as to cherish the hope that the affairs of the state will become prosperous instead of bad by the very same measures by which they have become bad instead of prosperous.* The irresistible logic of this passage is further enforced by the careful antithesis of the words and the rhetorical order of the two clauses. — 15. πολὺ γάρ, *for in the nature of things it is in all cases much easier to keep what you have than to get what you have not.* The commentators differ widely as to the construction of the words, some connecting πολὺ ῥᾷον adverbially with φυλάττειν, and making πάντα the subject of πέφυκεν, and others mak-

ing πολὺ ῥᾷον pred. after πέφυκεν and πάντα obj. of κτήσασθαι (πάντα, lit. all things, i. e. anything = in all cases). I have followed the latter. In Ol. I. 23, the orator seems to express just the opposite sentiment. But there he is speaking of the intoxicating influence of prosperity ; here only of what would otherwise be true in the *nature of the case :* hence, there he says it *oftentimes seems* more difficult to keep than to get ; here, *in the nature of things,* it is much easier to keep anything than to get it. Prudentibus quidem facilius est, sed imprudentibus difficilius. Dind.—17. ὅ τι…οὐδέν, *nothing whatever.* — 19. αὐτῶν…ἤδη, *this, therefore, is our own duty already.* ἤδη is emphatic = *and that immediately.* Cf. Phil. 1. 8 : ἢν ἀποθέσθαι φημὶ δεῖν ἤδη. — 27. 21. πρὶν…κρατήσητε, *before you shall have become masters of the position.* So Whiston. Heslop renders τῶν πραγμάτων *your objects,* sc. the deliverance of Olynthus. — 22. ἀπ' αὐτῶν τῶν ἔργων, *from the acts themselves,* not from the rumors and reports of them. — 23. τὰς προφάσεις, *to remove the excuses* (of the generals) *and the defaults on your own part* (which furnished the pretext for those excuses). — P. 20, l. 2, 3. φεύγειν… εὑρίσκειν. The Scholiast remarks that the orator is hinting especially at Chares. — 4. ἐνταῦθα, *here,* i. e. in the wars to which they were sent by the Athenians ; so ἐκεῖ below, *there,* sc. in their own private wars. — 5. Ἀμφίπολις Dindorf would change to Ἀμφίπολιν, as the obj. of κομιεῖσθε, and Franke, Rehdantz, Voemel, Westermann, and others agree with him and with the MSS. in omitting αὐτήν after παραχρῆμα. — 6. οἱ δὲ κίνδυνοι, κ. τ. λ., *and the dangers belong exclusively to the officers, and pay there is none.* — 8. λήμματα, *gains,* lit. gettings, or takings ; generally used in a bad sense. ἆθλα = prizes of honorable war ; λήμματα = the gains of piracy and freebooting. See Schaefer in loc. — 9. Lampsacus and Sigeum, cities on the Asiatic side of the Hellespont, the latter near the Ægean and the former near the mouth of the Propontis, were given to Chares by the Persian satrap Artabanus for some service rendered him. On the Athenian armaments at this time, see Grote, XI. 312, and the authorities cited in his notes. — 29. 12. ἀποβλέψητε, *look away, look only.* — 13. δόντες λόγον, *having given them the opportunity to speak for themselves,* or, as we say, having given them a hearing. — 17. πρότερον μέν, κ. τ. λ., *for formerly, gentlemen of Athens, you used to make your extraordinary contributions by classes, but now you administer the government by classes ; an*

*orator is at the head of either party, and a general under him, and
the men to shout, three hundred ;* al. οἱ τριακόσιοι, *the* three hundred.
1200 of the richest citizens of Athens (120 from each tribe) were
selected whose duty it was to bear the heaviest burdens of taxation,
and especially to advance money on any emergency, with the right,
however, to reimburse themselves in part by collections from other
citizens. These were divided into four classes (συμμορίαι), according
to their property, 300 in each class, each class having a ἡγεμών, or
chairman, at its head. These facts are sufficient to make the satire
or burlesque in the text intelligible. For further details, which,
however, are obscure and uncertain, see Dic. of Antiq. under εἰσφορά.
Scholars have perplexed themselves needlessly by seeking too close
an analogy between the symmorial and the political parties. Demosthenes was himself head of a symmoria for ten years. Or. con. Meidias, § 200. See also Or. περὶ Συμμορίων. — 21. προσνενέμησθε,
attach yourselves, or *are attached.* — ὡς = *to,* see Lex. and Gram. —
30. 22. ὑμῶν…γενομένους, *and having become now also still* (as formerly) *your own masters* (instead of letting your political and party
leaders be your lords and masters). — κοινόν, *alike free to all.* —
25 – 27. τοῖς μὲν…τοῖς δὲ…τοῖς δέ, sc. the politicians…the wealthy
and industrious citizens…and the mass of voters. — 25. ἀποδώσετε,
tanquam debitum (Franke), not merely *give,* but *give up* or *give over.*
— ὑμῶν limits τυραννίδος, and is objective genitive (cf. Or. de Cor.
66: τυραννίδα τῶν Ἑλλήνων) = *to give orders as if from a despotic government over you.* — 26. τριηραρχεῖν…στρατεύεσθαι. Heslop, Rehdantz, Funkhaenel, and some other editors omit the commas between
these infinitives, as all the editions and the orator himself omit the
connectives to emphasize the rapid list of services required of this
class. — P. 21, l. 4. περιέσται, *it will remain.* Some of the best
editors follow S, and read ἔξεσται, *you will have the opportunity.* —
31. κεφάλαιον, *I recommend, then, in sum that all.* Heslop. Observe
the emphatic recurrence three times over of this ALL, by which popular catchword the orator skilfully recommends the true democracy
of equal burdens and services. — 5. τὸ ἴσον, *that which is just and
equal,* that is, according to his property, as the preceding clause
defines it. — 6. κατὰ μέρος, *in turn,* that is, *in rotation.* The same
thing is expressed (Phil. I. 21) by ἐκ διαδοχῆς, *in succession.* —7. λόγον διδόναι, cf. note on δόντες λόγον, § 29. Render: *to give a hearing*
(continuously or successively is implied in the pres. inf.) *to all who*

3 *

the difficulty and perplexity. — P. 23, l. 3. **παρὼν καὶ ἀκούων,** *by personal knowledge and by hearsay.* — 4. **σύνοιδα,** sc. *ὑμῖν = as you also do.* So Franke and Rehdantz, although the word does not necessarily mean anything more than *full* knowledge. — **τὰ πλείω** is followed by **ἤ** as if the article were omitted ; lit. *the more of your advantages have slipped out of your hands by your unwillingness to do your duty than by your not understanding them.* **τὰ πλείω** usually means the greater *part,* the most. The Or. here compliments the intelligence of the Athenians at the expense of their patriotism, or, rather, their will and purpose (**βούλεσθαι**). See notes on Ol. II. 23, and I. 1. **μὴ βούλεσθαι** denotes want of resolution rather than want of disposition. — 6. **ἀξιῶ δέ,** *and I request you, if I address you with frankness, to bear with me, considering this whether I speak the truth and* (speak it) *for this purpose that the future may become better.* — **διά** here = *for* as in modern Greek. — 9. **πρὸς χάριν,** *for popular favor, popularity.* — 10. **πᾶν μοχθηρίας,** *complete demoralization.*

4. 11. **μικρά** is used adverbially = *briefly,* and **γεγενημένων** is gen. after **ὑπομνῆσαι.** So Westermann, Franke, Rehdantz, etc. Others (e. g. Schaefer, Dindorf, Heslop) make **μικρά** = **ὀλίγα,** *a few,* and obj. of **ὑπομνῆσαι,** which can govern either two acc. or an acc. and gen. — 13. **ὅτ᾽ ἀπηγγέλθη,** *when* Philip was reported, etc., i. e. you remember not merely the fact (**ὅτι**), but the time and the circumstances, which he proceeds to describe. — 14. **τρίτον...τουτί,** *now three or four years ago.* C. 482, c ; Cu. 405, Obs. 1 ; G. 161, N. ; H. 550 c. The time was more than three years, and less than four. See, however, Grote XI. 469, note, for a different view. — **Ἡραῖον Τεῖχος** was a fortress in Thrace near the Chersonese. It is identified by most commentators with a fortress of the same name near Perinthus ; but this is doubtful. See Grote, XI. 428. — **τότε τοίνυν,** well expressed by Heslop : *well it was then.* — **μαιμακτηριών,** November. — **πολλῶν δέ, κ. τ. λ.,** not *after* (Kennedy), which would require **γενομένου,** but *in the midst of much discussion and tumult,* that is, while it was going on, **γιγνομένου.** For the numb. of this part., see C. 497 ; H. 511 h ; G. 138, N. 2. — 16. **παρ᾽ ὑμῖν,** in your presence, that is, *in your assembly.* — 18. **μέχρι,** *up to,* more expressive of the exigency than *under.* This levy included all the citizens who were liable to military service beyond the bounds of Attica. — 19. **εἰσφέρειν,** *to raise a war-tax.* See Dic. Ant. **εἰσφορά.** — 20. **διελθόντος...ἐνιαυτοῦ,** *this year having passed away,* i. e. the

remaining seven months of it. The Attic year began with Heca-
tombeon, i. e. in July. Add the three months of the next year
named by the orator, and ten months elapse between the resolution
and its execution or rather abortion. He draws out the *picture* of
delay and final failure in sarcastic detail, counting them, as it were,
on his fingers. It is hardly necessary to supply a verb in English.
21. τούτου...μόγις, *in the course of this last-named month, hardly.* —
22. μετὰ τὰ μυστήρια. For these must of course be celebrated !
The sarcasm still continues. The Mysteries were celebrated during
nine days, from the 15th to the 23d of Boëdromion. For the time of
the Attic months, and the significance of the names, see Lex. and Dic.
Ant. — δέκα...ἀργυρίου. The failure, too, is drawn out in detail:
ten ships instead of *forty* — *empty*, i. e. unmanned, in contrast with
the levy of citizens *in mass* — and with *five* talents instead of *sixty*.
Charidemus was left to man the ships with mercenaries. Charidemus
was a native of Oreus in Bœotia, an adopted citizen of Athens, and a
commander of mercenary troops, especially in the Chersonese. See
Dic. of Biog. — 25. ἀμφότερα, both reports. — ἦλθε, raro usu de nun-
tiis. Schaefer. — 27. ἦν...αὐτός, *but this* WAS *the very opportunity*,
sc. when Philip was sick or dead. — P. 24, l. 2. ἠνώχλει. Observe
the force of the imp.: *would not have been preserved to be troubling
us as he now is.*

6. 3. οὐκ...ἔχοι, *cannot be altered*, strictly could not if we would.
— 4. ἑτέρου, sc. the Olynthiac. — τις = *a sort of*, not so good as
that we lost, but one of some considerable value. — δι᾽ ὅν, *by reason
of which*, really, for the sake of which. — 5. τί...τούτῳ. C. 478 ;
Cu. 401 ; Madv. 27. R. 1. — 7. θεάσασθε, *behold how* YOU *will have
conducted the whole war in behalf of Philip*, sc. as if you had been his
generals. — 7. 9. ὑπῆρχον. The series of clauses without connectives, extending through the section, explain the θεάσασθε ὃν τρόπον
by a rapid, distinct, and vivid enumeration of particulars descriptive
of the status at the beginning of the war : *there were, to begin with,
the Olynthians possessed of some power.* — 11. οὔτε...ἐθάρρει, *neither
Philip felt secure in regard to them, nor they in regard to Philip.*
θαρρεῖν τινι = to rely upon one, but θαρρεῖν τινα = to feel secure
(without anxiety) in regard to any one. — 12. ἐπράξαμεν...εἰρήνην,
we negotiated peace (with them) *and they with us.* It seems necessary
to supply πρὸς ἐκείνους, although Schaefer (followed apparently by
Whiston) makes πρὸς ἡμᾶς = πρὸς ἀλλήλους, which would certainly

require πρὸς ἡμᾶς αὐτούς. The peculiar form seems to be chosen to express the *mutual* readiness of the parties for peace. — 13. ὥσπερ... δυσχερές, *an obstruction, as it were, and an offence.* — 14. ἐφορμεῖν, lit. to lie at anchor, hence *to be on the watch for.* This clause explains τοῦτο. — τοῖς ἑαυτοῦ καιροῖς, *the opportunities which he gave.* — 15. ἐκπολεμῶσαι. See note Ol. I. 7, where we have the same thing in nearly the same words. — 17. ὁπωσδήποτε, *somehow or other*, the orator does not say how, but implies (what he *says* in Ol. I. 7, γέγονεν αὐτόματον) that it was without the agency of the Athenians. — 8. τί οὖν introduces the conclusion from the series of clauses without connectives in the foregoing section. — 19. ἐγὼ μέν. μέν solitarium, as the old grammarians called it, i. e. without a corresponding δέ expressed. It implies a counter-conception in the mind of the speaker, which *he* cannot entertain, however others may think. — χωρὶς γάρ, κ. τ. λ., *for aside from the disgrace which would encompass us.* The inf. and part. take ἄν, when it would belong to the finite verbs, of which they take the place. C. 618 ; Cu. 595 ; G. 211 ; H. 803. — 21. οὐδέ = καὶ οὐ, *I see that there is also no small reason to fear the consequences.* — 22. ἐχόντων...ἡμῖν, *the Thebans being affected towards us as they are*, sc. unkindly ; euphemism. As Heslop remarks, the feeling was fully reciprocated. Cf. De Cor. 18. — χρήμασιν, *in their resources*, sc. those derived from the plunder of the temple at Delphi. They had coined 10,000 talents ($10,000,000 in round numbers) from the consecrated vases and statues alone. — 24. μηδενὸς implies a supposition = *in case there was no one to prevent him after having subjected what he now has in hand* (Olynthus) *from turning his attention to things here* (in Athens). The reader will observe the euphemisms. — 9. 26. εἰς τοῦτο, *to this extent = till then.* The procrastination is emphasized by the use of the *future* inf. (ποιήσειν) instead of the pres. or aor. C. 660 ; H. 718 ; Madv. 171, R. 2 : *is putting off his going to do his duty.* — P. 25, l. 3. εἰς τοῦτο, *to this result.* Observe the emphatic position : *for that this is the result to which matters will come if we throw away our present advantages we are pretty well aware all of us, of course.*

10. 9. παράδοξον. He conciliates his hearers by this admission at the outset, that his proposal is contrary to their opinions and inclinations. — 10. καθίσατε, *appoint* (lit. cause to sit) *law-makers* ; al. καθίστατε ; but καθίσατε is the *regular* word, and the aorist tense seems to be required here. Special nomothetæ are here intended, for

of the laws should continue to enjoy the popularity (of a law) *which has injured the whole state, while the odium* (of legislation) *whereby we should all be benefited should damage him who has now given you the best advice.* The reader cannot fail to notice the nice adjustment of antithetic words and phrases even to the πᾶσαν and ἅπαντες, and the τότε and νῦν. — 7. **μηδαμῶς...ὑμῖν,** *do not by any means expect any man to be so powerful with you.*

14. 12. **Οὐ μὴν οὐδ'.** *Nay, more, you ought not to be ignorant of this, surely.* The statement is self-evident, and yet of vital moment; hence the emphatic combination of particles. — 13-15. **ἂν μὴ...ὑμᾶς,** *unless there be superadded the willingness to execute at least what you have resolved, heartily yourselves.* **ὑμᾶς** is emphatic; also **ποιεῖν.** — 16. **ἢ...διαπράξασθαι,** *or to accomplish the objects for which they may have been proposed.* **γραφῇ** is 2 aor. subj. pass. with ψηφίσματα for its subject. — 18. **μικρά,** few. — **ἐπράττετε,** *be performing,* distinctly bringing the action or rather inaction down to the present time: **ὑβρίκει,** *have insulted,* without any allusion to the present. **ἄν** influences both these verbs. — 20. **ἕνεκα** retains here essentially its original sense, *on account of:* so far as RESOLUTIONS *at least* could have *effected* the *result,* or, so far as it *depended* on RESOLUTIONS *at any rate.* — **15.** 21. **τὸ γὰρ πράττειν,** *for doing while it is posterior to speaking and voting in order of time is prior and superior to them in efficiency.* — 24. **τὰ δ' ἄλλα,** *and the others you have,* to wit, the speaking and voting, as explained in the following clause, viz. orators to give you the necessary advice, and of all men the quickest discernment to judge of what they say. A delicate compliment to season the sarcasm which precedes. — 26. **καὶ πράξαι δέ,** *yes, and you will be able to* DO *also now, if you act with proper efficiency,* or, perhaps, as Westermann explains, *if you begin it right,* lit. MAKE *it right.* **πράττειν** is to *do, practice, perform;* **ποιεῖν** *to make, effect,* or *create.* Phil. I. 11 : you will soon *create* (ποιήσετε) another Philip ; Phil. III. 52 : and they *create* (ποιοῦσιν) for him leisure to *do* (πράττειν) whatever he pleases. **πράττειν** is here opposed to λέγειν and χειροτονεῖν, and πρᾶξαι to εἰπεῖν and γνῶναι, as *doing* is to *speaking* and *voting,* and distinguished from ποιεῖν as *doing* from *making* an opportunity. The distinction between πράττειν and ποιεῖν is not always carefully observed. — **16.** P. 27, l. 4. **ἄνθρωπος,** Philip. Observe the emphasis on ἄνθρωπος and ἅπαντα in the reversal of the logical order of subject and object. — **ταύτης,** Olynthus and the Chalcidic peninsula. — 5. **πάν-**

army. ἕτερος with its comparative termination is always one of two; if plural, one of two groups or classes. Heslop compares Ol. I. 20 : λέγουσι δὲ καὶ ἄλλους τινὰς ἄλλοι πόρους, and says : there his proposition is counted in as one of several ways suggested for meeting the difficulty ; here ἕτεροι πόροι stand collectively on the one side, and the theoric fund on the other. — 2. εἴποι τις ἄν, *some one may ask.* — 3. φήμ᾽...ἔστιν, *yes, indeed, if there is any such man.* So Westermann and Rehdantz, and this corresponds with the εἴ τις which precedes and the εἴ τῳ which follows. Others render, *if it is possible.* — 4. ἀλλὰ θαυμάζω, κ. τ. λ., *but I wonder if it ever has happened or ever will happen to any human being when he has spent what he has for useless objects to find in what he has not abundant means for necessary purposes.* The conciseness and point of the original are imperfectly expressed in any translation. — 7. μέγα...λόγοις, *is a great help to such arguments.* Kennedy. *Powerfully seconds.* Heslop. — 8. διόπερ, *and for this very reason.* — 10. τὰ δὲ πράγματα, κ. τ. λ., *but the facts are often in reality very different.* πέφυκεν, are in their nature, are in reality. Such gnomes, full of common sense and obvious almost as axioms, yet laying bare the human heart, and illustrating history, often illuminate the pages of Demosthenes. — 20. 11. ὁρᾶτε, κ. τ. λ., *look at these things therefore in such light as the facts also* (and not your wishes merely) *allow, and then you will be able to serve and have pay.* Whiston extends the influence of ὅπως over the whole sentence, and renders, *and so that you will be able*, and Heslop places no comma after ἐνδέχεται. — 14. ἐλλείποντας...φέρειν, *failing for want of money in any of the duties required by the war, to bear tamely such reproaches,* sc. as are incurred by such conduct. — 16. οὐδ᾽ ἐπὶ μέν, κ. τ. λ., *no, nor after having seized arms and marched against Corinthians and Megarians to allow Philip to enslave Grecian cities for want of supplies for the soldiers.* The point of the passage lies in the *un-Hellenic* course which they pursued in resisting the petty warfare of Corinthians and Megarians (who were Greeks) upon one another or upon other Greeks, and allowing *Philip* (whom he stigmatizes as a barbarian) to *enslave* Grecian cities. "It is impossible to say with certainty to what events Demosthenes here alludes, nor need we conclude that his contemporaries were engaged in them." Whiston. It is generally supposed that he refers to events which occurred in the previous century, viz. the famous invasion of Megara by the Corinthians, B. C. 458,

than 10,000. It is an immense sum for a small state = more than $10,000,000 in gold, and in value ten times that sum. Cf. Böckh., Pub. Econ. 591. — εἰς...ἀνήγαγον, *brought up into the Acropolis,* sc. into the Opisthodomus, where the public moneys were kept under the guardianship of Athena. — 19. ὑπήκουε, *submitted to them;* hardly true, certainly exaggerated. Perdiccas II., the king who was then on the throne of Macedon (ὁ...ἔχων), was often at variance with the Athenians, and always glad to make up with them; in this sense only did he submit to them. Observe the juxtaposition of αὐτοῖς and βασιλεύς in emphatic contrast, a *king* to *them,* the Athenian *people.* — 22. αὐτοὶ στρατευόμενοι, *serving in person,* and not relying on mere mercenaries, — the point so often insisted on as the pivot of the whole Olynthiac question. — 25. 27. οἰκοδομήματα, *edifices,* such as the Propylæa, porticos, dock-yards, Piræus, etc. — κάλλη...ἱερῶν, *ornaments...of temples = beautiful temples,* such as the Theseum, Erechtheum, Parthenon, etc. — 26. P. 30, l. 3. ἰδίᾳ δέ, κ. τ. λ., *while as individuals* (in their private life) *they were so modest and so exceedingly steadfast in abiding by the spirit of the constitution,* sc. of the democracy. — 6. εἰ...ἐστίν, *if perchance any one of you knows at all what kind of a house it is.* εἰ ἄρα = si forte, *if now, if perchance.* ἄρα and ποτέ both add to the severity of the implication that it is very doubtful whether any of them know anything whatever about the great men of previous generations. — 8. εἰς περιουσίαν, *for personal advantage,* opposed to τὸ κοινόν. — 12. ἴσως, *fairly, impartially.* — εἰκότως, *naturally,* that is, as might have been expected. — 27. 13. τότε...προστάταις, *such now was the state of things with them at that time enjoying the leaders of whom I have spoken.* — 15. ὑπὸ... νῦν, *under the worthies of the present day.* — χρηστῶν, *excellent men!* is of course ironical. The reference is to the popular orators, who were the leading statesmen or politicians of the day. — 16. ἆρα... παραπλησίως, *are they in a way* (or state) *at all similar, or even resembling* that? — 17. τὰ μὲν...εἰπεῖν, *as to the rest I am silent, though I could say much.* The MSS. generally and the majority of the editions have οἷς before τὰ μέν; and as the more difficult reading it is entitled to the preference. But Schaefer and Sauppe explain the οἷς as a repetition by some copyist of the last syllable of the παραπλησίως which precedes; and there is no suitable reference or construction for it, — none on which commentators can at all agree, and none which is consistent with the simplicity, the gram-

matical regularity, and the clearness which belong to Demosthenes.
— 18. ἀλλ᾽ is opposed to τὰ μὲν ἄλλα, *I pass over everything else, but
I must speak of these.* — ὅσης, κ. τ. λ., *though favored with an ab-
sence of competitors so complete as you all see* (explained in the following specifications), *though the Lacedæmonians were ruined* (by the
battle of Leuctra and the loss of their prowess in the Peloponnese),
and the Thebans were fully occupied (by the Phocian war), *and of the
rest no one was competent to contest the supremacy with us.* So the
passage is well rendered by Heslop. — 22. ἐξὸν δέ, *and when it was
in our power.* These clauses are all circumstantial in reference to
ἀπεστερήμεθα and the succeeding clauses. δέ is omitted by Dindorf,
Franke, and Whiston. — 28. 24. χώρας οἰκείας, *territory that belongs
to us.* The Scholiast refers it particularly to Amphipolis. It may
also include other places of which Philip had robbed the Athenians. —
26. οὓς...οὗτοι, *and allies whom we had gained in the war, these men*
(the above-mentioned worthies) *have lost in time of peace,* that is,
when war was not openly declared. For the transfer of συμμάχους
from the antecedent to the relative clause, see C. 553 ; G. 154 ; H. 809.
— P. 31, l. 1. τηλικοῦτον ἠσκήκαμεν. Cf. I. 9 : ηὐξήσαμεν ἡμεῖς καὶ
κατεστήσαμεν τηλικοῦτον. See also II. 4. — 29. 2. ἀλλ᾽ ὦ τᾶν. A
remark interposed by an imagined respondent. This is not infre-
quent in Demosthenes. So Cicero often introduces by *ast* an objection which he would anticipate and forestall. — 5. τὰς ἐπάλξεις, *the
parapets which we are plastering, and the roads which we are repair-
ing, and fountains, and fooleries.* λήρους is thus used elsewhere also
by Demosthenes to throw contempt on a series of things previously
enumerated. Plato uses φλυαρίας in the same way. The omission
of the article with κρήνας and λήρους intensifies the contempt. Sauppe
charges the orator with injustice. The supply of a country so arid
as Attica with water was no trifling matter, and yet it was the merest
trifle relatively to the rights and liberties of the people. — 7. ἀπο-
βλέψατε, *turn your eyes.* — τοὺς...πολιτευομένους. *Those who direct
their statesmanship to these objects.* Eubulus and his associates seem
to have valued themselves on such improvements. — 8. οἱ μέν, e. g.
Demades, Æschines, Phryno, and Philocrates. — 9. οἱ δέ. Demades
rose from the rank of a sailor, Æschines was an inferior actor, etc.
— ἔνιοι. In the oration against Meidias, Demosthenes says that he
(Meidias) has built a house at Eleusis of such magnitude as to over-
shadow all others in the place.

30. 13. **τί δή ποτε**, *why in the world then.* δή referring the question directly to what precedes, and ποτέ emphasizing it. Al. δήποτε, and δή ποθ'. — 14. **τὸ μὲν πρῶτον**, *formerly indeed*, strictly, *at the first.* Al. πρότερον. — **τολμῶν**, *inasmuch as they dared.* It is the implied reason why they were masters of the politicians, etc. — **καὶ στρατεύεσθαι**, *to serve in the army also*, as well as to discharge their civil duties. — **αὐτός**, *in person.* — 16. **κύριος αὐτός**, *were themselves the disposers of all the emoluments.* — 17. **ἀγαπητὸν...ἑκάστῳ**, *and each of the others* (of the leading public men) *was well satisfied.* ἑκάστῳ is dative of the doer after ἀγαπητὸν ἦν. — 31. 21. **ἐκνενευρισμένοι** is understood by some as referring to material resources, which are the *nerves* and sinews of war, and so explained by the words which follow. But besides being somewhat tautological, that would leave out the main point. Better understood of the character of the Athenians, and opposed to στρατεύεσθαι τολμῶν αὐτός = *enervated.* — 23. **ἐν ὑπηρέτου...γεγένησθε**, *have sunk into the position of an underling and a hanger-on.* Cf. II. 14, and note there. — **ἀγαπῶντες** is antithetic to ἀγαπητόν above: not, like their ancestors, well satisfied with some share in the public honors and offices, but *delighted if these men* (Eubulus and company) *allow you to participate in the theoric money or exhibit the Boëdromia.* πέμψωσιν is here used in a pregnant sense, viz. to celebrate with processions and parade; hence our word *pomp.* The aorist denotes a special celebration (probably with unusual pomp by Eubulus the previous year): the present in μεταδιδῶσι denotes a customary action. The Boëdromia was a festival in honor of Apollo Boëdromius on the seventh day of the month Boëdromion (answering to latter half of September and first half of October, and named from this festival). For further particulars see Dic.' Antiq. Whiston reads βοΐδια. — 25. **ἀνδρειότατον**, *manliest of all.* It is, of course, ironical. Al. ἀνανδρότατον. — 26. **προσοφείλετε**, *you feel under obligations to them too.* προς- = *besides, too.* — 27. **καθείρξαντες**, *having cooped you up in the city itself*, as in a cage. — P. 32, l. 1. **τιθασεύουσι**, *keep you tame, making you submissive to themselves.* — **χειρόηθεις** = mansuetos. There is a manifest allusion throughout to wild beasts and their masters. — 32. **ἔστι δ' οὐδέποτ'**, *but it is never possible, I think, to form a great and noble spirit while engaged in small and mean pursuits ; for of what sort soever the occupations of men may be, such also must of necessity their spirit be.* The application of this great ethical maxim is to the

Athenians, who lived a life of pleasure and amusement. — 5. ταῦτα is the object of εἰπόντι and of πεποιηκότων. It is placed at the beginning for emphasis, and without a connective (asyndeton) as an illustration of the foregoing maxim: *these things, for instance — verily I should not be surprised if greater harm should come to me for having mentioned them than to those who have caused their existence.* — τῶν πεποιηκότων = ἢ τοῖς πεποιηκόσι. Cf. C. 511, b; H. 586, b.

33. 10. Ἐὰν...ἔτι. An abbreviation for ἐὰν οὖν, εἰ καὶ μὴ πρότερον ἠθελήσατε, ἀλλὰ νῦν γ᾽ ἔτι. *If then, though you would not before, yet now after all you will.* So Phil. I. 9. Whiston. — 13. ἀφορμαῖς ἐπί = *as means to obtain.* — ἴσως ἄν, ἴσως. Cf. note, I. 19. — 16. λημμά-των, *receipts,* here in contempt = *such paltry receipts as these,* described above, § 31. Cf. II. 28, and note there. — ἃ...ἔοικε, *which resemble delicate morsels given by physicians to the sick.* — σιτίοις may be regarded as a diminutive of σῖτος, and so rendered as above; it is rendered *delicacies* by Whiston; *diet* by Kennedy and Heslop; *gruel* by Champlin. — ἀσθενοῦσιν is erased or bracketed by several editors as standing between τοῖς and the emphatic word (σιτίοις), to which it should belong. — 17. καὶ γὰρ...καὶ = *for as...so.* — 18. ἐκεῖνα, sc. σίτια; ταῦτα, sc. these pittances from the theoric fund. — ταῦτα...νέμεσθε may be rendered, *these allowances,* with Heslop. — 20. οὔτ᾽...ἐᾷ, *nor permit you to renounce them, and do something else.* — 34. 22. οὐκοῦν...λέγεις, *well, then, you propose pay, do you not?* sc. for military service, instead of the allowances which the orator has just been satirizing. It is substantially the same question which he supposes some one to ask in I. 19 : σὺ γράφεις ταῦτ᾽ εἶναι στρατιω-τικά; but he answers the question more boldly here : *yes, and I also propose that there be immediately the same arrangement for all* the citizens, to wit, that you all do your duty, and then all receive the public money as freely as you now do, but receive it as pay for service. Thus the orator avoids any suggestion of *taking away* their receipts from the treasury. It was customary to pay citizen soldiers as well as mercenaries. — 24. τὴν αὐτὴν σύνταξιν, cf. I. 20 : μίαν σύνταξιν τὴν αὐτὴν τοῦ τε λαμβάνειν καὶ τοῦ ποιεῖν τὰ δέοντα; but then, in the first Oration, he only says it *ought* to be so, while here he directly proposes it. — 25. τὸ μέρος, *his share.* — τοῦθ᾽ is predicate after ὑπάρχοι, *may be that, whatever it be, which the state may require.* Al. παρέχοι. — ἔξεστιν, κ. τ. λ., *if we are allowed to be at peace, remaining at home better, because released from the necessity of doing*

551, c ; G. 154 ; H. 809. — 23. σχεδὸν = fere. Cf. Cic. de Nat. De. 1, 16 : exposui fere. — ἕλοισθε. This oration, like the First Ol., closes with a prayer. See note ibid. The attentive and appreciative reader cannot withhold his approval from the critical judgment of Grote, who, after giving a copious analysis, which fills several pages, laments that his space confines him to this brief and meagre abstract, and pronounces "the third Olynthiac of Demosthenes one of the most splendid harangues ever delivered."

THE

PHILIPPICS

OF

DEMOSTHENES.

With Introductions and Notes.

FOR THE USE OF COLLEGES.

By W. S. TYLER,

WILLISTON PROFESSOR OF GREEK IN AMHERST COLLEGE.

———————

BOSTON:
JOHN ALLYN, PUBLISHER.
1882.

University Press: John Wilson & Son,
Cambridge.

PREFACE.

This edition of the Philippics was intended to be the sequel and companion of the Olynthiacs, already published, and to be bound with that or in a separate volume, at the option of those who use it. Little, therefore, need now be added by way of preface. With comparatively few exceptions, sufficiently explained in the notes, it follows the same text, namely, that of Bekker in Tauchnitz's stereotyped edition; and the introductions and notes have been prepared for the same purpose, on the same general plan, and with substantially the same German and English editions before me for reference and comparison. The American edition of Dr. J. M. Smead has also been frequently consulted, and has never failed to impress me with a high respect for the faithful labors and the thorough scholarship of the editor. I take pleasure also in acknowledging my obligations, in common with all the teachers and students of Greek in our American colleges, to Dr. Champlin as the pioneer American editor of so many of the orations of Demosthenes.

My chief aim has been, not so much to trace out names

and dates and obscure facts, and settle disputed questions
in geography, history, archæology, or higher criticism, as
to help the student follow the argument, catch the spirit,
imbibe the sentiments, take on the style, enter into the
life and labors, of the great Athenian orator. It is hoped
that the general and special introductions, the analysis
of the argument, and the summary prefixed to each paragraph or division, will conduce not a little to this end. In
short, the design of the book is not criticism, but education, and that not to teach the teacher, but to guide and
inspire the pupil. I never read these orations, especially
since our late war, without a new and vivid impression of
their adaptation to warn and instruct us in our country
and our age, of their educational value to all countries and
all ages, of their fitness and their power to teach the young
especially, not only rhetorical and intellectual, but political
and moral lessons of unspeakable value. And if the young
men who read this edition of the Philippics may thus not
only be imbued with something of the eloquence of Demosthenes, but also inspired with his detestation of bribery,
corruption, oppression, and all wrong, and his supreme devotion to liberty, duty, honor, and right, my object will
have been accomplished, and I shall not have labored in
vain.

AMHERST COLLEGE, August, 1875.

INTRODUCTION.

ALTHOUGH the Olynthiacs stand first in the manuscripts and printed editions of the entire works of Demosthenes, the first Philippic preceded them some two or three years in the delivery, and is acknowledged to have been the earliest of his orations which have distinct reference to Philip of Macedon. Some twelve years had now elapsed since, on coming to his majority, he had prosecuted his guardians for maladministration, and, by his speeches against Aphobus in the dicastery, had not only won the verdict of the court, but, what was of more value, gained some confidence in himself and developed that hatred against wrong which ever after burned as a fire in his bones. Owing to his defective articulation and disagreeable delivery, he had ignominiously failed in his first appearance before the people ; but instructed by the comic actor, Satyrus, and encouraged by others of his audience, who saw in him the germs of an eloquence not inferior to that of Pericles, he withdrew, and, after several years of the most painstaking and persevering self-culture, returned to win a splendid triumph and chain victory to his car.

Three years before the first Philippic (B. C. 355) he had delivered his oration against Leptines, which, although a judicial oration, involved a public question of much interest, namely, that of the *Liturgies*, or charges for the public entertainments, and which was followed by the repeal of the law introduced by Leptines and opposed by Demosthenes. Two years before (B. C. 354) he had delivered his first parliamentary or popular harangue before the assembled people, the Oration De Symmoriis, in which, while he earnestly dissuades the Athenians from an aggressive, needless, and inexpedient war against the Persians, to which they were inclined, at the same time, with the insight and foresight of a true statesman, he urges them to the adoption of such a plan of *classification* and *contribution to the public service* as would prepare them for any and every public emergency, thus perhaps already intending (as Dionysius of Halicarnassus says, Rhet., VIII. 7), although he was too wise to make a premature disclosure of this chief end, to husband and rally the resources of his country for the great struggle with a nearer and more dangerous enemy, — Philip of Macedon. This earliest of the popular orations of Demosthenes, — though he was then a young man at the most of thirty-three years, according to Grote and Curtius only thirty years of age,* — thus shows much of the same practical wisdom and discernment of men and things which mark his whole career ; and from this time his history becomes identified with the history of Athens, and inseparably connected with that of all the other Grecian states. Curtius's admirable chapters on "Athens and King Philip" and the "Last Struggles for Independence" (Vol. V., Chap. III. and IV) are all strung,

---

* Authorities differ about the date of Demosthenes's birth by a period of four years, from B. C. 385 to 381. See (besides commentaries, lives of Demosthenes, and dictionaries of biography) Thirlwall's History of Greece, Chap. XLIII. ; Grote, Vol. XI., Chap. LXXXVII. ; and Curtius, Vol. V., Chap. III.

like beads on a thread, on the life of Demosthenes ; and
the same is substantially true of Thirlwall, Grote, and all the
best authorities on this portion of Grecian history. The
next year (B. C. 353) he made his speech Pro Megalopo-
litanis, in which he stems in like manner the popular cur-
rent of hatred against the Thebans, and advises the Athenians to maintain the existing status at Megalopolis and in
the Peloponnesus, thus consciously or unconsciously reserv-
ing the united strength of Athens and Thebes, and so far as
possible of all Greece, for the final conflict with their common enemy.

Philip had already been on the throne of Macedon seven
or eight years, and during six of these years he had been
steadily encroaching on the possessions or allies of Athens
in Northern Greece. Amphipolis, Pydna, Potidæa, and
Methone had all fallen into his hands ; Pheræ, Pagasæ,
all Thessaly, was virtually in his possession ; and the
Athenians were in a perpetual quarrel with him, if not
at open war. Yet in all this time we find no direct and
explicit mention of him in the extant orations of Demosthenes. The Athenians were slow to believe that a king
of Macedon, the disputed sovereign of a nation of Northern
barbarians who had hitherto been no match for the Olynthians and their immediate neighbors, and were scarcely
allowed access to the sea at any point, could be formidable to the military power of Athens or dangerous to
the liberties of Greece. But Greece, weakened by divisions, distracted by mutual jealousies, and almost exhausted
by civil wars, was no longer the Greece that hurled back
the millions of Persia, baffled and ruined. The Peloponnesian War (B. C. 431 – 404) had impaired the Hellenic
spirit and used up the resources of both the leading Grecian states. The Theban War, ending with the death

of Epaminondas, B. C. 362, had weakened and humbled Sparta. The Social War, between the Athenians and their allies, had stripped Athens of no small portion of its wealth and power. The Sacred or Phocian War, which was raging at this time, was still more fatal in its consequences, rousing almost all Greece to arms and opening the way for the direct and authorized interference of Philip in Grecian affairs. Strong in himself, in his person, his native genius, and his accidental training in the school of Epaminondas, strong in his autocratic power, his brave and disciplined army, and his growing navy, Philip was still stronger in the weakness and divisions of those whom he meant to subjugate. Athens, where he most feared resistance to his ambitious projects, was no longer the Athens that Miltiades, Themistocles, and Aristides animated to heroic sacrifices and led to glorious victories over the Persians. Arms had given place to arts. The Acropolis glittered with temples and theatres which excited the envy and tempted the cupidity of their neighbors, while the people were engrossed with a succession of spectacles and festivals. The military fund was alienated to the maintenance of magnificent shows, and it was made a crime even to propose its restoration. The poor clung tenaciously to the show-money which they drew from the public treasury, and the rich contributed reluctantly to the public service. Mercenary troops had been their reliance in war till they had almost forgotten that citizens ever went in person to the field of battle. From such a people Philip had little to fear, unless some master spirit of patriotism and eloquence could rouse them from their lethargy. He early saw and remarked that the battle was not with the Athenians, but with Demosthenes. If not the earliest to discover the danger, Demosthenes was the first to proclaim it openly and boldly to his sleeping

countrymen. The first great occasion of immediate alarm
for the liberty of Greece and their own safety was the
attempted march of Philip — now acting ostensibly as the
representative of the Amphictyonic Council and the aven-
ger of the god at Delphi in the Sacred War — through the
pass of Thermopylæ for the subjugation or extermination
of the sacrilegious Phocians. This was prevented by the
Athenians, who, awakened from their lethargy, despatched an
armament of such formidable strength, and so fortified and
guarded the pass, that Philip did not attempt to force his
way through it. But he went on strengthening his infantry
and cavalry, building up a navy, and extending his conquests in Thrace till his attack on the Ἡραῖον Τεῖχος, a fortress so near the Chersonese that the Athenian possessions
and colonists there were thus threatened, again aroused
their fears. Then they *voted* to equip a fleet of forty triremes, to man it with Athenian citizens, all persons up to
the age of forty-five being liable to serve in the expedition,
and to raise an extraordinary tax of sixty talents. But
while the armament was in preparation, news came to
Athens that Philip was sick, and then that he was dead;
and then they gave up the expedition (Ol., III. 4, 5). It
was under these circumstances * (B. C. 352, 351) that
Demosthenes ascended the bema and delivered his first
Philippic, in which he urged the Athenians to necessitate
the return of Philip to his own country and keep him
there by sending a fleet to hover along the coast, and also

---

* Grote and apparently Curtius suppose the oration to have been delivered in the interval between the magnificent vote and the almost farcical
execution of it, early in B. C. 351. Thirlwall places it prior to the vote
(352). But he is obliged to suppose the reports of Philip's sickness or
death alluded to in this oration (§ 10) to be different and at a different
time from those mentioned in the third Olynthiac (§ 5), which seems
hardly probable. See further, in Introduction to First Philippic.

1*

to raise another and larger armament and have it in constant readiness to sail at a moment's warning to the place of danger. From this time opposition to Philip's designs against the liberties of his country becomes the ruling idea of Demosthenes's life. This was the first of twelve orations, delivered in the course of about as many years (B. C. 352 – 340), all of which Dionysius calls Philippics, and which, whatever may have been their special subjects or occasions, were all in reality directed against the designs of Philip. The genius of Demosthenes has invested the name of this ambitious sovereign with an added interest, and the word "Philippic" has a place and a meaning in all the languages of the civilized world. The Oration De Symmoriis, as interpreted by Dionysius (Rhet., VIII. 7) and Curtius (V. p. 259, Amer. ed.), was a Philippic in disguise. The three Olynthiacs are expressly *called* Philippics by Dionysius (De Adm. Vi Dic. in Demos. 21 – 43), and are as fierce in their denunciation of the Macedonian as any of his orations. The Speech on the Chersonese is scarcely less bitter and severe against Philip than the third Philippic which was spoken about the same time. Franke classifies the De Chersoneso, the De Pace, and the Olynthiacs with the Philippics commonly so called in his edition of the "*Nine* Philippic Orations of Demosthenes." Only four orations, however, are usually called Philippics ; and one of these (the fourth) is so manifestly made up of portions of other orations of Demosthenes, strung together by another hand, that it is almost universally pronounced to be spurious, and we have not thought it worth while to include it in this edition.

If any one should infer from the title that the Philippics, whether those universally so called or those sometimes classified with them, are nothing but denunciation and invective against Philip, it would be as great a mistake as another which is quite extensively prevalent, namely, that Demosthenes is always harping on the ancestral glories of Athens. The fact is, that there is an almost infinite variety in these as there is in his other orations, — a variety in the contents and subject-matter, not only in different orations suited to the occasion and circumstances, but in the same oration, passing from the most vehement invective or the most glorious panegyric to the simplest facts and the driest details of business, — and a corresponding variety in style so that ancient critics were accustomed to ascribe to the style of Demosthenes the characteristic excellences of all the other masters in oratory, history, and philosophy, — the nervous conciseness of Thucydides, the graceful narrative of Plato, the rhythmical flow and cadence of Isocrates, the simplicity and clearness of Lysias, the dignity and strength of Isaeus, each in its proper place, — together with a logical force and a patriotic and moral earnestness all his own.

If we inquire what were the secrets of Demosthenes's power as an orator, the main points may perhaps be briefly enumerated under the following heads : —

1. He was not a mere orator : he was also a statesman. "I did not speak thus," he says in the just pride and splendid egotism of his Oration on the Crown, "and then not move a resolution ; and I did not move a resolution, and then not serve on the embassy ; and I did not serve on the embassy, and then not convince the Thebans : but from the beginning all through to the end I devoted myself absolutely to the dangers which encompassed the state." While this was his boast, it was also his strength. His oratory was the exact expression of the orator himself ; and the orator himself was the impersonation of the best elements

of his age and country, the guardian of the liberties of
Greece, the representative of the fame and glory of Athens.
He may perhaps be considered a man of one idea, but that
idea was the very soul and almost the substance of the
best periods of Grecian history. If he had but one object,
that object was the only one worthy of Athens and of
Greece. And he strove to accomplish that chief end of his
own life and his country's history by means as various as
the circumstances under which he spoke, by counsels and
measures just suited to the emergency, by facts or arguments, simple narrative or impassioned appeal, clear details
of plans and forces or urgent motives to immediate and
strenuous action, just such as the people needed, and as
each oration or part of an oration seemed to require. With
instruction, reproof, conviction, and persuasion thus coming
each in its proper time and place, and all pervaded, animated, and inspired by one idea and that idea the very life
and glory of Athenian history, it is not strange that he
carried with him the sympathies of the people, even when
they were smarting under defeat incurred in following his
advice.

2. Another secret of his power lay in the richness and
appropriateness of the materials and the strength and skilful arrangement of the arguments which constituted the
staple of his orations. It is a great mistake to suppose
that the chief merit of Demosthenes was in his style and
elocution. These greatly enhanced his power over those
who heard him ; but these cannot explain the charm that
still lingers in his orations when read and studied in a dead
language, and which is not lost in the most imperfect
translation. Just and vivid conceptions of the designs of
Philip, of the dangers of his country and the character
of his countrymen, broader views of human nature, max-

ims of prudence and sentiments of morality of universal application, arguments of every kind drawn from every possible source, informed and enforced by the very logic of common-sense and marshalled as Nestor advised Agamemnon to arrange his troops, — all these march in solid phalanx upon a single point and press upon it with overwhelming force.   Substance rather than show, breadth and depth rather than superficial polish, characterize the orations of Demosthenes.   Hence when, in the zenith of his glory, our orator was asked which he thought to be the better, his own orations or those of Callistratus, his answer was that those of Callistratus were the better if they were to be heard, but his own if they were to be read; thus showing that while he set a high value on delivery, he claimed the superiority in a more solid and enduring excellence.   Time has confirmed the truth and justice of that claim; the orations of Callistratus are all lost, but those of Demosthenes live and will live through all ages.

3. Passing now from the matter to the manner, we observe that the style of Demosthenes is chiefly remarkable for its adaptation to the subject-matter and occasion ; in other words, its perfect fitness to express his thoughts and accomplish his object.   This implies variety, flexibility, simplicity, clearness, transparency, — the highest excellences of style.   His style is highly artistic, but the art is concealed.   As compared with most of our modern popular orators, it is barren of tropes and bare of ornament. Beautiful figures of every kind are found in his orations ; but he never uses them merely for embellishment : he uses them to illustrate and enforce his ideas ; in other words, because the figure spontaneously suggests itself as the most obvious, natural, and forcible expression for the thought. Simple things in simple ways ; plain thoughts in plain

words; burning emotions in burning language; thunder only when there is lightning, and when there is no tempest, and no occasion for any, the tranquil liquid atmosphere and the clear blue sky, — in short, fit words in fit places is the one universal law in the style of Demosthenes. Simple narrative rises into sublime declamation, and that again subsides into simple narrative. Vehement bursts of passion are soon followed by a resumption of the chain of argument out of which they flashed like the spark from an electric communication momentarily interrupted. After prostrating his adversaries by his fiery logic, as Robert Hall happily says, " by his abrupt and terrible interrogations he tramples them in the mire." His sentences are seldom very long; and when they are longest, they are compact, condensed, with all the clauses duly co-ordinated or subordinated according to the Greek idea of a period, and connected with other sentences (usually shorter ones for the sake of variety) according to the strict rules of Geeek composition. As the oration grows more animated and impassioned, the sentences usually become shorter and more intense, following each other in quick succession, like the rapid firing in the heat of battle; though he seldom continues this for a great while without stopping, gathering up his forces in one mighty phalanx, and hurling them in massive form and irresistible force upon the enemy.

4. The soul of Demosthenes's eloquence was his political and moral earnestness. He was thoroughly, we might almost say terribly, in earnest. Even in his calmest moments his heart was all aglow, and, whenever his judgment approved and his will permitted, this set on fire his logic; this flashed out in his interrogations, and broke forth, like thunderbolts, in his invectives; this was the heat of passion which accompanied the light of reason, in all his speech

and action. His earnestness was partly, perhaps, professional and personal; hence his greatest oration, like the
greatest speech of Daniel Webster, was one in which his
own reputation was involved with the honor of his country. But it was chiefly that earnestness which springs from
great ideas and a noble object. It was patriotic, heroic,
martyr-like. Demosthenes was the embodiment of more
than Athenian character and history. He was the impersonation of those ideas of undying power and universal
influence, — the ideas of duty, liberty, and glory. To
breathe these ideas into his countrymen was the object of
his orations, the aim and end of his life. And while they
listened to him, for the time being, — alas, that it was only
for the time being, — he often succeeded in animating them
with his own spirit. And the most valuable lesson which
the young orator and scholar may learn from the orations
and the history of Demosthenes is that eloquence consists not
in fine words and beautiful figures, but in truth and earnestness, and the chief end of life is not success, but duty
and self-sacrificing devotion to some worthy end.

5. The delivery of Demosthenes was just that thought-
ful, soul-full, sublime, godlike "*action*" which he himself
declared to be the first, second, and third thing in oratory,
and by which he meant, not gesticulation or elocution, but
ὑπόκρισις (that was the orator's word), that is, the exact
representation or full and perfect *expression* of the thoughts,
emotions, wishes, and aspirations of the speaker. It was
those low undertones so expressive of depth and earnestness, and that compressed lip full and more than full of
determination and intensity, and the brow furrowed with
thought and care, and the eye moistened with tears, and
the form bent forward as if in eager pursuit, and the
clinched hands giving a terrible emphasis to the utterance

ΔΗΜΟΣΘΕΝΟΥΣ

ΚΑΤΑ ΦΙΛΙΠΠΟΥ Α.

Εἰ μὲν περὶ καινοῦ τινὸς πράγματος προυτίθετο, 1
ὦ ἄνδρες ᾿Αθηναῖοι, λέγειν, ἐπισχὼν ἂν ἕως οἱ
πλεῖστοι τῶν εἰωθότων γνώμην ἀπεφήναντο, εἰ μὲν
ἤρεσκέ τί μοι τῶν ὑπὸ τούτων ῥηθέντων, ἡσυχίαν ἂν
ἦγον, εἰ δὲ μή, τότ᾽ ἂν αὐτὸς ἐπειρώμην ἃ γιγνώσκω 5
λέγειν· ἐπειδὴ δὲ ὑπὲρ ὧν πολλάκις εἰρήκασιν οὗτοι
πρότερον συμβαίνει καὶ νυνὶ σκοπεῖν, ἡγοῦμαι καὶ
πρῶτος ἀναστὰς εἰκότως ἂν συγγνώμης τυγχάνειν.
εἰ γὰρ ἐκ τοῦ παρεληλυθότος χρόνου τὰ δέοντα οὗτοι
συνεβούλευσαν, οὐδὲν ἂν ὑμᾶς νῦν ἔδει βουλεύεσθαι. 10

Πρῶτον μὲν οὖν οὐκ ἀθυμητέον, ὦ ἄνδρες ᾿Αθη- 2
ναῖοι, τοῖς παροῦσι πράγμασιν, οὐδ᾽ εἰ πάνυ φαύλως ἔχειν δοκεῖ. ὃ γάρ ἐστι χείριστον αὐτῶν ἐκ
τοῦ παρεληλυθότος χρόνου, τοῦτο πρὸς τὰ μέλλοντα βέλτιστον ὑπάρχει. τί οὖν ἐστὶ τοῦτο; ὅτι 15
οὐδὲν, ὦ ἄνδρες ᾿Αθηναῖοι, τῶν δεόντων ποιούντων
ὑμῶν κακῶς τὰ πράγματα ἔχει, ἐπεί τοι εἰ πάνθ᾽ ἃ
προσῆκε πραττόντων οὕτως εἶχεν, οὐδ᾽ ἂν ἐλπὶς ἦν
αὐτὰ βελτίω γενέσθαι. ἔπειτα ἐνθυμητέον καὶ παρ᾽ 3

1   A

ἄλλων ἀκούουσι καὶ τοῖς εἰδόσιν αὐτοῖς ἀναμιμνησκομένοις, ἡλίκην ποτ᾽ ἐχόντων δύναμιν Λακεδαιμονίων,
ἐξ οὗ χρόνος οὐ πολύς, ὡς καλῶς καὶ προσηκόντως
οὐδὲν ἀνάξιον ὑμεῖς ἐπράξατε τῆς πόλεως, ἀλλ᾽ ὑπε-
5 μείνατε ὑπὲρ τῶν δικαίων τὸν πρὸς ἐκείνους πόλεμον. τίνος οὖν ἕνεκα ταῦτα λέγω; ἵν᾽ εἰδῆτε, ὦ
ἄνδρες Ἀθηναῖοι, καὶ θεάσησθε ὅτι οὐδὲν οὔτε φυλαττομένοις ὑμῖν ἐστὶ φοβερὸν οὔτ᾽, ἂν ὀλιγωρῆτε,
τοιοῦτον οἷον ἂν ὑμεῖς βούλοισθε, παραδείγμασι
10 χρώμενοι τῇ τότε ῥώμῃ τῶν Λακεδαιμονίων, ἧς ἐκρα-
τεῖτε ἐκ τοῦ προσέχειν τοῖς πράγμασι τὸν νοῦν, καὶ
τῇ νῦν ὕβρει τούτου, δι᾽ ἣν ταραττόμεθα ἐκ τοῦ
4 μηδὲν φροντίζειν ὧν ἐχρῆν. εἰ δέ τις ὑμῶν, ὦ ἄνδρες Ἀθηναῖοι, δυσπολέμητον οἴεται τὸν Φίλιππον
15 εἶναι, σκοπῶν τό τε πλῆθος τῆς ὑπαρχούσης αὐτῷ
δυνάμεως καὶ τὸ τὰ χωρία πάντα ἀπολωλέναι τῇ
πόλει, ὀρθῶς μὲν οἴεται, λογισάσθω μέντοι τοῦθ᾽,
ὅτι εἴχομέν ποτε ἡμεῖς, ὦ ἄνδρες Ἀθηναῖοι, Πύδναν
καὶ Ποτίδαιαν καὶ Μεθώνην καὶ πάντα τὸν τόπον
20 τοῦτον οἰκεῖον κύκλῳ, καὶ πολλὰ τῶν μετ᾽ ἐκείνου
νῦν ὄντων ἐθνῶν αὐτονομούμενα καὶ ἐλεύθερα ὑπῆρχε
καὶ μᾶλλον ἡμῖν ἐβούλετ᾽ ἔχειν οἰκείως ἢ ᾽κείνῳ.
5 εἰ τοίνυν ὁ Φίλιππος τότε ταύτην ἔσχε τὴν γνώμην,
ὡς χαλεπὸν πολεμεῖν ἐστὶν Ἀθηναίοις ἔχουσι το-
25 σαῦτα ἐπιτειχίσματα τῆς αὐτοῦ χώρας ἔρημον ὄντα
συμμάχων, οὐδὲν ἂν ὧν νυνὶ πεποίηκεν ἔπραξεν,
οὐδὲ τοσαύτην ἐκτήσατο δύναμιν. ἀλλ᾽ εἶδεν, ὦ

ἄνδρες Ἀθηναῖοι, τοῦτο καλῶς ἐκεῖνος, ὅτι ταῦτα
μέν ἐστιν ἅπαντα τὰ χωρία ἆθλα τοῦ πολέμου κείμενα ἐν μέσῳ, φύσει δ' ὑπάρχει τοῖς παροῦσι τὰ
τῶν ἀπόντων καὶ τοῖς ἐθέλουσι πονεῖν καὶ κινδυνεύειν τὰ τῶν ἀμελούντων. καὶ γάρ τοι ταύτῃ 6
χρησάμενος τῇ γνώμῃ πάντα κατέστραπται καὶ 6
ἔχει, τὰ μὲν ὡς ἂν ἑλών τις ἔχοι πολέμῳ, τὰ δὲ
σύμμαχα καὶ φίλα ποιησάμενος· καὶ γὰρ συμμα-
χεῖν καὶ προσέχειν τὸν νοῦν τούτοις ἐθέλουσιν
ἅπαντες οὓς ἂν ὁρῶσι παρεσκευασμένους καὶ πράτ- 10
τειν ἐθέλοντας ἃ χρή. ἂν τοίνυν, ὦ ἄνδρες Ἀθη- 7
ναῖοι, καὶ ὑμεῖς ἐπὶ τῆς τοιαύτης ἐθελήσητε γενέσθαι
γνώμης νῦν, ἐπειδήπερ οὐ πρότερον, καὶ ἕκαστος
ὑμῶν, οὗ δεῖ καὶ δύναιτ' ἂν παρασχεῖν αὐτὸν χρήσιμον τῇ πόλει, πᾶσαν ἀφεὶς τὴν εἰρωνείαν ἕτοιμος 15
πράττειν ὑπάρξῃ, ὁ μὲν χρήματ' ἔχων εἰσφέρειν, ὁ
δ' ἐν ἡλικίᾳ στρατεύεσθαι, — συνελόντι δ' ἁπλῶς
ἢν ὑμῶν αὐτῶν ἐθελήσητε γενέσθαι καὶ παύσησθε
αὐτὸς μὲν οὐδὲν ἕκαστος ποιήσειν ἐλπίζων, τὸν δὲ
πλησίον πάνθ' ὑπὲρ αὐτοῦ πράξειν, καὶ τὰ ὑμέτερ' 20
αὐτῶν κομιεῖσθε, ἂν θεὸς θέλῃ, καὶ τὰ κατερρᾳθυμημένα πάλιν ἀναλήψεσθε, κἀκεῖνον τιμωρήσεσθε.
μὴ γὰρ ὡς θεῷ νομίζετ' ἐκείνῳ τὰ παρόντα πεπηγέ- 8
ναι πράγματα ἀθάνατα, ἀλλὰ καὶ μισεῖ τις ἐκεῖνον
καὶ δέδιεν, ὦ ἄνδρες Ἀθηναῖοι, καὶ φθονεῖ, καὶ τῶν 25
πάνυ νῦν δοκούντων οἰκείως ἔχειν· καὶ ἅπανθ' ὅσα
περ καὶ ἐν ἄλλοις τισὶν ἀνθρώποις ἔνι, ταῦτα κἂν

καὶ τοῦτ᾽ ἐξεργάσαιτο, ἴσθ᾽ ὅτι πλησίον μὲν ὄντες,
ἅπασιν ἂν τοῖς πράγμασι τεταραγμένοις ἐπιστάντες
ὅπως βούλεσθε διοικήσαισθε, ὡς δὲ νῦν ἔχετε, οὐδὲ
διδόντων τῶν καιρῶν Ἀμφίπολιν δέξασθαι δύναισθ᾽
ἄν, ἀπηρτημένοι καὶ ταῖς παρασκευαῖς καὶ ταῖς 5
γνώμαις.

Ὡς μὲν οὖν δεῖ τὰ προσήκοντα ποιεῖν ἐθέλοντας 13
ὑπάρχειν ἅπαντας ἑτοίμως, ὡς ἐγνωκότων ὑμῶν καὶ
πεπεισμένων, παύομαι λέγων· τὸν δὲ τρόπον τῆς
παρασκευῆς ἣν ἀπαλλάξαι ἂν τῶν τοιούτων πραγ- 10
μάτων ὑμᾶς οἴομαι, καὶ τὸ πλῆθος ὅσον, καὶ πόρους οὕστινας χρημάτων, καὶ τἆλλα ὡς ἄν μοι βέλτιστα καὶ τάχιστα δοκεῖ παρασκευασθῆναι, καὶ δὴ
πειράσομαι λέγειν, δεηθεὶς ὑμῶν, ὦ ἄνδρες Ἀθηναῖοι,
τοσοῦτον. ἐπειδὰν ἅπαντα ἀκούσητε, κρίνατε, μὴ 14
πρότερον προλαμβάνετε· μηδ᾽ ἂν ἐξ ἀρχῆς δοκῶ 16
τινι καινὴν παρασκευὴν λέγειν, ἀναβάλλειν με τὰ
πράγματα ἡγείσθω. οὐ γὰρ οἱ ταχὺ καὶ τήμερον
εἰπόντες μάλιστα εἰς δέον λέγουσιν (οὐ γὰρ ἂν τά
γε ἤδη γεγενημένα τῇ νυνὶ βοηθείᾳ κωλῦσαι δυνη- 20
θείημεν), ἀλλ᾽ ὃς ἂν δείξῃ τίς πορισθεῖσα παρα- 15
σκευὴ καὶ πόση καὶ πόθεν διαμεῖναι δυνήσεται ἕως
ἂν ἢ διαλυσώμεθα πεισθέντες τὸν πόλεμον ἢ περι-
γενώμεθα τῶν ἐχθρῶν· οὕτω γὰρ οὐκέτι τοῦ λοιποῦ
πάσχοιμεν ἂν κακῶς. οἶμαι τοίνυν ἐγὼ ταῦτα λέ- 25
γειν ἔχειν, μὴ κωλύων εἴ τις ἄλλος ἐπαγγέλλεταί τι.
ἡ μὲν οὖν ὑπόσχεσις οὕτω μεγάλη, τὸ δὲ πρᾶγμα
ἤδη τὸν ἔλεγχον δώσει· κριταὶ δ᾽ ὑμεῖς ἔσεσθε.

16 Πρῶτον μὲν τοίνυν, ὦ ἄνδρες Ἀθηναῖοι, τριήρεις
πεντήκοντα παρασκευάσασθαί φημι δεῖν, εἶτ᾽ αὐτοὺς
οὕτω τὰς γνώμας ἔχειν ὡς, ἐάν τι δέῃ, πλευστέον
εἰς ταύτας αὐτοῖς ἐμβᾶσιν. πρὸς δὲ τούτοις τοῖς
5 ἡμίσεσι τῶν ἱππέων ἱππαγωγοὺς τριήρεις καὶ πλοῖα
17 ἱκανὰ εὐτρεπίσαι κελεύω. ταῦτα μὲν οἶμαι δεῖν
ὑπάρχειν ἐπὶ τὰς ἐξαίφνης ταύτας ἀπὸ τῆς οἰκείας
χώρας αὐτοῦ στρατείας εἰς Πύλας καὶ Χερρόνησον
καὶ Ὄλυνθον καὶ ὅποι βούλεται· δεῖ γὰρ ἐκείνῳ
10 τοῦτο ἐν τῇ γνώμῃ παραστῆσαι, ὡς ὑμεῖς ἐκ τῆς
ἀμελείας ταύτης τῆς ἄγαν, ὥσπερ εἰς Εὔβοιαν καὶ
πρότερόν ποτέ φασιν εἰς Ἁλίαρτον καὶ τὰ τελευ-
18 ταῖα πρῴην εἰς Πύλας, ἴσως ἂν ὁρμήσαιτε. οὗτοι
παντελῶς οὐδ᾽ εἰ μὴ ποιήσαιτ᾽ ἂν τοῦτο, ὡς ἔγωγέ
15 φημι δεῖν, εὐκαταφρόνητόν ἐστιν, ἵν᾽ ἢ διὰ τὸν φόβον εἰδὼς εὐτρεπεῖς ὑμᾶς (εἴσεται γὰρ ἀκριβῶς·
εἰσὶ γάρ, εἰσὶν οἱ πάντ᾽ ἐξαγγέλλοντες ἐκείνῳ παρ᾽
ἡμῶν αὐτῶν πλείους τοῦ δέοντος) ἡσυχίαν ἔχῃ, ἢ
παριδὼν ταῦτα ἀφύλακτος ληφθῇ, μηδενὸς ὄντος
20 ἐμποδὼν πλεῖν ἐπὶ τὴν ἐκείνου χώραν ὑμῖν, ἂν ἐνδῷ
19 καιρόν. ταῦτα μέν ἐστιν ἃ πᾶσι δεδόχθαι φημὶ
δεῖν καὶ παρεσκευάσθαι προσήκειν οἶμαι· πρὸς δὲ
τούτοις δύναμίν τινα, ὦ ἄνδρες Ἀθηναῖοι, φημὶ προχειρίσασθαι δεῖν ὑμᾶς, ἣ συνεχῶς πολεμήσει καὶ
25 κακῶς ἐκεῖνον ποιήσει. μή μοι μυρίους μηδὲ δισμυ-
ρίους ξένους, μηδὲ τὰς ἐπιστολιμαίους ταύτας δυνάμεις, ἀλλ᾽ ἣ τῆς πόλεως ἔσται, κἂν ὑμεῖς ἕνα κἂν

23 Τοσαύτην μὲν, ὦ ἄνδρες Ἀθηναῖοι, διὰ ταῦτα,
ὅτι οὐκ ἔνι νῦν ἡμῖν πορίσασθαι δύναμιν τὴν ἐκείνῳ
παραταξομένην, ἀλλὰ λῃστεύειν ἀνάγκη καὶ τούτῳ τῷ
τρόπῳ τοῦ πολέμου χρῆσθαι τὴν πρώτην· οὐ τοίνυν
5 ὑπέρογκον αὐτήν (οὐ γὰρ ἔστι μισθὸς οὐδὲ τροφή)
οὐδὲ παντελῶς ταπεινὴν εἶναι δεῖ. πολίτας δὲ παρεῖναι καὶ συμπλεῖν διὰ ταῦτα κελεύω, ὅτι καὶ πρότερόν
ποτ' ἀκούω ξενικὸν τρέφειν ἐν Κορίνθῳ τὴν πόλιν,
οὗ Πολύστρατος ἡγεῖτο καὶ Ἰφικράτης καὶ Χαβρίας
10 καὶ ἄλλοι τινές, καὶ αὐτοὺς ὑμᾶς συστρατεύεσθαι·
24 καὶ οἶδα ἀκούων ὅτι Λακεδαιμονίους παραταττόμε-
νοι μεθ' ὑμῶν ἐνίκων οὗτοι οἱ ξένοι καὶ ὑμεῖς μετ'
ἐκείνων. ἐξ οὗ δ' αὐτὰ καθ' αὑτὰ τὰ ξενικὰ ὑμῖν
στρατεύεται, τοὺς φίλους νικᾷ καὶ τοὺς συμμάχους,
15 οἱ δ' ἐχθροὶ μείζους τοῦ δέοντος γεγόνασιν. καὶ
παρακύψαντα ἐπὶ τὸν τῆς πόλεως πόλεμον, πρὸς
Ἀρτάβαζον καὶ πανταχοῖ μᾶλλον οἴχεται πλέοντα,
ὁ δὲ στρατηγὸς ἀκολουθεῖ, εἰκότως· οὐ γὰρ ἔστιν
25 ἄρχειν μὴ διδόντα μισθόν. τί οὖν κελεύω; τὰς
20 προφάσεις ἀφελεῖν καὶ τοῦ στρατηγοῦ καὶ τῶν
στρατιωτῶν, μισθὸν πορίσαντας καὶ στρατιώτας
οἰκείους ὥσπερ ἐπόπτας τῶν στρατηγουμένων παρα-
καταστήσαντας, ἐπεὶ νῦν γε γέλως ἔσθ' ὡς χρώ-
μεθα τοῖς πράγμασιν. εἰ γὰρ ἔροιτό τις ὑμᾶς,
25 εἰρήνην ἄγετε, ὦ ἄνδρες Ἀθηναῖοι; μὰ Δί' οὐχ
ἡμεῖς γε, εἴποιτ' ἄν, ἀλλὰ Φιλίππῳ πολεμοῦμεν.
26 οὐκ ἐχειροτονεῖτε δὲ ἐξ ὑμῶν αὐτῶν δέκα ταξιάρχους

καὶ στρατηγοὺς καὶ φυλάρχους καὶ ἱππάρχους δύο;
τί οὖν οὗτοι ποιοῦσιν; πλὴν ἑνὸς ἀνδρός, ὃν ἂν ἐκπέμψητε ἐπὶ τὸν πόλεμον, οἱ λοιποὶ τὰς πομπὰς
πέμπουσιν ὑμῖν μετὰ τῶν ἱεροποιῶν· ὥσπερ γὰρ οἱ
πλάττοντες τοὺς πηλίνους, εἰς τὴν ἀγορὰν χειροτο- 5
νεῖτε τοὺς ταξιάρχους καὶ τοὺς φυλάρχους, οὐκ ἐπὶ
τὸν πόλεμον.   οὐ γὰρ ἐχρῆν, ὦ ἄνδρες Ἀθηναῖοι, 27
ταξιάρχους παρ' ὑμῶν, ἵππαρχον παρ' ὑμῶν, ἄρ-.
χοντας οἰκείους εἶναι, ἵν' ἦν ὡς ἀληθῶς τῆς πόλεως
ἡ δύναμις; ἀλλ' εἰς μὲν Λῆμνον τὸν παρ' ὑμῶν ἵπ- 10
παρχον δεῖ πλεῖν, τῶν δ' ὑπὲρ τῶν τῆς πόλεως
κτημάτων ἀγωνιζομένων Μενέλαον ἱππαρχεῖν; καὶ
οὐ τὸν ἄνδρα μεμφόμενος ταῦτα λέγω, ἀλλ' ὑφ'
ὑμῶν ἔδει κεχειροτονημένον εἶναι τοῦτον, ὅστις
ἂν ᾖ.   15

Ἴσως δὲ ταῦτα μὲν ὀρθῶς ἡγεῖσθε λέγεσθαι, τὸ 28
δὲ τῶν χρημάτων, πόσα καὶ πόθεν ἔσται, μάλιστα
ποθεῖτε ἀκοῦσαι. τοῦτο δὴ καὶ περαίνω. χρήματα
τοίνυν, ἔστι μὲν ἡ τροφή, σιτηρέσιον μόνον τῇ δυ-
νάμει ταύτῃ, τάλαντα ἐνενήκοντα καὶ μικρόν τι 20
πρός, δέκα μὲν ναυσὶ ταχείαις τετταράκοντα τάλαντα,
εἴκοσιν εἰς τὴν ναῦν μναῖ τοῦ μηνὸς ἑκάστου, στρα-
τιώταις δὲ δισχιλίοις τοσαῦθ' ἕτερα, ἵνα δέκα τοῦ
μηνὸς ὁ στρατιώτης δραχμὰς σιτηρέσιον λαμβάνῃ,
τοῖς δ' ἱππεῦσι διακοσίοις οὖσιν, ἐὰν τριάκοντα 25
δραχμὰς ἕκαστος λαμβάνῃ τοῦ μηνός, δώδεκα τάλαντα.   εἰ δέ τις οἴεται μικρὰν ἀφορμὴν εἶναι σιτη- 29

1*

ρέσιον τοῖς στρατευομένοις ὑπάρχειν, οὐκ ὀρθῶς
ἔγνωκεν· ἐγὼ γὰρ οἶδα σαφῶς ὅτι, τοῦτ᾽ ἂν γένηται, προσποριεῖ τὰ λοιπὰ αὐτὸ τὸ στράτευμα ἀπὸ
τοῦ πολέμου, οὐδένα τῶν Ἑλλήνων ἀδικοῦν οὐδὲ
5 τῶν συμμάχων, ὥστ᾽ ἔχειν μισθὸν ἐντελῆ. ἐγὼ
συμπλέων ἐθελοντὴς πάσχειν ὁτιοῦν ἕτοιμος, ἐὰν
μὴ ταῦθ᾽ οὕτως ἔχῃ. πόθεν οὖν ὁ πόρος τῶν χρημάτων ἃ παρ᾽ ὑμῶν κελεύω γενέσθαι; τοῦτ᾽ ἤδη
λέξω.

ΠΟΡΟΥ ΑΠΟΔΕΙΞΙΣ.

30 Ἃ μὲν ἡμεῖς, ὦ ἄνδρες Ἀθηναῖοι, δεδυνήμεθα
11 εὑρεῖν, ταῦτά ἐστιν· ἐπειδὰν δ᾽ ἐπιχειροτονῆτε τὰς
γνώμας, ἃ ἂν ὑμῖν ἀρέσκῃ χειροτονήσατε, ἵνα μὴ
μόνον ἐν τοῖς ψηφίσμασι καὶ ἐν ταῖς ἐπιστολαῖς
πολεμῆτε Φιλίππῳ, ἀλλὰ καὶ τοῖς ἔργοις.

31 Δοκεῖτε δέ μοι πολὺ βέλτιον ἂν περὶ τοῦ πολέ-
16 μου καὶ ὅλης τῆς παρασκευῆς βουλεύσασθαι, εἰ τὸν
τόπον, ὦ ἄνδρες Ἀθηναῖοι, τῆς χώρας, πρὸς ἣν πολεμεῖτε, ἐνθυμηθείητε, καὶ λογίσαισθε ὅτι τοῖς πνεύ-
μασι καὶ ταῖς ὥραις τοῦ ἔτους τὰ πολλὰ προλαμ-
20 βάνων διαπράττεται Φίλιππος καὶ φυλάξας τοὺς
ἐτησίας ἢ τὸν χειμῶνα ἐπιχειρεῖ, ἡνίκ᾽ ἂν ἡμεῖς μὴ
32 δυναίμεθα ἐκεῖσε ἀφικέσθαι. δεῖ τοίνυν ταῦτ᾽ ἐνθυμουμένους μὴ βοηθείαις πολεμεῖν (ὑστεριοῦμεν
γὰρ ἁπάντων) ἀλλὰ παρασκευῇ συνεχεῖ καὶ δυνά-
25 μει. ὑπάρχει δ᾽ ὑμῖν χειμαδίῳ μὲν χρῆσθαι τῇ

τελευταῖα εἰς Μαραθῶνα ἀπέβη καὶ τὴν ἱερὰν ἀπὸ
τῆς χώρας ᾤχετ᾽ ἔχων τριήρη, ὑμεῖς δ᾽ οὔτε ταῦτα
ἠδύνασθε κωλύειν οὔτ᾽ εἰς τοὺς χρόνους οὓς ἂν προ-
35 θῆσθε βοηθεῖν. καίτοι τί δή ποτε, ὦ ἄνδρες Ἀθη-
5 ναῖοι, νομίζετε τὴν μὲν τῶν Παναθηναίων ἑορτὴν
καὶ τὴν τῶν Διονυσίων ἀεὶ τοῦ καθήκοντος χρόνου
γίγνεσθαι, ἄν τε δεινοὶ λάχωσιν ἄν τε ἰδιῶται οἱ
τούτων ἑκατέρων ἐπιμελούμενοι, εἰς ἃ τοσαῦτ᾽ ἀνα-
λίσκεται χρήματα ὅσα οὐδ᾽ εἰς ἕνα τῶν ἀποστόλων,
10 καὶ τοσοῦτον ὄχλον καὶ παρασκευὴν ὅσην οὐκ οἶδ᾽
εἴ τι τῶν ἁπάντων ἔχει, τοὺς δ᾽ ἀποστόλους πάντας
ὑμῖν ὑστερίζειν τῶν καιρῶν, τὸν εἰς Μεθώνην, τὸν
36 εἰς Παγασάς, τὸν εἰς Ποτίδαιαν; ὅτι ἐκεῖνα μὲν
ἅπαντα νόμῳ τέτακται, καὶ πρόοιδεν ἕκαστος ὑμῶν
15 ἐκ πολλοῦ τίς χορηγὸς ἢ γυμνασίαρχος τῆς φυλῆς,
πότε καὶ παρὰ τοῦ καὶ τί λαβόντα τί δεῖ ποιεῖν,
οὐδὲν ἀνεξέταστον οὐδ᾽ ἀόριστον ἐν τούτοις ἠμέλη-
ται, ἐν δὲ τοῖς περὶ τοῦ πολέμου καὶ τῇ τούτου
παρασκευῇ ἄτακτα, ἀδιόρθωτα, ἀόριστα ἅπαντα.
20 τοιγαροῦν ἅμα ἀκηκόαμέν τι καὶ τριηράρχους καθί-
σταμεν καὶ τούτοις ἀντιδόσεις ποιούμεθα καὶ περὶ
χρημάτων πόρου σκοποῦμεν, καὶ μετὰ ταῦτα ἐμ-
βαίνειν τοὺς μετοίκους ἔδοξε καὶ τοὺς χωρὶς οἰκοῦν-
37 τας, εἶτ᾽ αὐτοὺς πάλιν ἀντεμβιβάζειν, εἶτ᾽ ἐν ὅσῳ
25 ταῦτα μέλλεται, προαπόλωλε τὸ ἐφ᾽ ὃ ἂν ἐκπλέω-
μεν· τὸν γὰρ τοῦ πράττειν χρόνον εἰς τὸ παρασκευάζεσθαι ἀναλίσκομεν, οἱ δὲ τῶν πραγμάτων

καιροὶ οὐ μένουσι τὴν ἡμετέραν βραδυτῆτα καὶ εἰρωνείαν. ἃς δὲ τὸν μεταξὺ χρόνον δυνάμεις οἰόμεθ᾽
ἡμῖν ὑπάρχειν, οὐδὲν οἷαί τε οὖσαι ποιεῖν ἐπ᾽ αὐτῶν
τῶν καιρῶν ἐξελέγχονται. ὁ δ᾽ εἰς τοῦθ᾽ ὕβρεως
ἐλήλυθεν ὥστ᾽ ἐπιστέλλειν Εὐβοεῦσιν ἤδη τοιαύτας 5
ἐπιστολάς.

ΕΠΙΣΤΟΛΑΙ.

Τούτων, ὦ ἄνδρες Ἀθηναῖοι, τῶν ἀνεγνωσμένων 38
ἀληθῆ μέν ἐστι τὰ πολλά, ὡς οὐκ ἔδει, οὐ μὴν ἀλλ᾽
ἴσως οὐχ ἡδέα ἀκούειν. ἀλλ᾽ εἰ μέν, ὅσα ἄν τις
ὑπερβῇ τῷ λόγῳ ἵνα μὴ λυπήσῃ, καὶ τὰ πράγματα 10
ὑπερβήσεται, δεῖ πρὸς ἡδονὴν δημηγορεῖν· εἰ δ᾽ ἡ
τῶν λόγων χάρις, ἂν ᾖ μὴ προσήκουσα, ἔργῳ ζημία
γίγνεται, αἰσχρόν ἐστιν, ὦ ἄνδρες Ἀθηναῖοι, φενακίζειν ἑαυτούς, καὶ ἅπαντ᾽ ἀναβαλλομένους ἃ ἂν 39
ᾖ δυσχερῆ πάντων ὑστερίζειν τῶν ἔργων, καὶ μηδὲ 15
τοῦτο δύνασθαι μαθεῖν, ὅτι δεῖ τοὺς ὀρθῶς πολέμῳ
χρωμένους οὐκ ἀκολουθεῖν τοῖς πράγμασιν ἀλλ᾽ αὐτοὺς ἔμπροσθεν εἶναι τῶν πραγμάτων, καὶ τὸν αὐτὸν
τρόπον ὥσπερ τῶν στρατευμάτων ἀξιώσειέν τις ἂν
τὸν στρατηγὸν ἡγεῖσθαι, οὕτω καὶ τῶν πραγμάτων 20
τοὺς βουλευομένους, ἵν᾽ ἃ ἂν ἐκείνοις δοκῇ, ταῦτα
πράττηται καὶ μὴ τὰ συμβάντα ἀναγκάζωνται διώ-
κειν. ὑμεῖς δέ, ὦ ἄνδρες Ἀθηναῖοι, πλείστην δύνα- 40
μιν ἁπάντων ἔχοντες, τριήρεις, ὁπλίτας, ἱππέας,
χρημάτων πρόσοδον, τούτων μὲν μέχρι τῆς τήμερον 25

ἡμέρας οὐδενὶ πώποτε εἰς δέον τι κέχρησθε, οὐδὲν
δ᾽ ἀπολείπετε, ὥσπερ οἱ βάρβαροι πυκτεύουσιν,
οὕτω πολεμεῖν Φιλίππῳ. καὶ γὰρ ἐκείνων ὁ πλη-
γεὶς ἀεὶ τῆς πληγῆς ἔχεται, κἂν ἑτέρωσε πατάξῃς,
5 ἐκεῖσέ εἰσιν αἱ χεῖρες· προβάλλεσθαι δ᾽ ἢ βλέπειν
41 ἐναντίον οὔτ᾽ οἶδεν οὔτ᾽ ἐθέλει. καὶ ὑμεῖς, ἐὰν ἐν
Χερρονήσῳ πύθησθε Φίλιππον, ἐκεῖσε βοηθεῖν ψη-
φίζεσθε, ἐὰν ἐν Πύλαις, ἐκεῖσε, ἐὰν ἄλλοθί που,
συμπαραθεῖτε ἄνω κάτω, καὶ στρατηγεῖσθε μὲν ὑπ᾽
10 ἐκείνου, βεβούλευσθε δ᾽ οὐδὲν αὐτοὶ συμφέρον περὶ
τοῦ πολέμου, οὐδὲ πρὸ τῶν πραγμάτων προορᾶτε οὐδέν, πρὶν ἂν ἢ γεγενημένον ἢ γιγνόμενόν τι πύθησθε.
ταῦτα δ᾽ ἴσως πρότερον μὲν ἐνῆν· νῦν δὲ ἐπ᾽ αὐτὴν
42 ἥκει τὴν ἀκμήν, ὥστ᾽ οὐκέτ᾽ ἐγχωρεῖ. δοκεῖ δέ μοι
15 θεῶν τις, ὦ ἄνδρες Ἀθηναῖοι, τοῖς γιγνομένοις ὑπὲρ
τῆς πόλεως αἰσχυνόμενος τὴν φιλοπραγμοσύνην ταύτην ἐμβαλεῖν Φιλίππῳ. εἰ γὰρ ἔχων ἃ κατέστραπται καὶ προείληφεν ἡσυχίαν ἔχειν ἤθελε καὶ μηδὲν
ἔπραττεν ἔτι, ἀποχρῆν ἐνίοις ὑμῶν ἂν μοι δοκεῖ, ἐξ
20 ὧν αἰσχύνην καὶ ἀνανδρίαν καὶ πάντα τὰ αἴσχιστα
ὠφληκότες ἂν ἦμεν δημοσίᾳ· νῦν δ᾽ ἐπιχειρῶν ἀεί
τινι καὶ τοῦ πλείονος ὀρεγόμενος ἴσως ἂν ἐκκαλέ-
σαιθ᾽ ὑμᾶς, εἴπερ μὴ παντάπασιν ἀπεγνώκατε.
43 θαυμάζω δ᾽ ἔγωγε εἰ μηδεὶς ὑμῶν μήτ᾽ ἐνθυμεῖται
25 μήτ᾽ ὀργίζεται, ὁρῶν, ὦ ἄνδρες Ἀθηναῖοι, τὴν μὲν
ἀρχὴν τοῦ πολέμου γεγενημένην περὶ τοῦ τιμωρήσασθαι Φίλιππον, τὴν δὲ τελευτὴν οὖσαν ἤδη ὑπὲρ

τοῦ μὴ παθεῖν κακῶς ὑπὸ Φιλίππου. ἀλλὰ μὴν
ὅτι γε οὐ στήσεται, δῆλον, εἰ μή τις κωλύσει. εἶτα
τοῦτ᾽ ἀναμενοῦμεν, καὶ τριήρεις κενὰς καὶ τὰς παρὰ
τοῦ δεῖνος ἐλπίδας ἐὰν ἀποστείλητε, πάντ᾽ ἔχειν
οἴεσθε καλῶς; οὐκ ἐμβησόμεθα; οὐκ ἔξιμεν αὐτοὶ 44
μέρει γέ τινι στρατιωτῶν οἰκείων νῦν, εἰ καὶ μὴ 6
πρότερον; οὐκ ἐπὶ τὴν ἐκείνου πλευσόμεθα; ποῖ
οὖν προσορμιούμεθα, ἤρετό τις. εὑρήσει τὰ σαθρὰ,
ὦ ἄνδρες Ἀθηναῖοι, τῶν ἐκείνου πραγμάτων αὐτὸς
ὁ πόλεμος, ἂν ἐπιχειρῶμεν· ἂν μέντοι καθώμεθα 10
οἴκοι, λοιδορουμένων ἀκούοντες καὶ αἰτιωμένων ἀλλήλους τῶν λεγόντων, οὐδέποτ᾽ οὐδὲν ἡμῖν μὴ γένηται τῶν δεόντων. ὅποι μὲν γὰρ ἄν, οἶμαι, μέρος 45
τι τῆς πόλεως συναποσταλῇ, κἂν μὴ πᾶσα, καὶ τὸ
τῶν θεῶν εὐμενὲς καὶ τὸ τῆς τύχης συναγωνίζεται· 15
ὅποι δ᾽ ἂν στρατηγὸν καὶ ψήφισμα κενὸν καὶ τὰς
ἀπὸ τοῦ βήματος ἐλπίδας ἐκπέμψητε, οὐδὲν ὑμῖν
τῶν δεόντων γίγνεται, ἀλλ᾽ οἱ μὲν ἐχθροὶ καταγελῶσιν, οἱ δὲ σύμμαχοι τεθνᾶσι τῷ δέει τοὺς τοιούτους ἀποστόλους. οὐ γὰρ ἔστιν, οὐκ ἔστιν ἕνα 46
ἄνδρα δυνηθῆναί ποτε ταῦθ᾽ ὑμῖν πρᾶξαι πάνθ᾽ 21
ὅσα βούλεσθε· ὑποσχέσθαι μέντοι καὶ φῆσαι καὶ
τὸν δεῖνα αἰτιάσασθαι καὶ τὸν δεῖνα ἔστιν. τὰ
δὲ πράγματα ἐκ τούτων ἀπόλωλεν· ὅταν γὰρ
ἡγῆται μὲν ὁ στρατηγὸς ἀθλίων ἀπομίσθων ξέ- 25
νων, οἱ δ᾽ ὑπὲρ ὧν ἂν ἐκεῖνος πράξῃ πρὸς ὑμᾶς
ψευδόμενοι ῥᾳδίως ἐνθάδ᾽ ὦσιν, ὑμεῖς δ᾽ ἐξ ὧν

γάρ εἰσιν οἱ λογοποιοῦντες. ἀλλ' ἐὰν ἀφέντες ταῦτ' 50
ἐκεῖνο εἰδῶμεν, ὅτι ἐχθρὸς ἄνθρωπος καὶ τὰ ἡμέτερα
ἡμᾶς ἀποστερεῖ καὶ χρόνον πολὺν ὕβρικε, καὶ ἅπανθ'
ὅσα πώποτ' ἠλπίσαμέν τινα πράξειν ὑπὲρ ἡμῶν
καθ' ἡμῶν εὕρηται, καὶ τὰ λοιπὰ ἐν αὐτοῖς ἡμῖν 5
ἐστί, κἂν μὴ νῦν ἐθέλωμεν ἐκεῖ πολεμεῖν αὐτῷ,
ἐνθάδ' ἴσως ἀναγκασθησόμεθα τοῦτο ποιεῖν, ἂν
ταῦτα εἰδῶμεν, καὶ τὰ δέοντα ἐσόμεθα ἐγνωκότες
καὶ λόγων ματαίων ἀπηλλαγμένοι· οὐ γὰρ ἅττα
ποτ' ἔσται δεῖ σκοπεῖν, ἀλλ' ὅτι φαῦλ', ἂν μὴ προσ- 10
έχητε τοῖς πράγμασι τὸν νοῦν καὶ τὰ προσήκοντα
ποιεῖν ἐθέλητ', εὖ εἰδέναι.

Ἐγὼ μὲν οὖν οὔτ' ἄλλοτε πώποτε πρὸς χάριν 51
εἱλόμην λέγειν, ὅ τι ἂν μὴ καὶ συνοίσειν πεπεισμένος ὦ, νῦν τε ἃ γιγνώσκω πάνθ' ἁπλῶς, οὐδὲν ὑπο- 15
στειλάμενος, πεπαρρησίασμαι. ἐβουλόμην δ' ἄν,
ὥσπερ ὅτι ὑμῖν συμφέρει τὰ βέλτιστα ἀκούειν οἶδα,
οὕτως εἰδέναι συνοίσον καὶ τῷ τὰ βέλτιστα εἰπόντι·
πολλῷ γὰρ ἂν ἥδιον εἶπον. νῦν δ' ἐπ' ἀδήλοις
οὖσι τοῖς ἀπὸ τούτων ἐμαυτῷ γενησομένοις, ὅμως 20
ἐπὶ τῷ συνοίσειν, ἐὰν πράξητε, ταῦτα πεπεῖσθαι
λέγειν αἱροῦμαι. νικῴη δ' ὅ τι πᾶσιν ὑμῖν μέλλει
συνοίσειν.

ΚΑΤΑ ΦΙΛΙΠΠΟΥ Β.

1 Ὅταν, ὦ ἄνδρες Ἀθηναῖοι, λόγοι γίγνωνται περὶ
ὧν Φίλιππος πράττει καὶ βιάζεται παρὰ τὴν εἰρήνην, ἀεὶ τοὺς ὑπὲρ ἡμῶν λόγους καὶ δικαίους καὶ
φιλανθρώπους ὁρῶ φαινομένους, καὶ λέγειν μὲν
5 ἅπαντας ἀεὶ τὰ δέοντα δοκοῦντας τοὺς κατηγο-
ροῦντας Φιλίππου, γιγνόμενον δ᾽ οὐδὲν ὡς ἔπος
εἰπεῖν τῶν δεόντων οὐδ᾽ ὧν ἕνεκα ταῦτ᾽ ἀκούειν
2 ἄξιον· ἀλλ᾽ εἰς τοῦτο ἤδη προηγμένα τυγχάνει
πάντα τὰ πράγματα τῇ πόλει ὥσθ᾽, ὅσῳ τις ἂν
10 μᾶλλον καὶ φανερώτερον ἐξελέγχῃ Φίλιππον καὶ
τὴν πρὸς ὑμᾶς εἰρήνην παραβαίνοντα καὶ πᾶσι
τοῖς Ἕλλησιν ἐπιβουλεύοντα, τοσούτῳ τὸ τί χρὴ
3 ποιεῖν συμβουλεῦσαι χαλεπώτερον. αἴτιον δὲ τούτων ὅτι πάντας, ὦ ἄνδρες Ἀθηναῖοι, τοὺς πλεονεκ-
15 τεῖν ζητοῦντας ἔργῳ κωλύειν καὶ πράξεσιν οὐχὶ
λόγοις δέον, πρῶτον μὲν ἡμεῖς οἱ παριόντες τούτων
μὲν ἀφέσταμεν, καὶ γράφειν καὶ συμβουλεύειν, τὴν
πρὸς ὑμᾶς ἀπέχθειαν ὀκνοῦντες, οἷα ποιεῖ δέ, ὡς
δεινὰ καὶ χαλεπά, ταῦτα διεξερχόμεθα· ἔπειθ᾽ ὑμεῖς
20 οἱ καθήμενοι, ὡς μὲν ἂν εἴποιτε δικαίους λόγους καὶ
λέγοντος ἄλλου συνείητε, ἄμεινον Φιλίππου παρε-
σκεύασθε, ὡς δὲ κωλύσαιτ᾽ ἂν ἐκεῖνον πράττειν

ταῦτα ἐφ᾽ ὧν ἐστὶ νῦν, παντελῶς ἀργῶς ἔχετε.
συμβαίνει δὴ πρᾶγμα ἀναγκαῖον, οἶμαι, καὶ ἴσως 4
εἰκός· ἐν οἷς ἑκάτεροι διατρίβετε καὶ περὶ ἃ σπου-
δάζετε, ταῦτ᾽ ἄμεινον ἑκατέροις ἔχει, ἐκείνῳ μὲν αἱ
πράξεις, ὑμῖν δ᾽ οἱ λόγοι. εἰ μὲν οὖν καὶ νῦν λέ- 5
γειν δικαιότερα ὑμῖν ἐξαρκεῖ, ῥᾴδιον, καὶ πόνος
οὐδεὶς πρόσεστι τῷ πράγματι· εἰ δ᾽ ὅπως τὰ 6
παρόντ᾽ ἐπανορθωθήσεται δεῖ σκοπεῖν, καὶ μὴ
προελθόντα ἔτι πορρωτέρω λήσει πάντας ἡμᾶς,
μηδ᾽ ἐπιστήσεται μέγεθος δυνάμεως πρὸς ἣν οὐδ᾽ 10
ἀντᾶραι δυνησόμεθα, οὐχ ὁ αὐτὸς τρόπος ὅσπερ
πρότερον τοῦ βουλεύεσθαι, ἀλλὰ καὶ τοῖς λέγουσιν
ἅπασι καὶ τοῖς ἀκούουσιν ὑμῖν τὰ βέλτιστα καὶ τὰ
σώσοντα τῶν ῥᾴστων καὶ τῶν ἡδίστων προαιρετέον.

Πρῶτον μέν, εἴ τις, ὦ ἄνδρες Ἀθηναῖοι, θαρρεῖ 6
ὁρῶν ἡλίκος ἤδη καὶ ὅσων κύριός ἐστι Φίλιππος, 16
καὶ μηδένα οἴεται κίνδυνον φέρειν τοῦτο τῇ πόλει
μηδ᾽ ἐφ᾽ ὑμᾶς πάντα παρασκευάζεσθαι, θαυμάζω,
καὶ δεηθῆναι πάντων ὁμοίως ὑμῶν βούλομαι τοὺς
λογισμοὺς ἀκοῦσαί μου διὰ βραχέων, δι᾽ οὓς τά- 20
ναντία ἐμοὶ παρέστηκε προσδοκᾶν καὶ δι᾽ ὧν ἐχθρὸν
ἡγοῦμαι Φίλιππον, ἵν᾽ ἐὰν μὲν ἐγὼ δοκῶ βέλτιον
προορᾶν, ἐμοὶ πεισθῆτε, ἐὰν δ᾽ οἱ θαρροῦντες καὶ
πεπιστευκότες αὐτῷ, τούτοις προσθήσεσθε. ἐγὼ 7
τοίνυν, ὦ ἄνδρες Ἀθηναῖοι, λογίζομαι, τίνων ὁ Φί- 25
λιππος κύριος πρῶτον μετὰ τὴν εἰρήνην κατέστη;
Πυλῶν καὶ τῶν ἐν Φωκεῦσι πραγμάτων. τί οὖν;

ἀλλὰ καὶ τὰ πρὸ τούτων λογιζόμενος. εὑρίσκει 11
γάρ, οἶμαι, καὶ ἀκούει τοὺς μὲν ὑμετέρους προγό-
νους, ἐξὸν αὐτοῖς τῶν λοιπῶν ἄρχειν Ἑλλήνων ὥστ᾽
αὐτοὺς ὑπακούειν βασιλεῖ, οὐ μόνον οὐκ ἀνασχομέ-
νους τὸν λόγον τοῦτον, ἡνίκ᾽ ἦλθεν Ἀλέξανδρος ὁ 5
τούτων πρόγονος περὶ τούτων κῆρυξ, ἀλλὰ καὶ τὴν
χώραν ἐκλιπεῖν προελομένους καὶ παθεῖν ὁτιοῦν
ὑπομείναντας, καὶ μετὰ ταῦτα πράξαντας ταῦθ᾽ ἃ
πάντες μὲν ἀεὶ γλίχονται λέγειν, ἀξίως δ᾽ οὐδεὶς
εἰπεῖν δεδύνηται, διόπερ κἀγὼ παραλείψω δικαίως 10
(ἔστι γὰρ μείζω τἀκείνων ἔργα ἢ ὡς τῷ λόγῳ τις
ἂν εἴποι), τοὺς δὲ Θηβαίων καὶ Ἀργείων προγό-
νους τοὺς μὲν συστρατεύσαντας τῷ βαρβάρῳ, τοὺς
δ᾽ οὐκ ἐναντιωθέντας. οἶδεν οὖν ἀμφοτέρους ἰδίᾳ 12
τὸ λυσιτελοῦν ἀγαπήσοντας, οὐχ ὅ τι συνοίσει 15
κοινῇ τοῖς Ἕλλησι σκεψομένους. ἡγεῖτ᾽ οὖν, εἰ
μὲν ὑμᾶς ἕλοιτο φίλους, ἐπὶ τοῖς δικαίοις αἱρή-
σεσθαι, εἰ δ᾽ ἐκείνοις προσθεῖτο, συνεργοὺς ἕξειν
τῆς αὑτοῦ πλεονεξίας. διὰ ταῦτ᾽ ἐκείνους ἀνθ᾽ ὑμῶν
καὶ τότε καὶ νῦν αἱρεῖται. οὐ γὰρ δὴ τριήρεις γε 20
ὁρᾷ πλείους αὐτοῖς ἢ ὑμῖν οὔσας· οὐδ᾽ ἐν μὲν τῇ
μεσογείᾳ τιν᾽ ἀρχὴν εὕρηκε, τῆς δ᾽ ἐπὶ τῇ θαλάττῃ
καὶ τῶν ἐμπορίων ἀφέστηκεν· οὐδ᾽ ἀμνημονεῖ τοὺς
λόγους οὐδὲ τὰς ὑποσχέσεις ἐφ᾽ αἷς τῆς εἰρήνης
ἔτυχεν. 25

Ἀλλὰ νὴ Δί᾽ εἴποι τις ἂν ὡς πάντα ταῦτ᾽ εἰδὼς 13
οὐ πλεονεξίας ἕνεκεν οὐδ᾽ ὧν ἐγὼ κατηγορῶ τότε

ταῦτ᾽ ἔπραξεν, ἀλλὰ τῷ δικαιότερα τοὺς Θηβαίους
ἢ ὑμᾶς ἀξιοῦν. ἀλλὰ τοῦτον καὶ μόνον πάντων
τῶν λόγων οὐκ ἔνεστ᾽ αὐτῷ νῦν εἰπεῖν· ὁ γὰρ Μεσ-
σήνην Λακεδαιμονίους ἀφιέναι κελεύων πῶς ἂν
5 Ὀρχομενὸν καὶ Κορώνειαν τότε Θηβαίοις παρα-
δοὺς τῷ δίκαια νομίζειν ταῦτ᾽ εἶναι πεποιηκέναι
σκήψαιτο;

14 Ἀλλ᾽ ἐβιάσθη νὴ Δία (τοῦτο γάρ ἐσθ᾽ ὑπόλοιπον) καὶ παρὰ γνώμην, τῶν Θετταλῶν ἱππέων καὶ
10 τῶν Θηβαίων ὁπλιτῶν ἐν μέσῳ ληφθείς, συνεχώρησε ταῦτα. καλῶς. οὐκοῦν φασὶ μὲν μέλλειν
πρὸς τοὺς Θηβαίους αὐτὸν ὑπόπτως ἔχειν, καὶ λο-
γοποιοῦσι περιιόντες τινὲς ὡς Ἐλάτειαν τειχιεῖ·
15 ὁ δὲ ταῦτα μὲν μέλλει καὶ μελλήσει, ὡς ἐγὼ κρίνω,
15 τοῖς Μεσσηνίοις δὲ καὶ τοῖς Ἀργείοις ἐπὶ τοὺς
Λακεδαιμονίους συμβάλλειν οὐ μέλλει, ἀλλὰ καὶ
ξένους εἰσπέμπει καὶ χρήματ᾽ ἀποστέλλει καὶ δύναμιν μεγάλην ἔχων αὐτός ἐστι προσδόκιμος. τοὺς
μὲν ὄντας ἐχθροὺς Θηβαίων Λακεδαιμονίους ἀναι-
20 ρεῖ, οὓς δ᾽ ἀπώλεσεν αὐτὸς πρότερον Φωκέας νῦν
16 σώζει; καὶ τίς ἂν ταῦτα πιστεύσειεν; ἐγὼ μὲν
γὰρ οὐκ ἂν ἡγοῦμαι Φίλιππον, οὔτ᾽ εἰ τὰ πρῶτα
βιασθεὶς ἄκων ἔπραξεν οὔτ᾽ ἂν εἰ νῦν ἀπεγίγνωσκε
Θηβαίους, τοῖς ἐκείνων ἐχθροῖς συνεχῶς ἐναντιοῦ-
25 σθαι, ἀλλ᾽ ἀφ᾽ ὧν νῦν ποιεῖ, κἀκεῖνα ἐκ προαι-
ρέσεως δῆλός ἐστι ποιήσας. ἐκ πάντων δ᾽, ἄν
τις ὀρθῶς θεωρῇ, πάντα πραγματεύεται κατὰ τῆς

ἐδίδου τοὺς Ἀθηναίων ἀποίκους ἐκβαλών, καὶ τὴν
μὲν ἔχθραν τὴν πρὸς ἡμᾶς αὐτὸς ἀνήρητο, τὴν χώραν δ᾽ ἐκείνοις ἐδεδώκει καρποῦσθαι; ἆρα προσδοκᾶν αὐτοὺς τοιαῦτα πείσεσθαι, ἢ λέγοντος ἄν τινος
21 πιστεῦσαι οἴεσθε; ἀλλ᾽ ὅμως, ἔφην ἐγώ, μικρὸν
6 χρόνον τὴν ἀλλοτρίαν καρπωσάμενοι πολὺν τῆς
ἑαυτῶν ὑπ᾽ ἐκείνου στέρονται, αἰσχρῶς ἐκπεσόντες,
οὐ κρατηθέντες μόνον ἀλλὰ καὶ προδοθέντες ὑπ᾽
ἀλλήλων καὶ πραθέντες· οὐ γὰρ ἀσφαλεῖς ταῖς
10 πολιτείαις αἱ πρὸς τοὺς τυράννους αὗται λίαν ὁμι-
22 λίαι. τί δ᾽ οἱ Θετταλοί; ἆρ᾽ οἴεσθ᾽, ἔφην, ὅτ᾽
αὐτοῖς τοὺς τυράννους ἐξέβαλλε καὶ πάλιν Νίκαιαν
καὶ Μαγνησίαν ἐδίδου, προσδοκᾶν τὴν καθεστῶσαν
νῦν δεκαδαρχίαν ἔσεσθαι παρ᾽ αὐτοῖς, ἢ τὸν τὴν
15 πυλαίαν ἀποδόντα τοῦτον τὰς ἰδίας αὐτῶν προσό-
δους παραιρήσεσθαι; οὐκ ἔστι ταῦτα. ἀλλὰ μὴν
23 γέγονε ταῦτα καὶ πᾶσιν ἔστιν εἰδέναι. ὑμεῖς δ᾽,
ἔφην ἐγώ, διδόντα μὲν καὶ ὑπισχνούμενον θεωρεῖτε
Φίλιππον, ἐξηπατηκότα δ᾽ ἤδη καὶ παρακεκρουμέ-
20 νον ἀπεύχεσθε, εἰ σωφρονεῖτε δή, ἰδεῖν. ἔστι τοίνυν
νὴ Δί᾽, ἔφην ἐγώ, παντοδαπὰ εὑρημένα ταῖς πόλεσι
πρὸς φυλακὴν καὶ σωτηρίαν, οἷον χαρακώματα καὶ
24 τείχη καὶ τάφροι καὶ τἆλλα ὅσα τοιαῦτα. καὶ
ταῦτα μέν ἐστιν ἅπαντα χειροποίητα, καὶ δαπάνης
25 προσδεῖται· ἐν δέ τι κοινὸν ἡ φύσις τῶν εὖ φρο-
νούντων ἐν ἑαυτῇ κέκτηται φυλακτήριον, ὃ πᾶσι
μέν ἐστιν ἀγαθὸν καὶ σωτήριον, μάλιστα δὲ τοῖς

πλήθεσι πρὸς τοὺς τυράννους. τί οὖν ἐστὶ τοῦτο;
ἀπιστία. ταύτην φυλάττετε, ταύτης ἀντέχεσθε·
ἐὰν ταύτην σώζητε, οὐδὲν μὴ δεινὸν πάθητε. τί 25
ζητεῖτε; ἔφην. ἐλευθερίαν. εἶτ᾽ οὐχ ὁρᾶτε Φίλιππον ἀλλοτριωτάτας ταύτῃ καὶ τὰς προσηγορίας 5
ἔχοντα; βασιλεὺς γὰρ καὶ τύραννος ἅπας ἐχθρὸς
ἐλευθερίᾳ καὶ νόμοις ἐναντίος. οὐ φυλάξεσθ᾽ ὅπως,
ἔφην, μὴ πολέμου ζητοῦντες ἀπαλλαγῆναι δεσπότην εὕρητε;

Ταῦτ᾽ ἀκούσαντες ἐκεῖνοι, καὶ θορυβοῦντες ὡς 26
ὀρθῶς λέγεται, καὶ πολλοὺς ἑτέρους λόγους παρὰ 11
τῶν πρέσβεων καὶ παρόντος ἐμοῦ καὶ πάλιν ὕστερον ἀκούσαντες, ὡς ἔοικεν, οὐδὲν μᾶλλον ἀποσχή-
σονται τῆς Φιλίππου φιλίας οὐδ᾽ ὧν ἐπαγγέλλεται.
καὶ οὐ τοῦτό ἐστιν ἄτοπον, εἰ Μεσσήνιοι καὶ Πε- 15
λοποννησίων τινὲς παρ᾽ ἃ τῷ λογισμῷ βέλτισθ᾽
ὁρῶσί τι πράξουσιν· ἀλλ᾽ ὑμεῖς οἱ καὶ συνιέντες 27
αὐτοὶ καὶ τῶν λεγόντων ἀκούοντες ἡμῶν ὡς ἐπι-
βουλεύεσθε, ὡς περιστοιχίζεσθε, ἐκ τοῦ μηδὲν ἤδη
ποιῆσαι λήσεθ᾽, ὡς ἐμοὶ δοκεῖ, πάντα ὑπομείναν- 20
τες· οὕτως ἡ παραυτίχ᾽ ἡδονὴ καὶ ῥᾳστώνη μεῖζον
ἰσχύει τοῦ ποθ᾽ ὕστερον συνοίσειν μέλλοντος.

Περὶ μὲν δὴ τῶν ὑμῖν πρακτέων καθ᾽ ὑμᾶς αὐ- 28
τοὺς ὕστερον βουλεύεσθε, ἂν σωφρονῆτε· ἃ δὲ
νῦν ἀποκρινάμενοι τὰ δέοντ᾽ ἂν εἴητ᾽ ἐψηφισμένοι, 25
ταῦτ᾽ ἤδη λέξω. ἦν μὲν οὖν δίκαιον, ὦ ἄνδρες
Ἀθηναῖοι, τοὺς ἐνεγκόντας τὰς ὑποσχέσεις, ἐφ᾽ αἷς

29 ἐπείσθητε ποιήσασθαι τὴν εἰρήνην, καλεῖν· οὔτε
γὰρ αὐτὸς ἄν ποτε ὑπέμεινα πρεσβεύειν, οὔτ᾽ ἄν
ὑμεῖς οἶδ᾽ ὅτι ἐπαύσασθε πολεμοῦντες, εἰ τοιαῦτα
πράξειν τυχόντα εἰρήνης Φίλιππον ᾤεσθε· ἀλλ᾽ ἦν
5 πολὺ τούτων ἀφεστηκότα τὰ τότε λεγόμενα. καὶ
πάλιν γ᾽ ἑτέρους καλεῖν. τίνας; τοὺς ὅτ᾽ ἐγὼ
γεγονυίας ἤδη τῆς εἰρήνης ἀπὸ τῆς ὑστέρας ἥκων
πρεσβείας τῆς ἐπὶ τοὺς ὅρκους, αἰσθόμενος φενακι-
ζομένην τὴν πόλιν, προύλεγον καὶ διεμαρτυρόμην
30 καὶ οὐκ εἴων προέσθαι Πύλας οὐδὲ Φωκέας, λέ-
11 γοντας ὡς ἐγὼ μὲν ὕδωρ πίνων εἰκότως δύστροπος
καὶ δύσκολός εἰμί τις ἄνθρωπος, Φίλιππος δ᾽, ἅπερ
εὔξαισθ᾽ ἂν ὑμεῖς, ἐὰν παρέλθῃ, πράξει, καὶ Θεσπιὰς
μὲν καὶ Πλαταιὰς τειχιεῖ, Θηβαίους δὲ παύσει τῆς
15 ὕβρεως, Χερρόνησον δὲ τοῖς αὑτοῦ τέλεσι διορύξει,
Εὔβοιαν δὲ καὶ τὸν Ὠρωπὸν ἀντ᾽ Ἀμφιπόλεως
ὑμῖν ἀποδώσει· ταῦτα γὰρ ἅπαντα ἐπὶ τοῦ βήματος ἐνταῦθα μνημονεύετ᾽ οἶδ᾽ ὅτι ῥηθέντα, καίπερ
31 ὄντες οὐ δεινοὶ τοὺς ἀδικοῦντας μεμνῆσθαι. καὶ τὸ
20 πάντων αἴσχιστον, καὶ τοῖς ἐκγόνοις πρὸς τὰς ἐλπίδας τὴν αὐτὴν εἰρήνην εἶναι ταύτην ἐψηφίσασθε·
οὕτω τελέως ὑπήχθητε. τί δὴ ταῦτα νῦν λέγω καὶ
καλεῖν φημι δεῖν τούτους; ἐγὼ νὴ τοὺς θεοὺς τά-
ληθῆ μετὰ παῤῥησίας ἐρῶ πρὸς ὑμᾶς καὶ οὐκ ἀπο-
32 κρύψομαι. οὐχ ἵν᾽ εἰς λοιδορίαν ἐμπεσὼν ἐμαυτῷ
26 μὲν ἐξ ἴσου λόγον παρ᾽ ὑμῖν ποιήσω, τοῖς δ᾽ ἐμοὶ
προσκρούσασιν ἐξ ἀρχῆς καινὴν παράσχω πρόφα-

σιν τοῦ πάλιν τι λαβεῖν παρὰ Φιλίππου, οὐδ' ἵνα
ὡς ἄλλως ἀδολεσχῶ. ἀλλ' οἶμαί ποθ' ὑμᾶς λυπή-
σειν ἃ Φίλιππος πράττει, μᾶλλον ἢ τὰ νυνί· τὸ 33
γὰρ πρᾶγμα ὁρῶ προβαῖνον, καὶ οὐχὶ βουλοίμην
μὲν ἂν εἰκάζειν ὀρθῶς, φοβοῦμαι δὲ μὴ λίαν ἐγγὺς 5
ᾖ τοῦτ' ἤδη. ὅταν οὖν μηκέθ' ὑμῖν ἀμελεῖν ἐξου-
σία γίγνηται τῶν συμβαινόντων, μηδ' ἀκούηθ' ὅτι
ταῦτ' ἐφ' ὑμᾶς ἐστιν ἐμοῦ μηδὲ τοῦ δεῖνος, ἀλλ'
αὐτοὶ πάντες ὁρᾶτε καὶ εὖ εἰδῆτε, ὀργίλους καὶ τρα-
χεῖς ὑμᾶς ἔσεσθαι νομίζω. φοβοῦμαι δὴ μὴ τῶν 34
πρέσβεων σεσιωπηκότων ἐφ' οἷς αὐτοῖς συνίσασι 11
δεδωροδοκηκόσι, τοῖς ἐπανορθοῦν τι πειρωμένοις τῶν
διὰ τούτους ἀπολωλότων τῇ παρ' ὑμῶν ὀργῇ περι-
πεσεῖν συμβῇ· ὁρῶ γὰρ ὡς τὰ πολλὰ ἐνίους οὐκ
εἰς τοὺς αἰτίους ἀλλ' εἰς τοὺς ὑπὸ χεῖρα μάλιστα 15
τὴν ὀργὴν ἀφιέντας. ἕως οὖν ἔτι μέλλει καὶ συνί- 35
σταται τὰ πράγματα καὶ κατακούομεν ἀλλήλων,
ἕκαστον ὑμῶν, καίπερ ἀκριβῶς εἰδότα, ὅμως ἐπα-
ναμνῆσαι βούλομαι τίς ὁ Φωκέας πείσας καὶ Πύλας
ὑμᾶς προέσθαι, ὧν καταστὰς ἐκεῖνος κύριος τῆς ἐπὶ 20
τὴν Ἀττικὴν ὁδοῦ καὶ τῆς εἰς Πελοπόννησον κύριος
γέγονε, καὶ πεποίηχ' ὑμῖν μὴ περὶ τῶν δικαίων
μηδ' ὑπὲρ τῶν ἔξω πραγμάτων εἶναι τὴν βουλήν,
ἀλλ' ὑπὲρ τῶν ἐν τῇ χώρᾳ καὶ τοῦ πρὸς τὴν Ἀττικὴν πολέμου, ὃς λυπήσει μὲν ἕκαστον ἐπειδὰν παρῇ, 25
γέγονε δ' ἐν ἐκείνῃ τῇ ἡμέρᾳ. εἰ γὰρ μὴ παρε- 36
κρούσθητε τόθ' ὑμεῖς, οὐδὲν ἂν ἦν τῇ πόλει πρᾶγμα·

ΚΑΤΑ ΦΙΛΙΠΠΟΥ Γ.

Πολλῶν, ὦ ἄνδρες Ἀθηναῖοι, λόγων γιγνομένων 1
ὀλίγου δεῖν καθ᾽ ἑκάστην ἐκκλησίαν περὶ ὧν Φίλιππος, ἀφ᾽ οὗ τὴν εἰρήνην ἐποιήσατο, οὐ μόνον
ὑμᾶς ἀλλὰ καὶ τοὺς ἄλλους ἀδικεῖ, καὶ πάντων οἶδ᾽
ὅτι φησάντων γ᾽ ἄν, εἰ καὶ μὴ ποιοῦσι τοῦτο, καὶ 5
λέγειν δεῖν καὶ πράττειν ὅπως ἐκεῖνος παύσεται τῆς
ὕβρεως καὶ δίκην δώσει, εἰς τοῦθ᾽ ὑπηγμένα πάντα
τὰ πράγματα καὶ προειμένα ὁρῶ ὥστε δέδοικα μὴ
βλάσφημον μὲν εἰπεῖν ἀληθὲς δ᾽ ᾖ· εἰ καὶ λέγειν
ἅπαντες ἐβούλοντο οἱ παριόντες καὶ χειροτονεῖν 10
ὑμεῖς ἐξ ὧν ὡς φαυλότατ᾽ ἔμελλε τὰ πράγμαθ᾽
ἕξειν, οὐκ ἂν ἡγοῦμαι δύνασθαι χεῖρον ἢ νῦν διατεθῆναι. πολλὰ μὲν οὖν ἴσως ἐστὶν αἴτια τούτων, 2
καὶ οὐ παρ᾽ ἓν οὐδὲ δύο εἰς τοῦτο τὰ πράγματα
ἀφῖκται, μάλιστα δ᾽, ἄνπερ ἐξετάζητε ὀρθῶς, εὑρή- 15
σετε διὰ τοὺς χαρίζεσθαι μᾶλλον ἢ τὰ βέλτιστα
λέγειν προαιρουμένους, ὧν τινὲς μέν, ὦ ἄνδρες
Ἀθηναῖοι, ἐν οἷς εὐδοκιμοῦσιν αὐτοὶ καὶ δύνανται,
ταῦτα φυλάττοντες οὐδεμίαν περὶ τῶν μελλόντων
πρόνοιαν ἔχουσιν, ἕτεροι δὲ τοὺς ἐπὶ τοῖς πράγμα- 20
σιν ὄντας αἰτιώμενοι καὶ διαβάλλοντες οὐδὲν ἄλλο
ποιοῦσιν ἢ ὅπως ἡ μὲν πόλις αὐτὴ παρ᾽ αὑτῆς δίκην

λήψεται καὶ περὶ τοῦτ᾽ ἔσται, Φιλίππῳ δ᾽ ἐξέσται
3 καὶ λέγειν καὶ πράττειν ὅ τι βούλεται. αἱ δὲ
τοιαῦται πολιτεῖαι συνήθεις μέν εἰσιν ὑμῖν, αἴτιαι
δὲ τῶν κακῶν. ἀξιῶ δ᾽, ὦ ἄνδρες Ἀθηναῖοι, ἐάν
5 τι τῶν ἀληθῶν μετὰ παρρησίας λέγω, μηδεμίαν μοι
διὰ τοῦτο παρ᾽ ὑμῶν ὀργὴν γενέσθαι. σκοπεῖτε
γὰρ ὡδί. ὑμεῖς τὴν παρρησίαν ἐπὶ μὲν τῶν ἄλλων
οὕτω κοινὴν οἴεσθε δεῖν εἶναι πᾶσι τοῖς ἐν τῇ πόλει
ὥστε καὶ τρὶς ξένοις καὶ τοῖς δούλοις αὐτῆς μετα-
10 δεδώκατε, καὶ πολλοὺς ἄν τις οἰκέτας ἴδοι παρ᾽ ὑμῖν
μετὰ πλείονος ἐξουσίας ὅ τι βούλονται λέγοντας ἢ
πολίτας ἐν ἐνίαις τῶν ἄλλων πόλεων, ἐκ δὲ τοῦ
4 συμβουλεύειν παντάπασιν ἐξεληλάκατε. εἶθ᾽ ὑμῖν
συμβέβηκεν ἐκ τούτου ἐν μὲν ταῖς ἐκκλησίαις τρυ-
15 φᾶν καὶ κολακεύεσθαι πάντα πρὸς ἡδονὴν ἀκούουσιν, ἐν δὲ τοῖς πράγμασι καὶ τοῖς γιγνομένοις περὶ
τῶν ἐσχάτων ἤδη κινδυνεύειν. εἰ μὲν οὖν καὶ νῦν
οὕτω διάκεισθε, οὐκ ἔχω τι λέγω· εἰ δ᾽ ἃ συμφέρει
χωρὶς κολακείας ἐθελήσετε ἀκούειν, ἕτοιμος λέγειν.
20 καὶ γὰρ εἰ πάνυ φαύλως τὰ πράγματα ἔχει καὶ
πολλὰ προεῖται, ὅμως ἔστιν, ἐὰν ὑμεῖς τὰ δέοντα
ποιεῖν βούλησθ᾽, ἔτι πάντα ταῦτα ἐπανορθώσα-
5 σθαι. καὶ παράδοξον μὲν ἴσως ἐστὶν ὃ μέλλω
λέγειν, ἀληθὲς δέ· τὸ χείριστον ἐν τοῖς παρεληλυ-
25 θόσι, τοῦτο πρὸς τὰ μέλλοντα βέλτιστον ὑπάρχει.
τί οὖν ἐστι τοῦτο; ὅτι οὔτε μικρὸν οὔτε μέγα οὐδὲν
τῶν δεόντων ποιούντων ὑμῶν κακῶς τὰ πράγματα

ἔχει, ἐπεί τοι, εἰ πάνθ᾽ ἃ προσῆκε πραττόντων οὕτω
διέκειτο, οὐδ᾽ ἂν ἐλπὶς ἦν αὐτὰ γενέσθαι βελτίω.
νῦν δὲ τῆς μὲν ῥᾳθυμίας τῆς ὑμετέρας καὶ τῆς ἀμελείας κεκράτηκε Φίλιππος, τῆς πόλεως δ᾽ οὐ κεκρά-
τηκεν· οὐδ᾽ ἥττησθε ὑμεῖς, ἀλλ᾽ οὐδὲ κεκίνησθε.   5

Εἰ μὲν οὖν ἅπαντες ὡμολογοῦμεν Φίλιππον τῇ 6
πόλει πολεμεῖν καὶ τὴν εἰρήνην παραβαίνειν, οὐδὲν
ἄλλο ἔδει τὸν παριόντα λέγειν καὶ συμβουλεύειν ἢ
ὅπως ἀσφαλέστατα καὶ ῥᾷστα αὐτὸν ἀμυνούμεθα·
ἐπειδὴ δὲ οὕτως ἀτόπως ἔνιοι διάκεινται ὥστε πό- 10
λεις καταλαμβάνοντος ἐκείνου καὶ πολλὰ τῶν ὑμετέρων ἔχοντος καὶ πάντας ἀνθρώπους ἀδικοῦντος
ἀνέχεσθαι τινῶν ἐν ταῖς ἐκκλησίαις λεγόντων πολλάκις ὡς ἡμῶν τινές εἰσιν οἱ ποιοῦντες τὸν πόλεμον, ἀνάγκη φυλάττεσθαι καὶ διορθοῦσθαι περὶ 15
τούτου· ἔστι γὰρ δέος μή ποθ᾽ ὡς ἀμυνούμεθα 7
γράψας τις καὶ συμβουλεύσας εἰς τὴν αἰτίαν ἐμ-
πέσῃ τοῦ πεποιηκέναι τὸν πόλεμον. ἐγὼ δὴ τοῦτο
πρῶτον ἁπάντων λέγω καὶ διορίζομαι, εἰ ἐφ᾽ ἡμῖν
ἐστι τὸ βουλεύεσθαι περὶ τοῦ πότερον εἰρήνην ἄγειν 20
ἢ πολεμεῖν δεῖ. εἰ μὲν οὖν ἔξεστιν εἰρήνην ἄγειν 8
τῇ πόλει καὶ ἐφ᾽ ἡμῖν ἐστι τοῦτο, ἵν᾽ ἐντεῦθεν ἄρξω-
μαι, φημὶ ἔγωγε ἄγειν ἡμᾶς δεῖν, καὶ τὸν ταῦτα
λέγοντα γράφειν καὶ πράττειν καὶ μὴ φενακίζειν
ἀξιῶ· εἰ δ᾽ ἕτερος τὰ ὅπλα ἐν ταῖς χερσὶν ἔχων 25
καὶ δύναμιν πολλὴν περὶ αὑτὸν τοὔνομα μὲν τὸ τῆς
εἰρήνης ὑμῖν προβάλλει, τοῖς δ᾽ ἔργοις αὐτὸς τοῖς

τοῦ πολέμου χρῆται, τί λοιπὸν ἄλλο πλὴν ἀμύνεσθαι; φάσκειν δὲ εἰρήνην ἄγειν εἰ βούλεσθε, ὥσπερ
9 ἐκεῖνος, οὐ διαφέρομαι. εἰ δέ τις ταύτην εἰρήνην
ὑπολαμβάνει ἐξ ἧς ἐκεῖνος πάντα τἄλλα λαβὼν ἐφ'
5 ἡμᾶς ἥξει, πρῶτον μὲν μαίνεται, ἔπειτα ἐκείνῳ παρ'
ὑμῶν, οὐχ ὑμῖν παρ' ἐκείνου τὴν εἰρήνην λέγει·
τοῦτο δ' ἐστὶν ὃ τῶν ἀναλισκομένων χρημάτων
πάντων Φίλιππος ὠνεῖται, αὐτὸς μὲν πολεμεῖν ὑμῖν,
ὑφ' ὑμῶν δὲ μὴ πολεμεῖσθαι.

10 Καὶ μὴν εἰ μέχρι τούτου περιμενοῦμεν, ἕως ἂν
11 ἡμῖν ὁμολογήσῃ πολεμεῖν, πάντων ἐσμὲν εὐηθέστα-
τοι· οὐδὲ γὰρ ἂν ἐπὶ τὴν Ἀττικὴν αὐτὴν βαδίζῃ
καὶ τὸν Πειραιᾶ, τοῦτ' ἐρεῖ, εἴπερ οἷς πρὸς τοὺς
11 ἄλλους πεποίηκε δεῖ τεκμαίρεσθαι. τοῦτο μὲν γὰρ
15 Ὀλυνθίοις τετταράκοντ' ἀπέχων τῆς πόλεως στάδια
εἶπεν ὅτι δεῖ δυοῖν θάτερον, ἢ 'κείνους ἐν Ὀλύνθῳ
μὴ οἰκεῖν ἢ αὐτὸν ἐν Μακεδονίᾳ, πάντα τὸν ἄλλον
χρόνον, εἴ τις αὐτὸν αἰτιάσαιτό τι τοιοῦτον, ἀγα-
νακτῶν καὶ πρέσβεις πέμπων τοὺς ἀπολογησομέ-
20 νους· τοῦτο δ' εἰς Φωκέας ὡς πρὸς συμμάχους
ἐπορεύετο, καὶ πρέσβεις Φωκέων ἦσαν οἳ παρηκο-
λούθουν αὐτῷ πορευομένῳ, καὶ παρ' ἡμῖν ἤριζον
πολλοὶ Θηβαίοις οὐ λυσιτελήσειν τὴν ἐκείνου πάρ-
12 οδον. καὶ μὴν καὶ Φερὰς πρῴην ὡς φίλος καὶ
25 σύμμαχος εἰς Θετταλίαν ἐλθὼν ἔχει καταλαβών,
καὶ τὰ τελευταῖα τοῖς ταλαιπώροις Ὠρείταις τουτ-
οισὶ ἐπισκεψομένους ἔφη τοὺς στρατιώτας πεπομ-

φέναι κατ᾽ εὔνοιαν· πυνθάνεσθαι γὰρ αὐτοὺς ὡς
νοσοῦσι καὶ στασιάζουσι, συμμάχων δ᾽ εἶναι καὶ
φίλων ἀληθινῶν ἐν τοῖς τοιούτοις καιροῖς παρεῖναι.
εἶτ᾽ οἴεσθ᾽ αὐτόν, οἳ ἐποίησαν μὲν οὐδὲν ἂν κακόν, 13
μὴ παθεῖν δ᾽ ἐφυλάξαντ᾽ ἂν ἴσως, τούτους μὲν ἐξα- 5
πατᾶν αἱρεῖσθαι μᾶλλον ἢ προλέγοντα βιάζεσθαι,
ὑμῖν δ᾽ ἐκ προρρήσεως πολεμήσειν, καὶ ταῦθ᾽ ἕως
ἂν ἑκόντες ἐξαπατᾶσθε; οὐκ ἔστι ταῦτα· καὶ γὰρ 14
ἂν ἀβελτερώτατος εἴη πάντων ἀνθρώπων, εἰ τῶν
ἀδικουμένων ὑμῶν μηδὲν ἐγκαλούντων αὐτῷ, ἀλλ᾽ 10
ὑμῶν αὐτῶν τινὰς αἰτιωμένων, ἐκεῖνος ἐκλύσας τὴν
πρὸς ἀλλήλους ἔριν ὑμῶν καὶ φιλονεικίαν ἐφ᾽ ἑαυ-
τὸν προείποι τρέπεσθαι, καὶ τῶν παρ᾽ ἑαυτοῦ μισθο-
φορούντων τοὺς λόγους ἀφέλοιτο, οἷς ἀναβάλλουσιν
ὑμᾶς, λέγοντες ὡς ἐκεῖνός γε οὐ πολεμεῖ τῇ πόλει. 15

᾽Αλλ᾽ ἔστιν, ὦ πρὸς τοῦ Διός, ὅστις εὖ φρονῶν 15
ἐκ τῶν ὀνομάτων μᾶλλον ἢ τῶν πραγμάτων τὸν
ἄγοντ᾽ εἰρήνην ἢ πολεμοῦνθ᾽ ἑαυτῷ σκέψαιτ᾽ ἄν;
οὐδεὶς δήπου. ὁ τοίνυν Φίλιππος ἐξ ἀρχῆς, ἄρτι
τῆς εἰρήνης γεγονυίας, οὔπω Διοπείθους στρατη- 20
γοῦντος οὐδὲ τῶν ὄντων ἐν Χερρονήσῳ νῦν ἀπεσταλ-
μένων, Σέρριον καὶ Δορίσκον κατελάμβανε καὶ τοὺς
ἐκ Σερρίου τείχους καὶ Ἱεροῦ ὄρους στρατιώτας
ἐξέβαλλεν, οὓς ὁ ὑμέτερος στρατηγὸς κατέστησεν.
καίτοι ταῦτα πράττων τί ἐποίει; εἰρήνην μὲν γὰρ 25
ὀμωμόκει. καὶ μηδεὶς εἴπῃ, τί δὲ ταῦτ᾽ ἐστίν, ἢ 16
τί τούτων μέλει τῇ πόλει; εἰ μὲν γὰρ μικρὰ ταῦτα

23 καίτοι προστάται μὲν ὑμεῖς ἑβδομήκοντα ἔτη καὶ
τρία τῶν Ἑλλήνων ἐγένεσθε, προστάται δὲ τριάκοντα ἑνὸς δέοντα Λακεδαιμόνιοι· ἴσχυσαν δέ τι
καὶ Θηβαῖοι τουτουσὶ τοὺς τελευταίους χρόνους
5 μετὰ τὴν ἐν Λεύκτροις μάχην. ἀλλ' ὅμως οὔθ'
ὑμῖν οὔτε Θηβαίοις οὔτε Λακεδαιμονίοις οὐδεπώ-
ποτε, ὦ ἄνδρες Ἀθηναῖοι, συνεχωρήθη τοῦθ' ὑπὸ
τῶν Ἑλλήνων, ποιεῖν ὅ τι βούλοισθε, οὐδὲ πολλοῦ
24 δεῖ, ἀλλὰ τοῦτο μὲν ὑμῖν, μᾶλλον δὲ τοῖς τότ' οὖσιν
10 Ἀθηναίοις, ἐπειδή τισιν οὐ μετρίως ἐδόκουν προσ-
φέρεσθαι, πάντες ᾤοντο δεῖν, καὶ οἱ μηδὲν ἐγκαλεῖν
ἔχοντες αὐτοῖς, μετὰ τῶν ἠδικημένων πολεμεῖν, καὶ
πάλιν Λακεδαιμονίοις ἄρξασι καὶ παρελθοῦσιν εἰς
τὴν αὐτὴν δυναστείαν ὑμῖν, ἐπειδὴ πλεονάζειν ἐπε-
15 χείρουν καὶ πέρα τοῦ μετρίου τὰ καθεστηκότα
ἐκίνουν, πάντες εἰς πόλεμον κατέστησαν, καὶ οἱ
25 μηδὲν ἐγκαλοῦντες αὐτοῖς. καὶ τί δεῖ τοὺς ἄλλους
λέγειν; ἀλλ' ἡμεῖς αὐτοὶ καὶ Λακεδαιμόνιοι, οὐδὲν
ἂν εἰπεῖν ἔχοντες ἐξ ἀρχῆς ὅ τι ἠδικούμεθ' ὑπ' ἀλ-
20 λήλων, ὅμως ὑπὲρ ὧν τοὺς ἄλλους ἀδικουμένους
ἑωρῶμεν, πολεμεῖν ᾠόμεθα δεῖν. καίτοι πάνθ' ὅσα
ἐξημάρτηται καὶ Λακεδαιμονίοις ἐν τοῖς τριάκονт'
ἐκείνοις ἔτεσι καὶ τοῖς ἡμετέροις προγόνοις ἐν τοῖς
ἑβδομήκοντα, ἐλάττονά ἐστιν, ὦ ἄνδρες Ἀθηναῖοι,
25 ὧν Φίλιππος ἐν τρισὶ καὶ δέκα οὐχ ὅλοις ἔτεσιν
οἷς ἐπιπολάζει ἠδίκηκε τοὺς Ἕλληνας, μᾶλλον δὲ
26 οὐδὲ πέμπτον μέρος τούτων ἐκεῖνα. Ὄλυνθον μὲν

δὴ καὶ Μεθώνην καὶ Ἀπολλωνίαν καὶ δύο καὶ τριάκοντα πόλεις ἐπὶ Θρᾴκης ἐῶ, ἃς ἁπάσας οὕτως
ὠμῶς ἀνῄρηκεν ὥστε μηδ᾽ εἰ πώποτ᾽ ᾠκήθησαν
προσελθόντ᾽ εἶναι ῥᾴδιον εἰπεῖν· καὶ τὸ Φωκέων
ἔθνος τοσοῦτον ἀνῃρημένον σιωπῶ. ἀλλὰ Θεττα- 5
λία πῶς ἔχει; οὐχὶ τὰς πολιτείας καὶ τὰς πόλεις
αὐτῶν παρῄρηται καὶ τετραρχίας κατέστησεν, ἵνα
μὴ μόνον κατὰ πόλεις ἀλλὰ καὶ κατ᾽ ἔθνη δουλεύωσιν; αἱ δ᾽ ἐν Εὐβοίᾳ πόλεις οὐκ ἤδη τυραννοῦν- 27
ται, καὶ ταῦτα ἐν νήσῳ πλησίον Θηβῶν καὶ Ἀθη- 10
νῶν; οὐ διαρρήδην εἰς τὰς ἐπιστολὰς γράφει "ἐμοὶ
δ᾽ ἐστὶν εἰρήνη πρὸς τοὺς ἀκούειν ἐμοῦ βουλομένους"; καὶ οὐ γράφει μὲν ταῦτα, τοῖς δ᾽ ἔργοις οὐ
ποιεῖ, ἀλλ᾽ ἐφ᾽ Ἑλλήσποντον οἴχεται, πρότερον
ἧκεν ἐπ᾽ Ἀμβρακίαν, Ἦλιν ἔχει τηλικαύτην πόλιν 15
ἐν Πελοποννήσῳ, Μεγάροις ἐπεβούλευσε πρῴην,
οὔθ᾽ ἡ Ἑλλὰς οὔθ᾽ ἡ βάρβαρος τὴν πλεονεξίαν χωρεῖ τἀνθρώπου. καὶ ταῦθ᾽ ὁρῶντες οἱ Ἕλληνες 28
ἅπαντες καὶ ἀκούοντες οὐ πέμπομεν πρέσβεις περὶ
τούτων πρὸς ἀλλήλους καὶ ἀγανακτοῦμεν, οὕτω δὲ 20
κακῶς διακείμεθα καὶ διορωρύγμεθα κατὰ πόλεις
ὥστ᾽ ἄχρι τῆς τήμερον ἡμέρας οὐδὲν οὔτε τῶν συμφερόντων οὔτε τῶν δεόντων πρᾶξαι δυνάμεθα, οὐδὲ
συστῆναι, οὐδὲ κοινωνίαν βοηθείας καὶ φιλίας οὐδεμίαν ποιήσασθαι, ἀλλὰ μείζω γιγνόμενον τὸν 29
ἄνθρωπον περιορῶμεν, τὸν χρόνον κερδᾶναι τοῦ- 26
τον ὃν ἄλλος ἀπόλλυται ἕκαστος ἐγνωκώς, ὥς γ᾽

36 Τί οὖν αἴτιον τουτωνί; οὐ γὰρ ἄνευ λόγου καὶ
δικαίας αἰτίας οὔτε τόθ' οὕτως εἶχον ἑτοίμως πρὸς
ἐλευθερίαν οἱ Ἕλληνες, οὔτε νῦν πρὸς τὸ δουλεύειν.
ἦν τι τότ', ἦν, ὦ ἄνδρες Ἀθηναῖοι, ἐν ταῖς τῶν πολ-
5 λῶν διανοίαις ὃ νῦν οὐκ ἔστιν, ὃ καὶ τοῦ Περσῶν
ἐκράτησε πλούτου καὶ ἐλευθέραν ἦγε τὴν Ἑλλάδα
καὶ οὔτε ναυμαχίας οὔτε πεζῆς μάχης οὐδεμιᾶς ἡττᾶτο, νῦν δ' ἀπολωλὸς ἅπαντα λελύμανται καὶ ἄνω
37 καὶ κάτω πεποίηκε τὰ τῶν Ἑλλήνων πράγματα. τί
10 οὖν ἦν τοῦτο; τοὺς παρὰ τῶν ἄρχειν βουλομένων
ἢ διαφθείρειν τὴν Ἑλλάδα χρήματα λαμβάνοντας
ἅπαντες ἐμίσουν, καὶ χαλεπώτατον ἦν τὸ δωροδο-
κοῦντα ἐξελεγχθῆναι, καὶ τιμωρίᾳ μεγίστῃ τοῦτον
38 ἐκόλαζον. τὸν οὖν καιρὸν ἑκάστου τῶν πραγμάτων,
15 ὃν ἡ τύχη πολλάκις παρασκευάζει, οὐκ ἦν πρίασθαι
παρὰ τῶν λεγόντων οὐδὲ τῶν στρατηγούντων, οὐδὲ
τὴν πρὸς ἀλλήλους ὁμόνοιαν, οὐδὲ τὴν πρὸς τοὺς
τυράννους καὶ τοὺς βαρβάρους ἀπιστίαν, οὐδ' ὅλως
39 τοιοῦτον οὐδέν. νῦν δ' ἅπανθ' ὥσπερ ἐξ ἀγορᾶς
20 ἐκπέπραται ταῦτα, ἀντεισῆκται δὲ ἀντὶ τούτων ὑφ'
ὧν ἀπόλωλε καὶ νενόσηκεν ἡ Ἑλλάς. ταῦτα δ'
ἐστὶ τί; ζῆλος, εἴ τις εἴληφέ τι, γέλως, ἂν ὁμο-
λογῇ, μῖσος, ἂν τούτοις τις ἐπιτιμᾷ, τἆλλα πάνθ'
40 ὅσα ἐκ τοῦ δωροδοκεῖν ἤρτηται. ἐπεὶ τριήρεις γε
25 καὶ σωμάτων πλῆθος καὶ χρημάτων καὶ τῆς ἄλλης
κατασκευῆς ἀφθονία, καὶ τἆλλα οἷς ἄν τις ἰσχύειν
τὰς πόλεις κρίνοι, νῦν ἅπασι καὶ πλείω καὶ μείζω

ἐστὶ τῶν τότε πολλῷ. ἀλλ᾽ ἅπαντα ταῦτ᾽ ἄχρηστα,
ἄπρακτα, ἀνόνητα ὑπὸ τῶν πωλούντων γίγνεται.

Ὅτι δ᾽ οὕτω ταῦτ᾽ ἔχει, τὰ μὲν νῦν ὁρᾶτε δήπου 41
καὶ οὐδὲν ἐμοῦ προσδεῖσθε μάρτυρος· τὰ δ᾽ ἐν τοῖς
ἄνωθεν χρόνοις ὅτι τἀναντία εἶχεν, ἐγὼ δηλώσω, 5
οὐ λόγους ἐμαυτοῦ λέγων, ἀλλὰ. γράμματα τῶν
προγόνων τῶν ὑμετέρων, ἃ ᾽κεῖνοι κατέθεντο εἰς
στήλην χαλκῆν γράψαντες εἰς ἀκρόπολιν. Ἄρθ- 42
μιος, φησίν, ὁ Πυθώνακτος Ζελείτης ἄτιμος καὶ
πολέμιος τοῦ δήμου τοῦ Ἀθηναίων καὶ τῶν συμμά- 10
χων αὐτὸς καὶ γένος. εἶθ᾽ ἡ αἰτία γέγραπται δι᾽
ἣν ταῦτ᾽ ἐγένετο· ὅτι τὸν χρυσὸν τὸν ἐκ Μήδων
εἰς Πελοπόννησον ἤγαγεν. ταῦτ᾽ ἐστὶ τὰ γράμματα. λογίζεσθε δὴ πρὸς θεῶν, τίς ἦν ποθ᾽ ἡ διά- 43
νοια τῶν Ἀθηναίων τῶν τότε ταῦτα ποιούντων, ἢ 15
τί τὸ ἀξίωμα. ἐκεῖνοι Ζελείτην τινὰ Ἄρθμιον
δοῦλον βασιλέως (ἡ γὰρ Ζέλειά ἐστι τῆς Ἀσίας),
ὅτι τῷ δεσπότῃ διακονῶν χρυσίον ἤγαγεν εἰς Πελοπόννησον, οὐκ Ἀθήναζε, ἐχθρὸν αὐτῶν ἀνέγραψαν
καὶ τῶν συμμάχων αὐτὸν καὶ γένος, καὶ ἀτίμους. 20
τοῦτο δ᾽ ἐστὶν οὐχ ἣν ἄν τις οὑτωσὶ φήσειεν ἀτι- 44
μίαν· τί γὰρ τῷ Ζελείτῃ, τῶν Ἀθηναίων κοινῶν εἰ
μὴ μεθέξειν ἔμελλεν; ἀλλ᾽ ἐν τοῖς φονικοῖς γέγραπται νόμοις, ὑπὲρ ὧν ἂν μὴ διδῷ φόνου δικάσασθαι,
καὶ ἄτιμός φησι τεθνάτω. τοῦτο δὴ λέγει, καθα- 25
ρὸν τὸν τούτων τινὰ ἀποκτείναντα εἶναι. οὐκοῦν 45
ἐνόμιζον ἐκεῖνοι τῆς πάντων τῶν Ἑλλήνων σωτη-

οὐδενὸς οὐδέν, ἀλλ᾽ εἶναι νόμιμόν τινα καὶ προφανῆ
τὸν πόλεμον. νυνὶ δ᾽ ὁρᾶτε μὲν δήπου τὰ πλεῖστα 49
τοὺς προδότας ἀπολωλεκότας, οὐδὲν δ᾽ ἐκ παρατάξεως οὐδὲ μάχης γιγνόμενον· ἀκούετε δὲ Φίλιππον
οὐχὶ τῷ φάλαγγα ὁπλιτῶν ἄγειν βαδίζονθ᾽ ὅποι 5
βούλεται, ἀλλὰ τῷ ψιλοὺς, ἱππέας, τοξότας, ξένους,
τοιοῦτον ἐξηρτῆσθαι στρατόπεδον. ἐπειδὰν δ᾽ ἐπὶ 50
τούτοις πρὸς νοσοῦντας ἐν αὑτοῖς προσπέσῃ καὶ
μηδεὶς ὑπὲρ τῆς χώρας δι᾽ ἀπιστίαν ἐξίῃ, μηχανή-
ματ᾽ ἐπιστήσας πολιορκεῖ. καὶ σιωπῶ θέρος καὶ 10
χειμῶνα, ὡς οὐδὲν διαφέρει, οὐδ᾽ ἔστιν ἐξαίρετος
ὥρα τις ἣν διαλείπει. ταῦτα μέντοι πάντας εἰδό- 51
τας καὶ λογιζομένους οὐ δεῖ προσέσθαι τὸν πόλεμον εἰς τὴν χώραν, οὐδ᾽ εἰς τὴν εὐήθειαν τὴν τοῦ
τότε πρὸς Λακεδαιμονίους πολέμου βλέποντας ἐκ- 15
τραχηλισθῆναι, ἀλλ᾽ ὡς ἐκ πλείστου φυλάττεσθαι
τοῖς πράγμασι καὶ ταῖς παρασκευαῖς, ὅπως οἴκοθεν
μὴ κινήσεται σκοποῦντας, οὐχὶ συμπλακέντας δια-
γωνίζεσθαι. πρὸς μὲν γὰρ πόλεμον πολλὰ φύσει 52
πλεονεκτήμαθ᾽ ἡμῖν ὑπάρχει, ἄν περ, ὦ ἄνδρες 20
Ἀθηναῖοι, ποιεῖν ἐθέλωμεν ἃ δεῖ, ἡ φύσις τῆς ἐκείνου χώρας, ἧς ἄγειν καὶ φέρειν ἔστι πολλὴν καὶ
κακῶς ποιεῖν, ἄλλα μυρία· εἰς δὲ ἀγῶνα ἄμεινον
ἡμῶν ἐκεῖνος ἤσκηται.

Οὐ μόνον δὲ δεῖ ταῦτα γιγνώσκειν, οὐδὲ τοῖς 53
ἔργοις ἐκεῖνον ἀμύνεσθαι τοῖς τοῦ πολέμου, ἀλλὰ 26
καὶ τῷ λογισμῷ καὶ τῇ διανοίᾳ τοὺς παρ᾽ ὑμῖν

ὑπὲρ αὑτοῦ λέγοντας μισῆσαι, ἐνθυμουμένους ὅτι
οὐκ ἔνεστι τῶν τῆς πόλεως ἐχθρῶν κρατῆσαι, πρὶν
ἂν τοὺς ἐν αὐτῇ τῇ πόλει κολάσητε ὑπηρετοῦντας
54 ἐκείνοις. ὃ μὰ τὸν Δία καὶ τοὺς ἄλλους θεοὺς οὐ
5 δυνήσεσθε ὑμεῖς ποιῆσαι, ἀλλ᾽ εἰς τοῦτο ἀφῖχθε
μωρίας ἢ παρανοίας ἢ οὐκ ἔχω τί λέγω (πολλάκις
γὰρ ἔμοιγ᾽ ἐπελήλυθε καὶ τοῦτο φοβεῖσθαι, μή τι
δαιμόνιον τὰ πράγματα ἐλαύνῃ), ὥστε λοιδορίας,
φθόνου, σκώμματος, ἧς τινος ἂν τύχητε ἕνεκ᾽ αἰτίας
10 ἀνθρώπους μισθωτούς, ὧν οὐδ᾽ ἂν ἀρνηθεῖεν ἔνιοι
ὡς οὐκ εἰσὶ τοιοῦτοι, λέγειν κελεύετε, καὶ γελᾶτε
55 ἄν τισι λοιδορηθῶσιν. καὶ οὐχί πω τοῦτο δεινόν,
καίπερ ὂν δεινόν· ἀλλὰ καὶ μετὰ πλείονος ἀσφα-
λείας πολιτεύεσθαι δεδώκατε τούτοις ἢ τοῖς ὑπὲρ
15 ὑμῶν λέγουσιν. καίτοι θεάσασθε ὅσας συμφορὰς
παρασκευάζει τὸ τῶν τοιούτων ἐθέλειν ἀκροᾶσθαι.
λέξω δ᾽ ἔργα ἃ πάντες εἴσεσθε.
56   Ἦσαν ἐν Ὀλύνθῳ τῶν ἐν τοῖς πράγμασι τινὲς
μὲν Φιλίππου καὶ πάνθ᾽ ὑπηρετοῦντες ἐκείνῳ, τινὲς
20 δὲ τοῦ βελτίστου καὶ ὅπως μὴ δουλεύσουσιν οἱ πο-
λῖται πράττοντες. πότεροι δὴ τὴν πατρίδα ἐξώλε-
σαν; ἢ πότεροι τοὺς ἱππέας προύδοσαν, ὧν προ-
δοθέντων Ὄλυνθος ἀπώλετο; οἱ τὰ Φιλίππου
φρονοῦντες καὶ ὅτ᾽ ἦν ἡ πόλις τοὺς τὰ βέλτιστα
25 λέγοντας συκοφαντοῦντες καὶ διαβάλλοντες οὕτως
ὥστε τόν γ᾽ Ἀπολλωνίδην καὶ ἐκβαλεῖν ὁ δῆμος ὁ
τῶν Ὀλυνθίων ἐπείσθη.

Οὐ τοίνυν παρὰ τούτοις μόνοις τὸ ἔθος τοῦτο 57
πάντα κακὰ εἰργάσατο, ἄλλοθι δ' οὐδαμοῦ· ἀλλ'
ἐν Ἐρετρίᾳ, ἐπειδὴ ἀπαλλαγέντος Πλουτάρχου καὶ
τῶν ξένων ὁ δῆμος εἶχε τὴν πόλιν καὶ τὸν Πορθμόν,
οἱ μὲν ἐφ' ὑμᾶς ἦγον τὰ πράγματα, οἱ δ' ἐπὶ Φί- 5
λιππον. ἀκούοντες δὲ τούτων τὰ πολλὰ μᾶλλον
οἱ ταλαίπωροι καὶ δυστυχεῖς Ἐρετριεῖς τελευτῶντες ἐπείσθησαν τοὺς ὑπὲρ αὑτῶν λέγοντας ἐκβαλεῖν. καὶ γάρ τοι πέμψας Ἱππόνικον ὁ σύμμαχος 58
αὐτοῖς Φίλιππος καὶ ξένους χιλίους, τὰ τείχη πε- 10
ριεῖλε τοῦ Πορθμοῦ καὶ τρεῖς κατέστησε τυράννους,
Ἵππαρχον, Αὐτομέδοντα, Κλείταρχον· καὶ μετὰ
ταῦτ' ἐξελήλακεν ἐκ τῆς χώρας δὶς ἤδη βουλομένους σώζεσθαι, τότε μὲν πέμψας τοὺς μετ' Εὐρυλό-
χου ξένους, πάλιν δὲ τοὺς μετὰ Παρμενίωνος. 15

Καὶ τί δεῖ τὰ πολλὰ λέγειν; ἀλλ' ἐν Ὠρεῷ Φι- 59
λιστίδης μὲν ἔπραττε Φιλίππῳ καὶ Μένιππος καὶ
Σωκράτης καὶ Θόας καὶ Ἀγαπαῖος, οἵπερ νῦν
ἔχουσι τὴν πόλιν (καὶ ταῦτ' ᾔδεσαν ἅπαντες), Εὐφραῖος δέ τις, ἄνθρωπος καὶ παρ' ἡμῖν ποτ' ἐνθάδε 20
οἰκήσας, ὅπως ἐλεύθεροι καὶ μηδενὸς δοῦλοι ἔσον-
ται. οὗτος τὰ μὲν ἄλλα ὡς ὑβρίζετο καὶ προεπη- 60
λακίζετο ὑπὸ τοῦ δήμου, πολλὰ ἂν εἴη λέγειν·
ἐνιαυτῷ δὲ πρότερον τῆς ἁλώσεως ἐνέδειξεν ὡς προ-
δότην τὸν Φιλιστίδην καὶ τοὺς μετ' αὐτοῦ, αἰσθό- 25
μενος ἃ πράττουσιν. συστραφέντες δὲ ἄνθρωποι
πολλοὶ καὶ χορηγὸν ἔχοντες Φίλιππον καὶ πρυτα-

πράγματ' ἀνάγκη σκοπεῖν ὅπως σωθήσεται· οἱ δ'
ἐν αὑτοῖς οἷς χαρίζονται Φιλίππῳ συμπράττουσιν.
εἰσφέρειν ἐκέλευον, οἱ δ' οὐδὲν δεῖν ἔφασαν· πο- 64
λεμεῖν καὶ μὴ πιστεύειν, οἱ δ' ἄγειν εἰρήνην, ἕως
ἐγκατελήφθησαν. τἆλλα τὸν αὐτὸν τρόπον οἶμαι 5
πάνθ', ἵνα μὴ καθ' ἕκαστα λέγω· οἱ μέν, ἐφ' οἷς
χαριοῦνται, ταῦτ' ἔλεγον, οἱ δ' ἐξ ὧν ἔμελλον σω-
θήσεσθαι. πολλὰ δὲ καὶ τὰ τελευταῖα οὐχ οὕτως
οὔτε πρὸς χάριν οὔτε δι' ἄγνοιαν οἱ πολλοὶ προΐεντο,
ἀλλ' ὑποκατακλινόμενοι, ἐπειδὴ τοῖς ὅλοις ἡττᾶσθαι 10
ἐνόμιζον. ὃ νὴ τὸν Δία καὶ τὸν Ἀπόλλω δέδοικα 65
ἐγὼ μὴ πάθητε ὑμεῖς, ἐπειδὰν ἴδητε ἐκλογιζόμενοι
μηδὲν ὑμῖν ἐνόν. καίτοι μὴ γένοιτο μὲν τὰ πράγματ' ἐν τούτῳ· τεθνάναι δὲ μυριάκις κρεῖττον ἢ
κολακείᾳ τι ποιῆσαι Φιλίππου. καλήν γ' οἱ πολ- 66
λοὶ νῦν ἀπειλήφασιν Ὠρειτῶν χάριν, ὅτι τοῖς Φι- 16
λίππου φίλοις ἐπέτρεψαν αὑτούς, τὸν δ' Εὐφραῖον
ἐώθουν· καλήν γ' ὁ δῆμος ὁ Ἐρετριέων, ὅτι τοὺς
μὲν ὑμετέρους πρέσβεις ἀπήλασε, Κλειτάρχῳ δ'
ἐνέδωκεν αὑτόν· δουλεύουσί γε μαστιγούμενοι καὶ 20
σφαττόμενοι. καλῶς Ὀλυνθίων ἐφείσατο τῶν τὸν
μὲν Λασθένη ἵππαρχον χειροτονησάντων, τὸν δὲ
Ἀπολλωνίδην ἐκβαλόντων. μωρία καὶ κακία τοι- 67
αῦτα ἐλπίζειν, καὶ κακῶς βουλευομένους καὶ μηδὲν
ὧν προσήκει ποιεῖν ἐθέλοντας, ἀλλὰ τῶν ὑπὲρ τῶν 25
ἐχθρῶν λεγόντων ἀκροωμένους, τηλικαύτην ἡγεῖσθαι πόλιν οἰκεῖν τὸ μέγεθος ὥστε μηδέν, μηδ'

ἐπειδὴ γάρ ἐστι πρὸς ἄνδρα καὶ οὐχὶ συνεστώσης 72
πόλεως ἰσχὺν ὁ πόλεμος, οὐδὲ τοῦτ᾽ ἄχρηστον, οὐδ᾽
αἱ πέρυσι πρεσβεῖαι περὶ τὴν Πελοπόννησον ἐκεῖ-
ναι καὶ κατηγορίαι, ἃς ἐγὼ καὶ Πολύευκτος ὁ
βέλτιστος ἐκεινοσὶ καὶ Ἡγήσιππος καὶ οἱ ἄλλοι 5
πρέσβεις περιήλθομεν, καὶ ἐποιήσαμεν ἐπισχεῖν
ἐκεῖνον καὶ μήτ᾽ ἐπ᾽ Ἀμβρακίαν ἐλθεῖν μήτ᾽ ἐς Πελοπόννησον ὁρμῆσαι.   οὐ μέντοι λέγω μηδὲν αὐ- 73
τοὺς ὑπὲρ αὑτῶν ἀναγκαῖον ἐθέλοντας ποιεῖν τοὺς
ἄλλους παρακαλεῖν· καὶ γὰρ εὔηθες τὰ οἰκεῖα αὐ- 10
τοὺς προεμένους τῶν ἀλλοτρίων φάσκειν κήδεσθαι,
καὶ τὰ παρόντα περιορῶντας ὑπὲρ τῶν μελλόντων
τοὺς ἄλλους φοβεῖν.   οὐ λέγω ταῦτα, ἀλλὰ τοῖς
μὲν ἐν Χερρονήσῳ χρήματ᾽ ἀποστέλλειν φημὶ δεῖν
καὶ τἄλλα ὅσα ἀξιοῦσι ποιεῖν, αὐτοὺς δὲ παρα- 15
σκευάζεσθαι, τοὺς δ᾽ ἄλλους Ἕλληνας συγκαλεῖν,
συνάγειν, διδάσκειν, νουθετεῖν· ταῦτ᾽ ἐστὶ πόλεως
ἀξίωμα ἐχούσης ἡλίκον ὑμῖν ὑπάρχει.   εἰ δ᾽ οἴεσθε 74
Χαλκιδέας τὴν Ἑλλάδα σώσειν ἢ Μεγαρέας, ὑμεῖς
δ᾽ ἀποδράσεσθαι τὰ πράγματα, οὐκ ὀρθῶς οἴεσθε· 20
ἀγαπητὸν γὰρ ἂν αὐτοὶ σώζωνται τούτων ἕκαστοι.
ἀλλ᾽ ὑμῖν τοῦτο πρακτέον· ὑμῖν οἱ πρόγονοι τοῦτο
τὸ γέρας ἐκτήσαντο καὶ κατέλιπον μετὰ πολλῶν
καὶ μεγάλων κινδύνων.   εἰ δ᾽ ὃ βούλεται ζητῶν 75
ἕκαστος καθεδεῖται, καὶ ὅπως μηδὲν αὐτὸς ποιήσει 25
σκοπῶν, πρῶτον μὲν οὐδὲ μή ποθ᾽ εὕρῃ τοὺς ποιή-

3   D

FIRST PHILIPPIC.

INTRODUCTION.

THE First Philippic was delivered late in the year 352 B. C., or early in the year 351. The progress of Philip's conquests and aggressions, which furnished the occasion for it, and whose rapid succession our orator himself has sketched in more than one of his orations (e. g. *Ol.*, I. 12, 13; *Phil.*, I. 4; *De Cor.*, 69), may be registered chronologically thus: Amphipolis, on the Strymonic Gulf, so tenaciously held by the Athenians as a colony, and so eagerly coveted as a source of supply of timber for their ships, was captured by Philip in 358 (Curtius, V. p. 52; Grote, XI. 328), and from that time was held up for many years as a bribe to purchase peace or a rod to compel compliance. Pydna, Potidæa, and Methone, all clustering about the Thermaic Gulf, which lay nearer to Athens (Methone being the last possession of the Athenians on the Macedonian coast), were taken severally in the years 357, 356, and 353. Pagasæ, Pheræ, and Magnesia, lying on or about the still nearer Pagasæan Gulf, and guarding the approaches towards Thermopylæ, all fell into his hands in 353. The same year witnessed also his attempt to pass through Thermopylæ for the destruction of the Phocians. Most of these important places had stood in more or less intimate relations to the Athenians, and were wrested more or less directly from their hands. With his fleet gathered or largely increased by his conquest of these maritime cities, he now plundered the merchantmen of the allies of Athens (as we learn from the oration itself, § 34), landed his troops on the Athenian islands Lemnos and Imbros, carrying off Athenian citizens as prisoners, and even seized their ships at Geræstus in Eubœa, levied immense sums of money from them, and finally bore away the sacred trireme from Marathon on the coast of Attica over against Athens. "And all this," the orator says, "you were unable to prevent, neither could you despatch succors at the times when you proposed to send them." It was not till Philip, after his successes in Thessaly, marched into Thrace, ejecting some of the kings there, and setting up others as he chose (*Ol.*, I. 13), and commenced the siege of Heræon Teichos (cf. *Phil.*, I. 10, 11, 41 with *Ol.*, III. 4, 5 and Grote, XI. p. 429, note), that the Athenians, alarmed for the safety of their possessions in that quarter, voted to raise an army adequate to oppose any effectual resistance to his encroachments. And when, on the report of Philip's death, or, at any rate, that he was sick, this expedition lingered and dwindled till it finally turned out a miserable abortion (*Ol.*, III. 5, and note there), Demosthenes, then only about thirty years of age, and not yet one of the accepted, still less one of the popular advisers of the Athenian demus, broke silence, and, giving them the counsel which should rather have come from their older and more admired political orators, delivered his first Philippic oration.

In the Argument which is prefixed to this oration in many editions, Libanius says : "The Athenians, unsuccessful in their war with Philip [the war about Amphipolis, so called, which commenced soon after Philip's capture of the city, and *formally* ended only with the Peace of Philocrates, B. C. 346], have convened in assembly in a state of discouragement. The orator accordingly endeavors, in the first place, to remove this discouragement by telling them it is no wonder that they have been defeated, they have been so slothful and negligent of their duty ; and, in the second place, he instructs them how they can best carry on the war. He moves them to arm and equip two forces, one larger, consisting of citizens, which shall remain at home and be ready for the exigencies which arise from time to time ; the other smaller, consisting partly of citizens and partly of mercenaries, to hover along the coast of Macedonia, and carry on the war incessantly, and thus put an end to Philip's privateering and conquering expeditions."

many different roads to the main conviction which the orator wishes to impress, profoundly animated with genuine Pan-hellenic patriotism and with the dignity of that free Grecian world now threatened by a monarch from without. It has other merits besides, not less important in themselves, and lying more immediately within the scope of the historian. We find Demosthenes, yet only thirty years old, young in political life, and thirteen years before the battle of Chæronea, taking accurate measure of the political relations between Athens and Philip ; examining those relations during the past, pointing out how they had become every year more unfavorable, and foretelling the dangerous contingencies of the future, unless better precautions were taken ; exposing with courageous frankness, not only the past mismanagement of public men, but also defective dispositions of the people themselves, wherein such management had its root ; lastly, after fault found, adventuring on his own responsibility to propose specific measures of correction, and urging upon reluctant citizens a painful imposition of personal hardship as well as of taxation. We shall find him insisting on the same obligation, irksome alike to the leading politicians and to the people (§ 51), throughout all the Olynthiacs and Philippics. We note his warnings given at this early day, when timely prevention would have been practicable ; and his superiority to older politicians, like Eubulus and Phocion, in prudent appreciation, in foresight, and in the courage of speaking out unpalatable truths. The first Philippic alone is sufficient to prove how justly Demosthenes lays claim to the merit of ' having seen events in their beginnings,' and given timely warning to his countrymen (*De Cor.*, 246). It will also go to show, along with other proofs hereafter to be seen, that he was not less honest and judicious in his attempts to fulfil the remaining portion of a statesman's duty, that of working up his countrymen to unanimous and resolute enterprise ; to the pitch requisite not merely for speaking and voting, but for acting and suffering, against the common enemy."

Before reading this first Philippic of Demosthenes, the student should endeavor to reproduce in his mind's eye, not only the circumstances, but the scene, the time, the place, the audience, and the orator ; for they were all quite extraordinary.

The time was extraordinary. It was a decisive moment in the history of Athens and of Greece. Nay, more, it was a great crisis in the history of the world. A power was rising in the North and rapidly advancing southward, which threatened, first, to subvert the liberties of Greece, and then to bestride Europe, Asia, and Africa like a colossus, obliterating old empires, changing the fate of nations, and introducing a new epoch in human history. It was the same power which rose up in prophetic vision before the eyes of Hebrew seers in the form now of a winged leopard, and now of a he-goat, coming from the west, overrunning the East, traversing the face of the whole earth without touching the ground, and casting down and trampling under foot whatever came in its way. At the time when this oration was delivered, as we have seen, city after city, which were but lately the possessions or the allies of Athens, had already fallen into the hands of the king of Macedon ; and now to name them was to mark the successive steps of his progress, now they were so many magazines and batteries for new assaults, so many ἐπιτειχίσματα, as the Greeks would call them, for further conquests. He had indeed met with a temporary check at Thermopylæ, and was now in Thrace. But he was still extending his acquisitions, and threatening the possessions of Athens in that quarter ; and the Athenians, disheartened, but by no means awake to the extent of their danger, were just now in that strange state of mingled anxiety and apathy from which only a prophet's foresight and eloquence could arouse them, and only the wisdom and guidance of a faithful and trusted statesman could deliver them.

The place was extraordinary. It was Athens, the watch-tower of old Hellas ; but, alas ! her most trusted watchmen were now asleep, if some of them were not even in sympathy and alliance with the enemy, — Athens, immortalized at Marathon and Platæa and Artemisium and Salamis as the defender of the liberties of Greece, but now, alas ! degenerate, if some of the leading men were not even false to the principles and spirit of their illus-

trious ancestors. The particular spot which was the scene of
this oration, and the centre of political influence in Athens, was
the Pnyx. And this was no ordinary senate-house, no parlia-
ment-house, or congressional chamber, or other common hall of
assembly. The Pnyx was one of the four hills on and around
which Athens was built, and not less famous or sacred in its
way than the Areopagus or the Acropolis itself, being the representative of the politics and government of Athens as those
other world-renowned hills were the representatives severally of
its law and its religion. The Pnyx proper was a large semi-
circular area, partly hewn out of the solid rock and partly built
up on a massive Pelasgic wall upon the abrupt face of this hill,
where all the citizens of Athens and Attica were wont to assem-
ble, beneath no roof but the clear blue sky, and within no walls
but the distant, lofty, bold and purple-tinted mountains, — there,
not by their representatives, but in person, not in a council
consisting at most of a few hundreds, but in an assembly of
thousands, to deliberate on public affairs and transact the business of the state. The rostra or bema from which the orator
spoke, and to which he ascended by eight or ten steps, hewn out
of the rock, was a square platform, a dozen or fifteen feet high,
itself also hewn out of the solid rock, in the middle of the chord
of that semicircle, to speak mathematically, or, speaking more
exactly and popularly, occupying the same position in reference
to the area of the Pnyx and the seats of the assembly which the
hand and eye of the archer do when he takes hold of the string
and begins to draw it back and round out the bow, and takes
sight along the arrow before he lets it fly. That bema looked
directly down upon the Pnyx, and more remotely upon the
agora and the whole city. It looked over to the Areopagus with
its venerable council and court, and to the Acropolis, crowned
with temples and statues of the gods. It looked around upon
Athens and Attica, upon Hymettus and Pentelicus, just behind
which was the plain of Marathon ; upon Parnes and Cithæron,
beyond which were Platæa and Artemisium and Thermopylæ ;
upon Piræus and Salamis and Eleusis and Megara and Corinth
and Argolis and all the cities and islands and harbors and prom-

Demosthenes as read to them by his rival, "You should have heard the monster himself!" In like manner Dionysius of Halicarnassus says : "When I read one of the speeches of Isocrates, I am disposed to serene and tranquil thought, like those who listen to spondaic measures or Dorian or Lydian melodies ; but when I take up an oration of Demosthenes, I am inspired like the Corybants at the Mysteries of Cybele, and I am borne hither and thither with anxiety, fear, contempt, hatred, pity, anger, good-will, and all the varied passions of the orator."

This matchless orator was now a young man, at the very commencement of his remarkable public life. From early childhood to mature manhood he has had to contend with difficulties which would have discouraged and overwhelmed any ordinary character. Orphanage, dishonest guardians, imperfect education, constitutional defects and impediments, jealous rivals and bitter personal enemies, — everything has been against him. He has conquered all these difficulties, baffled his enemies, mastered himself, triumphed over nature and adverse circumstances, turned failure and opposition into helps and means of victory. But now he is to enter upon the great battle of his life. Now he has to contend not only with Philip and his conquering legions. The ablest generals, the most eloquent orators, the oldest and most experienced statesmen, the most admired and trusted counsellors of Athens, are for the most part against him. The Athenians themselves, in their character and habits, are against him. The spirit of the people, all the tendencies of the age, not only at Athens but in all Greece, are against him. In order to succeed he must work a miracle ; he must breathe life into the ribs of death itself. He knows this, he feels it in his inmost soul. Yet he does not despair, he does not even hesitate. The people have gathered in crowds from the city and the country and filled the Pnyx. The Κήρυξ cries, "Who wishes to speak ?" Without waiting for any of the older orators and usual leaders of the people, Demosthenes rises from his seat, comes forward, ascends the bema, and delivers the oration which we are about to read. We know it was not successful ; the orator failed to accomplish his object. We know that he was destined to fail in his heroic struggle for the liberties of his country. But he fell as heroes fall, he died as martyrs die, not with those miserable words profit and success on his lips, but with his banner blazoned all over with duty, honor, liberty, and glory. Few scenes in history are more striking, few more suggestive of the moral sublime, few more fruitful in lessons of wisdom and duty to young men, than the appearance of Demosthenes on the Athenian bema for the delivery of his First Philippic.

ANALYSIS.

The following skeleton exhibits an outline of the plan and general divisions of the oration : —

A. Exordium (§ 1).

B. Encouragement drawn from discouragement and from the past history of Athens and of Philip (2 – 12).

C. Measures recommended. Plan of the campaign (13 – 22).

D. Reasons for this plan (23 – 27).

E. Ways and Means (28 – 30).

F. Topographical suggestions (31, 32).

G. The probable results of this course, in contrast with the wretched state of things now existing at Athens (33 – 46).

H. How shall this state of things be brought to an end (47 – 50)?

I. Conclusion (51).

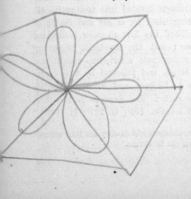

NOTES.

A. Exordium: Apology for speaking first (1).

§ 1. IF THE SUBJECT UNDER DISCUSSION HAD BEEN A NEW ONE, I WOULD HAVE WAITED FOR YOUR USUAL ADVISERS TO SPEAK FIRST. BUT SINCE THEY HAVE OFTEN GIVEN THEIR ADVICE ON THIS VERY SUBJECT, AND THAT NOT SATISFACTORY, ELSE THERE WOULD BE NO NEED OF YOUR PRESENT CONSULTATION, I MAY REASONABLY EXPECT TO BE PARDONED FOR OPENING THE DEBATE.

1. Page 1, line 1. Both in thought and in language this introductory sentence is a good illustration of the art which is so perfect that it conceals the art. Under cover of a modest and harmless apology for himself and a graceful compliment to his audience, the orator, in his very first sentence, lets fly a polished shaft at the policy of their favorite counsellors. At the same time, while the sentence seems to be perfectly simple and natural, the words are selected with exquisite taste, the clauses are measured as it were with square and compass, and the whole period is constructed with consummate skill. In the first place, the whole sentence is divided into two antithetic and well-balanced members distinguished by εἰ μέν and ἐπειδὴ δέ (C. 685 c ; Cu. 628 ; H. 862). Then the first member is divided into a protasis and an apodosis ; and the apodosis, beginning with ἐπισχὼν ἄν, contains two subordinate alternative conditions, distinguished by εἰ μέν and εἰ δὲ μή, and followed by two corresponding alternative conclusions (...ἂν ἦγον, and ἂν ἐπειρώμην...), each of which is marked by the particle ἄν. ἐπισχὼν ἄν is equivalent to ἐπέσχον ἂν καί (C. 658 a ; Cu. 595 ; G. 211 ; H. 803),*

---

* The grammars of Crosby, Curtius, Goodwin, and Hadley are thus referred to, as in the Notes on the Olynthiacs and the De Corona.

only the participle ἐπισχών is distinctly *preliminary* to the verb
ἦγον. The past tenses of the indicative with εἰ in the protasis and
ἄν in the apodosis express a supposition contrary to the fact (C. 631, b;
Cu. 537; G. 222; H. 746). The use of the imperfect (instead of the
pluperfect or aorist) throughout the protasis and the apodosis (προὐ-
τίθετο, ἤρεσκε, ἦγον, ἐπειρώμην) expresses a *continued* action or state
instead of a completed or momentary one. The prytanes or proëdri,
or whoever *brought forward* the subject or *laid* the question *before*
the people, gave an opportunity to speak not only at the moment
when the herald cried, τίς ἀγορεύειν βούλεται, but *during the whole*
time that the subject was under consideration. See Sauppe ad loc.
— Εἰ...προὐτίθετο, *if it were some new subject, gentlemen of Athens,
which was laid* (and is still lying) *before us for discussion, I should
have waited until the most of those who are accustomed* to do so *had
expressed their opinion, and then, if*, etc. It was the especial prerog-
ative of the prytanes and particularly of the *proëdri* to bring matters before the ecclesia for their consideration and action. Dic. of
Antiq. art. βουλή. Cf. Isoc., VIII. 15: περὶ ὧν οἱ πρυτάνεις προτι-
θέασι. But the state, and the people, and even private individuals,
are sometimes said in a more general sense προτιθέναι λόγον. After
εἰωθότων supply γνώμην ἀποφήνασθαι from γνώμην ἀπεφήναντο. The
reference is to Eubulus and Phocion and other leaders of the peace-
party, who were older than Demosthenes, and had been accustomed
to guide the Athenian populace (Curtius, V. 142, 444; Grote, XI.
443). Demosthenes was now only thirty, and might well apologize
for proposing a plan of his own without waiting for or even consulting orators who had so long swayed the people, and who were advocates of a more popular policy. According to the law of Solon, persons of over fifty years of age were called upon to speak first in the
assemblies of the people. Æsch. con. Ctes. 4. This had become
obsolete. Aristoph. Acharn. 43. Still, for the sake of good order
and good feeling, the older statesmen would usually speak first. We
have in *De Cor.*, 170 a graphic description of the herald calling again
and again τίς ἀγορεύειν βούλεται, and when all the orators and all the
generals were speechless, Demosthenes comes forward not only first
but alone to give his advice in the perilous emergency. — 5. ἃ γιγνώσκω = γνώμην, *my sentiments.* — 6. ἐπειδὴ δέ introduces the second
member of the antithesis, and sets over against the supposition and
conclusion of the first member a similarly balanced fact and inference

from it. — ὑπὲρ ὧν, al. περὶ ὧν. The former has the preference as the more difficult or improbable reading, besides being found in the best MSS. and editions. The difference is not essential, and the prepositions are used almost interchangeably. Properly περί is *about*, hence *in regard to*, and ὑπέρ is *over*, hence *in behalf of* : *but since it so happens that we are now considering interests in behalf of which these men have spoken many times before, I am led to believe that though I have risen first I may reasonably expect to meet with indulgence.* For ἀναστάς, the participle expressing condition, see C. 635; Cu. 583; G. 226; H. 751. For καί = *even though*, C. 674, f; Cu. 537, 5; H. 795, f. — 9. ἐκ...χρόνου, strictly *from* past time, having reference to the *beginning* of the time; but in usage = *in* or *during*.

B. Encouragement and exhortation to united and vigorous action (2–12).

2–12. YOU SHOULD DRAW ENCOURAGEMENT FROM THE VERY WRETCHEDNESS OF YOUR STATE; FOR IT IS ALL THE RESULT OF YOUR INACTION, AND THEREFORE CAN BE REMEDIED BY ACTION. REMEMBER HOW NOBLY AND SUCCESSFULLY YOU RESISTED THE LACEDÆMONIANS AT THE HEIGHT OF THEIR POWER. SEE HOW PHILIP HAS WON HIS CONQUESTS, AND RECOVER YOUR LOST POSSESSIONS AND ALLIES BY SIMILAR ENERGY. THEY INCLINE TO YOU RATHER THAN TO HIM. GIVE THEM A CHANCE, AND THEY WILL SOON SLIP AWAY FROM HIM. HELP YOURSELVES, AND GODS AND MEN WILL HELP YOU. WHEN *WILL* YOU DO YOUR DUTY IF NOT NOW ? TO FREE MEN THERE IS NO NECESSITY SO DIRE AS DISHONOR, AND NO DISHONOR LIKE BEING SUBJECT TO A MAN OF MACEDON.

2. 11. Πρῶτον μέν, correlative to ἔπειτα, § 3. Take courage, *first*, from the very wretchedness of your state; *secondly*, from your past history, etc. — οὖν, not inferential, but continuative or transitional from the exordium to the body of the speech. So *Ol.*, I. 2; II. 3; III. 3, and often. — 12. τοῖς...πράγμασιν, *at* or *by the present state of things*. Verbs expressing an emotion of pleasure, displeasure, or the like are followed by a dative of the object, cause, or ground of the emotion. Madv.* 44; C. 456; Cu. 439; H. 611. — οὐδ' = *not even*. — 13. ὃ γὰρ...ὑπάρχει, *for that which is the worst in regard to them in the past, this promises to become* (or *is capable of becoming*) *the best for the future*. This logic of common-sense, so paradoxical and yet so just and *well put*, is repeated in *Phil.*, III. 5; and in *Ol.*, I. 4,

* Madvig's Syntax.

the orator extracts encouragement from the most formidable of Philip's resources by a similar argument. — 15. τί...τοῦτο. The superior vivacity and force of this rhetorical question (which the orator asks himself or supposes his hearers to ask) over the logical γάρ, which might have connected the two clauses, is observed by Greek rhetoricians. Demosthenes is fond of this figure. — ὅτι οὐδέν, κ. τ. λ., *it is that your affairs are in a bad condition, because you do* (lit. *while you are doing*) *nothing that ought to be done.* — 17. ἐπεί τοι, κ. τ. λ., *for verily, if, while you were performing your whole duty, they were thus, there would be no hope of their becoming better.* — 3. 19. ἔπειτα, κ.τ.λ., *in the second place, you ought to consider both you who hear it from others and you who know it from personal remembrance,* i. e. both the younger and the older members of the assembly. — ὑμῖν is understood as the agent of ἐνθυμητέον. C. 458, 682 ; Cu. 434 ; G. 281 ; H. 600. — ἀναμιμνησκομένοις denotes the manner and means of knowing. C. 674 ; Cu. 581 ; G. 277 ; H. 789.

P. 2, l. 2. ἡλίκην...ὡς, lit. *when the Lacedæmonians once were in possession of how much power, how nobly and becomingly,* etc. The use of the double relative or interrogative in a single clause is not unfrequent in Greek. We make two clauses, and use a verb instead of the participle: *how much power the Lacedæmonians once possessed and yet how nobly and becomingly,* etc. — 3. ἐξ οὗ...πολύς, *not long since,* a kind of adverbial clause, hence the verb ἔστι is usually omitted, but not always, as Heslop affirms. See Franke in loc. The historical reference is perhaps to the repulse of Agesilaus, king of Sparta, by the combined forces of the Athenians and Thebans under Chabrias and Gorgidas. "These events would doubtless be in the recollection of many of the hearers of Demosthenes, when twenty-seven years after he delivered his first Philippic." Whiston. — ὡς προσηκόντως, i. e. how *befitting* them as the professed and acknowledged champions of the rights and liberties of the Greeks. — 5. ὑπὲρ τῶν δικαίων, *in behalf of the rights.* Ἑλληνικῶν is of course understood, but need not be expressed. It is found in *Ol.,* II. 24, and is added here in some MSS. and editions, but not the most or the best. — ἐκείνους, more emphatic than αὐτούς, THEM, powerful as they were. — 6. εἰδῆτε... καὶ θεάσησθε, *that you may know and see clearly,* as it were with the clearness of ocular vision. Demosthenes was so fond of such *pairs* of kindred words, that Greek critics censured and ridiculed him for it. Cf. Rehdantz in loc. See also *De Cor.,* 4, and note there. It is a

species of rhetorical amplification and emphasis which suited the intensity of the orator's mind and the earnestness of his spirit. The interposition of ὦ ἄνδρες Ἀθηναῖοι between the two words is also frequent, as
Whiston suggests, and adds to the emphasis. — 7. ουδὲν οὔτε...οὔτ'.
οὐδέν is the subject of both clauses, and the correlation and contrast
of the two is emphasized by οὔτε...οὔτ': *both that nothing is to be
feared by you while you are on your guard, and that nothing will be
as you would have it if you are negligent.*—**φυλαττομένοις**, lit. *being
on your guard,* implies condition. C. 635; Cu. 583; G. 226; H.
751.—9. **παραδείγμασι.** The success of the Athenians in overcom-
ing the Lacedæmonians *illustrated* the first proposition, viz. that they
had nothing to fear so long as they were on the watch; and the present insolence of Philip demonstrated the second, to wit, that nothing
would be as they would have it if they were negligent. — 10. **τῇ τότε,
τῇ νῦν,** C. 526; Cu. 381; H. 534. —13. **ὧν ἐχρῆν,** sc. φροντίζειν, *from
our caring nothing for what we ought,* sc. to have cared.—4. 15. **σκοπῶν, κ. τ. λ.,** *when he looks at the greatness of his present military
power on the one hand and on the other* (τε...καί) *at the loss of all the
places by our state.*—**δυνάμεως** is usually *force, army,* in Demosthenes.
Philip was at this time (in the Sacred War) at the head of an army
of 20,000 foot and 3,000 horse. Grote, XI. 410; Thirlwall, II. 98;
Curtius, V. 77. —16. **τὰ χωρία,** *the* places so well known and soon
to be named. — 17. **ὀρθῶς μὲν οἴεται, κ. τ. λ.** See a similar argument
and construction, *Ol.,* II. 22, σώφρονος μέν, κ. τ. λ., and elsewhere. —
μέντοι, *yet,* or *however,* opposed to μέν. So *Ol.,* III. 2. See note,
De Cor., 12. — 18. **Πύδναν, Ποτίδαιαν, Μεθώνην,** often named as *sore*
places in the orations of Demosthenes, and always in the order of
their capture by Philip. See special Introduction, p. 51, for the
places and dates. — **καὶ...καὶ...καί.** Franke calls attention to the
polysyndeton, i. e. the repetition of the connective. Asyndeton, entire
omission of the connective, is more frequent. *Ol.,* I. 9; *De Cor.,* 69,
237, et al. The former gives weight and magnitude, the latter vivacity and rapidity. — **πάντα...κύκλῳ,** i. e. the whole country about the
Thermaic Gulf. See Map.—**οἰκεῖον,** *as our own.* Literally and with
the order and emphasis of the Greek: WE once...*held all that region*
AS OUR OWN *round about.* Placed before κύκλῳ, according to Rehdantz,
to avoid hiatus and rhythmical feebleness. — 20. **μετ' ἐκείνου,** *on his
side.* —21. **αὐτονομούμενα καὶ ἐλεύθερα.** Observe the pair: *independent and free.* The Pæonians and Illyrians are specified as such nations

in *Ol.*, I. 23, where see the same words and the same argument. —
5. 23. ἔσχε τὴν γνώμην, *got the idea* (Heslop) ; *taken it into his head*
(Kennedy), quite different from εἶχε. — 25. ἐπιτειχίσματα, *fortresses
held as points of attack*.   Pydna, Potidæa, and Methone were on the
coast of Macedon, and commanded the country.   So in *De Cor.*, 87,
Eubœa is called κατὰ τῆς πόλεως ἐπιτειχισμόν, and so Deceleia was
held by the Lacedæmonians as an ἐπιτείχισμα against Athens in the
hence called Decelean War.   See Whiston's note ad loc. — χώρας is
objective genitive = *against* or *in respect to his own country*. —
26. πεποίηκεν ἔπραξεν, *he would have done nothing of what he has
now accomplished*.   For the distinction between these words, see note
Ol., III. 15.

P. 3, l. 2. κείμενα ἐν μέσῳ, a metaphor drawn from the games
where the prizes are placed in some central and conspicuous place in
the arena.   Hom., *Il.*, XVIII. 507, XXIII. 273.   Heslop renders :
offered to competition. — 3. φύσει ὑπάρχει, *naturally belong*.   Such
apothegms, or *gnomes*, abound in our orator, and are expressed with
much brevity and point. — 6. 6. χρησάμενος, *by acting* on this principle, strictly *having* acted on it, the aor. part. distinctly implying
that such action or application was *preliminary* to the conquests. —
7. τὰ μέν, lit. *some as one would hold places after having taken them
in war;* more concisely and idiomatically : *some as military conquests,
others as allies and friends.* — 9. καὶ προσέχειν…ἅπαντες.   The
commentators generally notice these words as forming a hexameter
line.   Such lines, of which they instance not a few, probably slipped
from him unconsciously.   See Cic., *Or.*, 56, 169. — 7. 11 – 13. ἂν…
νῦν, *if therefore you also will adopt the same principle now.* — 13. καὶ
ἕκαστος, *and if each one of you, giving up all evasion, would be ready
to act where he ought and wherever he can make himself useful to the
state.* — 16. εἰσφέρειν.   This is the technical word for the extraordinary war-tax or contribution (εἰσφοραί) which was paid by the 1,200
richest Athenians, who were divided into classes (συμμορίαι) for that
purpose.   See note *Ol.*, II. 29, and references there. — 17. ἐν ἡλικίᾳ,
in (of) the military age, sc. from 18 to 60.   See *Ol.*, I. 28. — συνελόντι δ' ἁπλῶς, *to speak concisely*.   ὡς often precedes the part. when
thus used.   See explanation in Lex. L. & S.; C. 671 c ; Cu. 435 ;
G. 184, 5 ; H. 601 ; Madv. 38 c. — 18. ὑμῶν αὐτῶν…γένεσθαι, *become your own masters*.   Cf. *Ol.*, II. 30, and note there.   Gen. of possession.   C. 443 ; H. 572, c. — 19. οὐδέν instead of μηδέν in a con-

ditional clause, because the force of the conditional particle (ἄν) is
intended to fall chiefly on the next clause, while this clause states a
fact = while each one hopes to do nothing himself. — 20. **καὶ**...
κομιεῖσθε, *you will both secure your own possessions, if God will, and
get back again what has been thrown away by sheer neglect.* For κομιεῖσθε, cf. *Ol.,* II. 28, where it is said of securing or receiving back
Amphipolis. On ἂν θεὸς θέλῃ, see *Ol.,* II. 20 and note there. Heslop
reads ἐθέλῃ here, but the editions generally have θέλῃ, and the editors generally agree that the shorter form of this verb is used of the
gods even after a word ending with a consonant. Cf. Sauppe and
Dindorf in loc. Several commentators call attention to the contrast
between the κατά in κατερρᾳθυμημένα and the ἀνά in ἀναλήψεσθε and
the pleonasm in πάλιν with the ἀνά. The two clauses of the apodosis
are not tautology, but an emphatic reduplication of kindred ideas,
resembling the pairs of kindred words which our author is so fond of
using. — 8. 24. **ἀθάνατα,** proleptic : *that his present power is secured
to him as to a god in everlasting possession.* Heslop. — **ἀλλὰ καὶ
μισεῖ τις,** nay, *many a one even of those who seem to be very friendly
to him both hates and fears and envies him.* τις, our *many a one,* as
often in Homer, e. g. *Il.,* III. 297. The reference is to the Illyrians,
Pæonians, and other allies of Philip. Cf. *Ol.,* I. 23 ; II. 15. —
26. **ἅπανθ' ὅσα περ** take their true meaning and interpretation from
the μισεῖν, δέδιεν, and φθονεῖ which precede : all the hates and fears
and envies and jealousies, — all the feelings, passions, and motives, —
ALL *the elements of human nature,* WHATEVER THEY MAY BE, *which
exist in other men.* The omission of the substantive makes the language more comprehensive and emphatic without making it obscure
in its connection. The fact that the orator felt under the necessity
of making such remarks as this, and that which immediately precedes,
shows the almost superstitious awe and dread which Philip had inspired at Athens.

P. 4, l. 1. **κατέπτηχε μέντοι,** *now, however, all these are cowed
down, having no place of refuge.* Observe the emphatic position of
κατέπτηχε. It is especially applied to timid animals *crouching* in
their lair. See Whiston in loc. — **ἤδη,** emphatic in position as well
as in signification, *forthwith.* Heslop renders *at once;* Whiston
immediately. — 9. 5. **ἀσελγείας,** here *insolence.* Partitive gen. denoting degree. C. 416 ; Cu. 412 ; G. 168 ; H. 559 c. — **ἄνθρωπος,**
the man, bitter with a mixture of hatred and contempt. — 6. **ὃς οὐδ',**

who does not even. — 7. ἄγειν ἡσυχίαν, almost exactly our idiom:
keep quiet. — 8. ὡς φασιν. So in *Ol.,* I. 22, he reports what he *hears*
from others in regard to Philip. — 8. οὐχ οἷός ἐστιν, *and is not the
man to rest in the possession of what he has conquered,* but *is ever trying
to compass something more, and is throwing his net round about us on
every side while we procrastinate and sit still.* οἷος is different from οἷός
τε. οἷος ἐστιν = βούλεται καὶ προῄρηται, οἷός τ᾽ ἐστιν = δύναται. Harpo-
crates cited by Franke, cf. οἷαί τε, § 37. — περιστοιχίζεται is a metaphor drawn from hunters who fix poles or stakes (στοῖχοι) in the
ground and then stretch their nets upon them to prevent the escape
of the wild beasts they are pursuing. So all the commentators.
Heslop finds in προσπεριβάλλεται also a hunting metaphor. But
Whiston says, it is apparently borrowed from a person wrapping a
mantle or cloak about himself. This is the prevailing use of περι-
βάλλεσθαι. Thucydides (V. 2) uses προσπεριβάλλειν, of throwing a
wall about a city; and Isocrates (198 E) uses the middle voice of
throwing a wall about one's self. — 10. 11. πότ᾽...πότε, cf. ἔστιν...
ἔστιν, *Ol.,* I. 19, and note there. Observe the increase of the emphasis
by the interposition of ὦ ἄνδρες Ἀθηναῖοι. So also between *pairs* of
kindred words, cf. note, § 3, above. — ἐπειδὰν τί γένηται, *when what
shall have happened,* sc. will you do your duty = what event, what
disaster *will* rouse you ? The double interrogative again, cf. note § 3
above. The rapid series of interrogations in this section well illustrates the remark of Robert Hall quoted in the general Introduction,
p. xiv. — 13. ἐπειδὰν...ᾖ, *whenever there is a necessity, forsooth.* — νὴ
Δία is ironical. Heslop and Kennedy render it, *I suppose.* — νῦν δέ.
νῦν qualifies γιγνόμενα especially, but influences also the whole question by its emphatic position at the beginning : *but* NOW *what ought
we to think of things that are now taking place.* — 14. ἐγὼ μέν, *I for
my part,* whatever may be the opinion of others. L. & S. Lex. μέν, 7.
— 16. ἤ, interrogative, involves the antithesis to the preceding μέν :
or if you do not think so, do you wish ? See explanation and examples in Lex. ἤ interrogative, 2. — εἰπέ like ἄγε and φέρε is used irre-
spective of the number of persons addressed. C. 656. It brings the
question home to each hearer. — 17. αὐτῶν is gen. of source after πυνθάνεσθαι, and is used instead of ἀλλήλων, as it often is. So in English we can say, *inquire among yourselves,* or *inquire of one another.*
Longinus (18) quotes the passage, doubtless from memory, with ἀλλήλων instead of αὐτῶν. Some editions (Bekker, Dindorf, Whiston, but

ὅσον and πόρους οὕστινας in the same way as with τρόπον ἦν: *the kind*
of armament and the number of men and the supplies of money which
I think would deliver us from such a state, and how the other requisites
might, as it seems to me, be best and most expeditiously provided, I
will now also (or *even now,* i. e. *at once,* Heslop ; Franke, *statim*) en-
deavor to tell. — 14. 15. κρίνατε (aor.) denotes a momentary, προ-
λαμβάνετε (pres.) a continued action : *form your judgment when you*
have heard all I have to say : don't be prejudging as I go on. Madv.
141. Heslop. Some copies insert καί before μή. — πρότερον, sc. before you have heard, defines as well as emphasizes the προ-. —
16. μηδ᾽...λέγειν, *nor if I seem to any one to be recommending an*
entirely new force. — ἐξ ἀρχῆς, lit. *from the beginning* = *entirely.*
The novelty of the proposed force consisted in its being made up of
citizens instead of mercenaries, and being constantly maintained instead of being raised anew for every new emergency (τῇ νυνὶ βοηθείᾳ.)
It might take longer to raise such a force and provide for its subsistence, hence some might charge him with the very *delay* (ἀναβάλλειν)
which he deprecated. But it would prove the most expeditious in
the end ; *for,* he proceeds to say, *it is not those who cried "Quick !"*
and " To-day !" that speak most to the purpose. — οἱ εἰπόντες is past ;
those who have spoken on former occasions, and ταχύ and τήμερον
were the very words which they spoke. — 19. οὐ γὰρ ἄν, κ. τ. λ., *for*
we could not prevent what has already happened by present succor, sc.
if we should render it ever so immediately (implied protasis, C. 658 a ;
Cu. 575 ; G. 211 ; H. 783). The maxim is so obvious as to be almost
common-place in itself ; but it is so well put, and in such a connection as to form (sit venia verbo) *a knock-down argument.* —
15. 21. ἀλλ᾽ ὃς ἄν, *but he speaks most to the purpose who can show.* —
τίς...πόση...πόθεν answer to the ἦν...ὅσον...οὕστινας of the thirteenth
section (τίς having reference to the kind of troops, πόση to the number, and πόθεν to the ways and means of support, cf. § 20 below), and
πορισθεῖσα belongs with each of the interrogatives and denotes the
preliminary action or condition which will enable the troops to *hold*
out : what force, and how great, and from what source provided and
supplied (i. e. in case it be provided and supplied, C. 635 ; Cu. 583 ;
G. 226 ; H. 751) *will be able to keep the field.* The conciseness and
flexibility of the Greek is seen in such sentences. — 23. πεισθέντες,
of our own accord. —24. τοῦ λοιποῦ, C. 433 a ; Cu. 426 ; H. 591. —
26. μὴ κωλύων, *not, however, wishing to oppose.* μή, not οὐ, because

nant signification of *awake* and *start off: that* YOU *may perhaps awake
from this your excessive apathy, and start off, just as you did to Eubœa.* After ὥσπερ understand ὡρμήσατε. — 11. **εἰς Εὔβοιαν.** This
expedition was sent to aid the Eubœans against the Thebans, B. C.
358, and was successful in compelling the latter to evacuate the
island. It was a frequent subject of glorification with the Athenians.
Demosthenes himself was one of the trierarchs (*De Cor.*, 99), and Grote
suggests (XI. 307) that he doubtless heard the appeal of Timotheus,
whose eloquence moved the Athenians to undertake the expedition,
and whose generalship conducted it to so successful an issue. —
12. **εἰς ῾Αλίαρτον.** This happened B. C. 395, before the birth of
Demosthenes; hence πρότερόν ποτέ φασιν. The Athenians under
Thrasybulus marched to assist the Thebans against the Spartans, and
arrived just in season to turn the scale and compel the Spartans to
withdraw from Bœotia. This expedition is also mentioned, *De Cor.*,
96. — 12. **τὰ τελευταῖα,** *finally,* as the last instance. — 13. **πρῴην,**
recently. It was two or three years previous to this oration, B. C.
353–2. — 18. 13. **οὗτοι παντελῶς, κ. τ. λ.,** *and even if you should
not achieve this as* I *say you ought, it* (the preparation which I recommend) *is by no means a thing to be despised in order that either through
the fear* which it would cause, etc. — 17. **εἰσί…εἰσίν,** cf. πότ᾿…πότε,
§ 10, and note there. — **ἐξαγγέλλοντες** denotes a customary action,
who are in the habit of reporting, carrying *abroad* intelligence, ἐξ-. —
18. **πλείους τοῦ δέοντος,** *more than there should be;* in eo numero fue-
runt Philocrates, Phryno, Aristodemus, Neoptolemus, Ctesiphon, alii.
Sauppe. — 19. **μηδενός,** not οὐδενός, on account of ἵνα, says Franke;
but better with Rehdantz, because it is an implied condition; *if
there were nothing to prevent you sailing against his country,* as there
would not be, if you raise a permanent force and take advantage of the
winds and the situation (cf. § 31) as I recommend. — 20. **ἂν ἐνδῷ
καιρόν,** *should he* (Philip) *give you an opportunity.* — 19. 21. **ταῦτα
μέν…πρὸς δέ,** cf. note, § 17, above. — **δεδόχθαι…καὶ παρεσκευάσθαι,**
immediately voted and at once provided. C. 599; Cu. 506; G. 202, 2;
H. 715. — **πρὸς τούτοις,** *besides this* (Bekker, Dindorf, Heslop, Whiston, etc.), al. πρὸ τούτων, *before this* (Franke, Sauppe, Rehdantz, etc.).
The former reading, found in good MSS., accords better with the
sentence immediately preceding, and is confirmed by πρὸς τούτοις,
§ 22. — 23. **προχειρίσασθαι,** *to get ready to hand.* Whiston. —
25. **μή μοι,** *none of your ten thousand, nor twice ten thousand merce-*

naries. The acc. and dat. depend on λέγητε or some such verb implied in μή. — 26. **ἐπιστολιμαίους**, *on paper,* defined by ἐν τοῖς ψηφίσμασιν below, § 30. — **ταύτας**, sc. with which you are so familiar. — 27. **ἀλλ' ἣ...ἔσται**, *but a force which shall belong to the state,* i. e. consisting, not of mercenaries alone, but largely of citizens, and therefore fully subject to the command and at the disposal of the state, instead of running off to fight their own battles, 24 below. This is the reading of most of the editions. Some MSS. read ἀλλ' ἥ. — **κἂν...ἀκολουθήσει**, *and which, whether you elect one or more, or this or that man, or any one whatever as general, will obey and follow him.* — **τὸν δεῖνα**, cf. note, *Ol.,* II. 31 ; III. 35.

20. P. 7, l. 3. **τίς...πόση...πόθεν**, cf. note, § 15 above. — **πῶς... ποιεῖν**, i. e. how the force can be so constituted that it will cheerfully obey the commander and fight the battles of the country. — 5. **καθ'** is distinctive, *one by one.* — 6. **ξένους μὲν λέγω**, *mercenaries I do indeed propose.* Lest the remark in the previous section, "none of your ten thousand, or twice ten thousand mercenaries," should be misunderstood, and prejudice the minds of his hearers, for whom it was much easier and pleasanter to *vote any number of mercenaries* than to take the field themselves, he takes the earliest opportunity to suggest that he does not propose to dispense entirely with this usual and popular species of troops. At the same time he intimates by the word μέν that this is not the only force which he proposes. Instead, however, of proceeding at once to state the number of mercenaries, — a number which they would deem contemptibly small for them to vote,—he stops to warn them against their pernicious habit of voting large and doing little or nothing ; in other words, as soon as he has relieved their minds by this popular suggestion, he returns to his main point, "*none of your myriads,*" etc., and insists that they shall vote no more than they can and will execute. If any reader sees in this not only rhetorical art, but *artifice,* he should remember that the Athenian people would not listen to an orator who did not please their tastes and yield more or less to their prejudices. — 7. **καὶ ὅπως**, *and beware how you do what has many times harmed you.* For the construction, see C. 626 ; Cu. 553, Obs.; G. 218, N. 2 ; H. 756 a. — **ποιήσετε**, al. *ποιήσητε.* But the fut. ind. is more common than the subj., especially with Dem., in such warnings. Cf. Vömel in loc. — 9. **ἐπὶ...ποιεῖτε**, *when it comes to* (ἐπί with the dative) *the doing* (action, business, agendum), *you do not execute* (effect, accomplish, faci-

4

tis) *even the smallest.* Cf. note, *Ol.,* III. 15. — 10. ἀλλὰ...φαίνηται,
*but after you have executed and provided the small, add to these from
time to time* (imper. pres.), *if they prove* (not merely *seem,* but *are
shown) to be too small.* C. 514 ; H. 662. — 21. 12. λέγω δή resumes
the ξένους μὲν λέγω above, emphasizing λέγω, however, instead of
ξένους, *I propose then.* δή resumptive = *then,* or *I say.* — στρατιώτας here means *foot-soldiers ; the cavalry* are spoken of below, ἱππέας.
So below, §§ 28, 33. — ἐξ ἧς...ἡλικίας, *of whatever age you may think
advisable.* It was customary to specify in the bill some age as the
limit of an enlistment. — 15. μὴ μακρόν. The orator sweetens the
bitter draught as often and as much as possible. — 17. ἀλλήλοις is dative after ἐξ διαδοχῆς, *relieving one another.* — 18. διακοσίους...πεντή-
κοντα. One tenth of the whole force was to be cavalry, — the usual
proportion in the Greek service, — and at least one fourth of the infantry and the cavalry were to be Athenians. — 19. ὥσπερ is correlative to τὸν αὐτὸν τρόπον in *Ol.,* I. 15, also, where see note : *in the
same manner as the foot-soldiers,* i. e. for the same length of time,
and relieving each other in the same way. — ἱππαγωγούς, sc. εἶναι
κελεύω. Ad rem, see note on τριήρεις, § 16, above. — 22. 22. ταχείας
τριήρεις, see note § 16. — 23. ναυτικόν shows that these swift triremes, war-galleys, were emphatically the *navy.* On Philip's navy,
see Grote, XI. 424. — τριήρων ἡμῖν, gen. of want and dat. of advantage after δεῖ. C. 414, 453 ; Cu. 431 ; H. 575, or dat. of the person
and gen. of the thing. G. 184, N. 1.— καί, *too,* i. e. besides the
transports. — ὅπως...πλέῃ, i. e. the swift ships are to serve as a con-
voy. — 26. τηλικαύτην, *of such amount,* as named above, i. e. here, *so
small* = tantillam. — 27. Καὶ πολίτας...κελεύω, *and why I recommend* (move) *that those who serve should be* CITIZENS. As only one
fourth of the soldiers were to be citizens, various suggestions have
been made to get over the difficulty, such, e. g. as making πολίτας,
or πολίτας τοὺς στρατευομένους, the subject, and εἶναι =, παρεῖναι (§ 23).
But the above is the only translation of which the Greek will admit.
συστρατευομένους has been proposed as an amendment, instead of
στρατευομένους, so as to correspond with the actual constitution of
the force as above recommended. But even then the article would
not be right. And as the reading is, it corresponds with the *characteristic feature* of the recommendation : *a potiori nomen fit.*

D. Reasons for this recommendation (23–27).

23–27. I RECOMMEND THIS COMPARATIVELY SMALL FORCE, BE-

CAUSE IT IS IMPRACTICABLE FOR US NOW TO PROVIDE AN ARMY THAT
CAN MEET PHILIP'S ARMY ON THE FIELD OF BATTLE. AND I URGE
THAT A CONSIDERABLE PART OF THE FORCE CONSIST OF ATHENIANS,
BECAUSE IT IS NO NEW THING FOR CITIZENS TO SERVE IN YOUR
ARMIES, AND BECAUSE, SINCE MERCENARY SOLDIERS, OFFICERED,
TOO, MORE OR LESS, BY FOREIGNERS, HAVE CARRIED ON YOUR WARS,
THEY CONQUER YOUR FRIENDS, AND FIGHT THEIR OWN BATTLES FOR
THEIR OWN INTEREST, WHILE YOU AND YOUR GENERALS ARE EN-
GROSSED WITH SPORTS AND FESTIVALS.

23. P. 8, l. 1. Τοσαύτην here takes the place of τηλικαύτην in the
previous section, with the same meaning and the same construction,
sc. ἀποχρῆν οἶμαι, or possibly εἶναι κελεύω. — τοσαύτην μὲν...πολίτας
δέ, so small in the first place — in the second place citizens. C. 701 q.
— 2. ἐκείνῳ, as usual, refers to Philip. — 3. λῃστεύειν, as opposed to
παραταξομένην = to carry on a guerilla warfare. — 4. τὴν πρώτην,
in the first place = for the present. Cf. Ol., III. 2. — 5. ὑπέρογκον
...ταπεινήν, it must not be over-large nor on the other hand altogether
contemptible. — 7. καὶ πρότερόν ποτ' ἀκούω. Compare the καὶ πρότερόν
ποτέ φασιν of § 17. The reference in both sections is to the same
war, often called the Corinthian War, B. C. 395. Curtius, IV. 245;
Grote, IX. 454. Little is known of Polystratus. He is mentioned
also in the Or. con. Leptinem, § 84. The other two generals here
named were among the ablest and most distinguished of the Athenian
generals. Iphicrates gained especial distinction by defeating (in the
Corinthian War) a Lacedæmonian mora (about 600 men) of heavy
infantry with the light-armed πελτασταί which he organized and
trained. Whiston in loc.; Curtius, IV. 263; Thirlwall, I. 571, Amer.
ed.; Grote, IX. 482. Chabrias was scarcely less famous. Curtius,
IV. 459, V. 93; Thirlwall, II. 20, 82. — 24. οἶδα ἀκούων. The
orator still refers to the same war, and now adds a reference to its
successes which, of course, he knows only by what he has heard. Cf.
ἀκούων σύνοιδα, Ol., III. 3. — 11. Λακεδαιμονίους...ὑμεῖς μετ' ἐκείνων.
These are the words which the orator wishes to emphasize: that
these mercenaries fighting by your side and YOU BY THEIRS conquered
the LACEDÆMONIANS. It is curious and instructive to see Demosthenes thus referring to the service of Athenian citizens in their
armies as a matter of hearsay beyond the personal knowledge of himself and his hearers, so long and so entirely had they come to rely on
mercenaries. See on this subject Curtius, IV. 310; Grote, XI. 390.

— 14. **νίκᾳ,** *they are continually conquering your* FRIENDS, *while your* ENEMIES, *etc.* — 16. **παρακύψαντα,** *after a passing glance.* — 17. **πρὸς Ἀρτάβαζον.** See *Ol.,* II. 28, where the orator asks why all their generals run away from the service on which they are sent and seek out wars of their own. The allusion there and here is probably to Chares, who, in the Social War, having no money to pay his troops, lent them to the Persian satrap Artabazus, who was then in rebellion against the king. He gained a victory for the satrap, and was well paid for the service, but came very near involving the Athenians in a war with the king of Persia. Diod., XVI. 22 ; Grote, XI. 324. — 17. **μᾶλλον,** *rather* than to **τὸν τῆς πόλεως πόλεμον.** — 18. **εἰκότως,** *of course,* followed by **γάρ,** which assigns the reason in the form of a *gnome* or apothegm. — 19. **μὴ διδόντα,** conditional negative = *if he does not find them pay.* — 25. 21. **πορίσαντας...παρακαταστήσαντας,** *by providing pay and by attaching citizen soldiers as eye-witnesses of the conduct of your generals.* C. 674 ; Cu. 581 ; G. 277, 2 ; H. 789, 6. **μάρτυρας** is used below, § 47, instead of **ἐπόπτας.** — 23. **ἐπεὶ νῦν γε,** *for the way we manage things now certainly is ridiculous,* **γέλως** being the predicate in an emphatic position. — 25. **μὰ Δί'...γε,** *no indeed, not we.* — 26. **πολεμοῦμεν,** in the war of Amphipolis. — 26. 27. **οὐκ ἐχειροτονεῖτε,** *and did you not* (lately, this very year, according to your custom in time of war) *elect from among yourselves taxiarchs and generals and phylarchs ten of each, and two hipparchs? What, then, are all these doing,* and why, when you have such an ample supply of Athenian officers, do you not only employ mercenary troops, but let foreign officers command them ? Such seems to be the spirit of the argument in this and the following sections. The Athenian army was organized and officered, according to the democratic constitution of the state, with ten generals, ten taxiarchs (division commanders), and ten phylarchs (cavalry officers), one from each tribe ; and in the earlier and better days of Athenian history, as, for example, at the battle of Marathon, these were all in the field and at their post of duty. But now in this degenerate age, Demosthenes says, with the exception of one man, whom they *may perchance* send out to the war (**ὃν ἂν ἐκπέμψητε ἐπὶ τὸν πόλεμον**), they were all in the city helping the sacrificial magistrates conduct the sacred processions (**μετὰ τῶν ἱεροποιῶν**) ! Ten of these ἱεροποιοί were elected each year, one from each tribe, as masters of religious ceremonies.

P. 9, l. 4. **ὥσπερ γάρ**, *for you elect your taxiarchs and your
phylarchs not for the war, but for the agora, just like those who
model generals in plaster*, that is, you make your military officers
mere statuettes, puppets, and figure-heads for your shows and ceremonies. These would of course be *in* and *for the agora*. — **27. 7. οὐ
γὰρ ἐχρῆν**, *for ought not taxiarchs to have been* FROM AMONG YOUR-
SELVES, *a hippareh* FROM AMONG YOURSELVES, *officers of* YOUR OWN
(Athenian citizens), *in order that the army might have been really at
the disposal of the state?* Observe the emphatic repetition. — 9. **ἵν'
ἦν**. **ἵνα** with a past tense of the ind. to denote the unattained end
of an unfulfilled condition. G. 216, 3 ; C. 624, d ; H. 742 ; Madv.
131 b, 3. — **ἀλλ'**, *nay*. Kennedy renders it *or*. — 10. **εἰς Δῆμνον**.
From a lately discovered fragment of Hyperides we learn that one of
the two hipparchs was sent every year to Lemnos, for the purpose,
as we may conclude from this passage, of taking part in some proces-
sion of the Cleruchs (Athenian settlers), or other sacred solemnity,
rather than for the discharge of military duty. Heslop. — 12. **τῶν
δ' ὑπὲρ...ἱππαρχεῖν**, *while Menelaus* (a foreigner) *is hipparch of those
who are contending for the possessions of the state* (Athens). Of this
Menelaus nothing is *known* except that he was not an Athenian ;
the statement of Harpocration that he was half-brother of Philip is
scarcely probable. — 13. **ἀλλ'...κεχειροτονημένον**, *but this man, whatever his character may be, ought to have been elected by you,* i. e. he
ought to have been an *Athenian*, for a foreigner might be *hired*, but
could not be truly and properly *elected*. See Schaefer in loc.

E. Ways and Means (28 – 30).

28 – 30. I RECOMMEND THAT YOU RAISE NINETY-TWO TALENTS AS
MEANS OF SUBSISTENCE FOR THE ARMY AND NAVY. THE REST THE
ARMY ITSELF WILL SUPPLY FROM THE WAR. FROM WHAT SOURCES
THIS SUM CAN BE RAISED WILL APPEAR FROM THE SCHEDULE HERE-
WITH SUBMITTED.

28. 16. **ταῦτα μέν**, sc. the kind of armament and the number of
troops ; the first and second topics suggested § 13 ; **τὸ δὲ τῶν χρημάτων**,
the third part of his exposition, which he there calls **πόρους οὕστινας
χρημάτων**. — 18. **περαίνω**, pres. ind. = *I proceed to despatch*. — **χρήματα τοίνυν**, *as to supplies, then, the* (cost of) *subsistence, ration-money
only for this force, is ninety talents and a little over.* The items sum
up ninety-two talents, it will be seen. With this adverbial use of
πρός compare our *too*, which is only an emphatic *to*. — 22. **τοῦ μηνὸς**

ἑκάστου. The calculation is for the year of twelve months, for it is
to be a permanent force. — 23. τοσαῦθ' ἕτερα, *as much more*, sc. forty
talents. The *budget* (for these estimates remind us of the yearly budget
laid before the British Parliament, and the Athenian orator's office at
this time was scarcely less complex than that of the British Minister,
who is the leader in the House of Commons) is made up as follows: —

For the ships, 10 ships × 20 minæ × 12 months = 2,400 minæ   . = 40 talents
For the foot-soldiers, 2,000 foot × 10 drachmas × 12 months
   = 240,000 drachmas . . . . = 40   "
For the horse, 200 horsemen × 30 drachmas × 12 mths. = 72,000 dr. = 12 "

          Sum total for the year . . . . 92 talents

A talent was nominally a little less than $1,000, and a drachma
somewhat less than a Massachusetts shilling ($\frac{1}{6}$ of $1). The student
may aid his memory by keeping in mind this standard of comparison,
and for practical purposes generally it will be sufficiently accurate.
It should be remembered, however, that the *value* of money, as esti-
mated in the corn or other means of subsistence it would buy, was
many times its present value. Böckh, *Pub. Econ.* B. I., passim ;
Dic. Antiq., Talentum. Demosthenes's allowance, therefore (of 30
drachmas a month, a shilling a day), for the subsistence of the horse-
man with his horse, and a third of that sum (less than 6 cents a day)
for the foot-soldier, is not so scanty as with the present value of
money it would seem to be. — 25. οὖσιν, being, i. e. *numbering.* —
26. λαμβάνῃ, pres. subj. *receive statedly*, from month to month. —
29. 27. ἀφορμήν is literally a starting-point. Heslop renders it
start here ; Whiston, *provision : but if any one thinks it to be a small
outfit that ration-money only be furnished to begin with, he is mistaken.* — For γιγνώσκω in the sense of think, or judge, see § 1 and
note there.

    P. 10, l. 3. προσποριεῖ, *will provide what else* (προς-) *is required
from the war* (i. e. not for itself, which would require the middle,
but so that you will not have to provide it, cf. πορίσωσιν, *Ol.*, II. 16).
Böckh remarks on this passage in his *Pub. Econ.*, B. II., Ch. 22, " this
proposal is worthy of remark as having no parallel in any Grecian
author ; it is the outline of a plan for embodying a military force to
maintain itself at free quarters and at the same time to form a permanent standing army, though its continuance was indeed limited to
the duration of the war." Heslop. — ΠΟΡΟΥ ΑΠΟΔΕΙΞΙΣ.
Exposé of Ways and Means. A schedule of resources available

in the Ægean during that season." Leake's *Northern Greece*, quoted
by Whiston. — 21. ἡνίκ' ἂν ἡμεῖς μὴ δυναίμεθα is subjective, giving
the view of Philip: ἡνίκα ἡμεῖς οὐ δυνάμεθα would be objective, stat-
ing the fact as accepted by the speaker and generally understood.
The latter would mean, *when we cannot;* the former may be rendered,' *when he thinks we cannot,* or, more exactly, *whenever in his
opinion we should not be able.* C. 643 e, 686 n; L. & S. *Lex.* This
form also expresses a *repeated* condition negatively, answering to the
customary action expressed by ἐπιχειρεῖ. — 32. 23. ὑστεριοῦμεν, *for
we shall be too late for everything,* as, e. g. in the cases of Methone,
Pagasæ, and Potidæa, mentioned below, § 35. — 25. ὑπάρχει δ' ὑμῖν,
and you are at liberty (licet, Franke) *to use as a winter station for the
force Lemnos,* etc.   The islands here named, together with Scopelus,
Halonesus, Peparethus, etc., were at this time subject to Athens.

P. 11, l. 3. ὑπάρχει, *are in readiness;* ὑπάρχειν is understood with
χρή. — τὴν δ' ὥραν, *and during* (acc.) *the season of the year when it
is both easy to land* (come to the land and remain there, dat.) *and the
winds are safe.* — 5. τὸ τῶν πνευμάτων, strictly the matter of the winds,
is a more general expression for the winds themselves.   Cf. τὰ τῆς
τύχης, § 12, and τὸ τῶν θεῶν, and τὸ τῆς τύχης, 45. — 5. πρὸς αὐτῇ,
κ. τ. λ., *they will easily take their station near his country and at the
entrances of his ports,* sc. to land troops to carry out the system of
λῃστεία recommended in § 23 and to interfere with commerce.

G.   The probable results of this course, in contrast with the wretched
state of things now existing at Athens (33 – 46).

33 – 46.   Provide the money and enlist the army for the
war, as I recommend, and you will cease to be always deliberating, and accomplishing nothing.   You will also take
away from Philip his chief resources, for he supports his
army by plundering you and your allies.   And you will no
longer be always too late.   Why is it that your festivals
always come off at the appointed time, while your military
expeditions are always behind the time?   Because in the
former everything is fixed by law, whereas in the latter
there is nothing settled.   You should not follow events,
but lead them, as you expect your generals to lead your
armies.   But you fight just as barbarians box, always cov-
ering the place after you are hit, and following Philip
hither and thither as if he were the commander of your

ARMIES. DO YOU ASK WHERE WE SHOULD ATTACK HIM? HAVE
YOUR FORCE IN THE FIELD, AND YOU WILL SOON FIND HIS WEAK
POINTS. SEND OUT EVEN A SMALL FORCE OF ATHENIAN CITIZENS,
AND THE FAVOR OF THE GODS AND OF FORTUNE WILL GO WITH
THEM.

33. P. 11, l. 7. Ἅ = *How*, adverbial accusative. C. 483, b ; Cu.
201 ; G. 160 ; H. 552. — παρά, alongside of, hence *at the time of and
according to.* It might be rendered *from* or *through*, as in § 11. —
κύριος is pred. after κατστάς. Render : *How, therefore, and when he
shall use the force, the general who is put in command of this matter
will decide as occasion may arise.* — 10. γέγραφα, sc. in my motion. —
12. παρασκευάσαντες…κατακλείσητε, *and then, after having furnished
the other things required, the foot-soldiers, the triremes, the cavalry, in
short, the whole force complete, you bind them by law to remain at the
war.* So Sauppe and Dindorf, governing δύναμιν by παρασκευάσαντες
and repeating it after κατακλείσητε. Franke and Rehdantz separate
ἐντελῆ from δύναμιν and make it agree with τἄλλα, thus summing up
the particulars. Whatever be the construction, it is proleptic = *so as
to be complete.* — 14. τῶν μὲν χρημάτων, *becoming (as you are not now)
the receivers and providers of the money yourselves and requiring from
the general the due (τόν) account of his doings.* — πορισταί, *providing
it yourselves instead of letting your generals take it perchance from
your friends and allies* (§ 24), just as ἐπὶ τῷ πολέμῳ, l. 14, means the
war to which they are sent in contrast with wars of their own to enrich
or at least to support themselves. — 18. πλέον…ποιοῦντες, *and making
no progress*, L. & S. under πλείων. — 34. 19. πρῶτον μέν is correlative to ἔπειτα, l. 23 = *in the first place…in the second place.* — 21. ὑμετέρων ὑμῖν, emphatic juxtaposition : *he carries on war with* YOU *by
means of what he gets from* YOUR OWN *allies.* — 22. ἄγων καὶ φέρων
= agere et ferre, is explained in the *Lex.*, which see. — 22. τοὺς
πλέοντας, sc. of your allies = *their merchantmen*, their commerce. —
23. αὐτοί, *yourselves as well as your allies will be saved from robbery
and plunder.* — 24. οὐχ, *and he (Philip) will not do as he has done in
time past, when he made a descent upon Lemnos and Imbrus and carried away captive your citizens* (Athenian settlers, cf. note, § 32),
when he seized the ships at Geræstus and levied, etc. The verbs in
these specifications are all to be understood in the future with οὐχ.
These are the things which he will no longer be permitted to do.
Observe that these clauses have no connectives, cf. note § 4. Geræs-

tus was a promontory and town in the South of Eubœa. It was a convenient point for corn-ships and other vessels to touch at on their way from the Levant to Attica. Grote, X. 176.

P. 12, l. 1. τὴν ἱερὰν...τριήρη, probably the Paralus. There was also another sacred vessel called the Salaminia, and indeed still others of less distinction in the time of Demosthenes. Besides going on the sacred embassies (θεωρίαι) to Delos and elsewhere, these vessels carried despatches, embassadors, and other officers of state. See art. Salaminia, *Dic. Antiq.* — 3. ἠδύνασθε, al. δύνασθε. — εἰς τοὺς χρόνους, strictly, *to* or *for* the times, to correspond with the *sending* succor expressed by βοηθεῖν. — 5. Παναθηναίων...Διονυσίων. There were two Panathenaic festivals, the Less observed annually, and the Greater celebrated once in four years, and four Dionysiac festivals, all annual, observed at different times and places in honor of the god Dionysus, at the greatest of which, observed in the city, crowds of strangers as well as citizens were present, and the new tragedies were exhibited. See the documents in *De Cor.*; L. & S. *Lex.*; and more fully, *Dic. Antiq.* — 6. τοῦ καθήκοντος χρόνου, *at the proper time.* C. 433; Cu. 426; G. 179; H. 591. — 7. ἰδιῶται, properly private individuals as distinguished from public and professional men ; here, the inexperienced, laymen as it were, in distinction from experts, δεινοί. — 8. εἰς ἅ, κ. τ. λ., *for which you are in the habit of expending more money than for any one of your military expeditions, and which are more numerously attended and more magnificent than any I know of anywhere.* — τοσαῦτα...ὅσα οὐδ' ἕνα, lit. so much as none = *more than any*, with an emphasis, however, on the τοσαῦτα which might be expressed in English by combining the two forms = *so much* money...more than for any, etc. — Μεθώνην. Cf. special Introduction, p. 51. Observe the asyndeton, cf. note § 4. — 36. 15. ἐκ πολλοῦ, *long beforehand.* — χορηγός. It was the duty of the choragus, who was one of the rich men of the state, to provide, maintain, and train the dramatic choruses at the Dionysiac festivals. — γυμνασίαρχος, gymnasiarch of his tribe. Each tribe appointed its own gymnasiarchs. It was their office to provide, maintain, and train athletes for the games at the festivals. See *Dic. Antiq.* — 16. τί λαβόντα τί δεῖ ποιεῖν, *what* money he is to *receive and what he must do* in return for it. The action denoted by the part. being preliminary to that expressed by the verb, and the two questions being condensed into one clause in the Greek, cf. note § 3. — 19. ἄτακτα...ἀόριστα, *un-*

Cu. 374; G. 142, N. 3; H. 528 n.—ὡς οὐκ ἔδει = *unhappily.* Whiston. — οὐ μὴν ἀλλ' ἴσως οὐχ, *although, perhaps, not at all.* — 9. εἰ
μὲν...δημηγορεῖν, *if indeed all that we may pass over in speaking to
avoid giving offence would pass over as matters of fact, we ought to
speak so as to please you.* — τὰ πράγματα is the subject of ὑπερβήσεται, lit. *the things* (as well as the words) *will pass over.* So Westermann, Whiston, Rehdantz. Others, as Franke and Heslop, make
τις the subject, and give ὑπερβήσεται a causative sense, *if he could
thereby cause the things to pass over.* — 11. εἰ δ' ἡ, κ. τ. λ., *but if gra-
ciousness of speech when it is ill-timed becomes a damage in action, it
is a shame,* etc. It is difficult to express our orator's favorite contrast of λόγος and ἔργον or πρᾶγμα in good English. — 39. 15. μηδὲ
τοῦτο, κ. τ. λ., *and not be able to learn so much as this even, that
they who would carry on war successfully must not follow in the
wake of events, but must themselves march in advance of events.* —
20. τῶν πραγμάτων depends on ἡγεῖσθαι to be supplied from the previous clause : *so also must they who sit in council* (consult for the
public good) *take the lead of events* (guide circumstances). — τὰ συμβάντα...διώκειν is only a stronger expression for ἀκολουθεῖν τοῖς πράγμασιν, lit. *to be continually pursuing what has happened,* and so is
already past and gone. — 40. 24. ἁπάντων, *of all the Greek states.*
Cf. 24, 216 : τριήρεις ὅσας οὐδεμία πόλις Ἑλληνὶς κέκτηται, κ. τ. λ.
On the Mil. and Nav. Force of Athens, see Böckh. *Pub. Econ.,* B. II.
c. 21, and the Revenue, B. III. — 25. μέχρι...ἡμέρας, *to this very day.*

P. 14, l. 1. οὐδὲν δ' ἀπολείπετε, *and you fail in no particular*
(lit. you leave off nothing) *to carry on war with Philip just as the
barbarians box.* Al. οὐδενὸς ἀπολείπεσθε, which Schaefer and Whiston render, *and yet there is nothing in which you do not interfere,* and
other editors in other ways. But most editors have adopted the
reading of our text, and justify the reading and construction by reference to Plato's *Phædo,* 69 B. Barbarians, of course, represent un-
skilful boxers as compared with the practised Greeks. Instead of
πολεμεῖν, Schaefer and Whiston read πολεμεῖτε. — 4. τῆς πληγῆς
ἔχεται, *always feels for the blow,* lays hold of it as it were. So Heslop,
Kennedy, and Whiston. Or πληγῆς may mean *the wound,* the part
struck : *when stricken, he always lays hold of the part struck.* —
ἐκεῖσέ...χεῖρες, lit. *thither are his hands,* with a singular mixture of
motion and rest in the expression, which is doubtless intended to
heighten the burlesque. — 41. 6. καὶ ὑμεῖς, *so you.* Cf. καὶ περὶ τῶν

πραγμάτων, *Ol.*, I. 11, and note there. — 9. **στρατηγεῖσθε,** *you are commanded by him,* as if he were your general. — 11. **πρὸ...προορᾶτε... πρίν,** triple emphasis, well rendered by Heslop: *nor before events take place do you foresee anything till you hear that something has happened or is happening.* — 42. 14. **δοκεῖ,** personal for impersonal. Cf. note, *Ol.*, I. 10, where also there is an equally distinct recognition of the providence of the gods. — 16. **τοῖς γιγνομένοις,** dat. after αἰσχυνόμενος, cf. τοῖς πράγμασιν, § 2 and note there. — 19. **ἀποχρῆν,** *I think some of you would be satisfied with a state of things in consequence of which we should as a state have incurred dishonor and the reproach of cowardice and the deepest disgrace of every kind.* The subject of ἀποχρῆν is contained in the relative clause ἐξ ὧν, κ. τ. λ. C. 571, f. — **εἴπερ...ἀπεγνώκατε,** *if, that is, you have not altogether given up in despair.* — 43. 26. **ἀρχήν.** "Though they had begun the war in the hope of punishing him for his duplicity in appropriating Amphi- olis, they had been themselves the losers by the capture of Pydna, Potidæa, Methone, etc.; and they were now thrown upon the defen- sive, without security for their maritime allies, their commerce, or their coasts." Grote, XI. p. 427. — 26. **περί** = *about* ; **ὑπέρ,** l. 27 = *for the sake of.* It is a good illustration of the difference between the words.

P. 15, l. 2. **ὅτι γε οὐ στήσεται,** *that, to say the least, he will not stop,* sc. in his conquests and encroachments on our possessions. — **εἶτα** expresses surprise or indignation : *shall we then wait for this,* sc. for some one else to stop him. — 3. **τριήρεις κενάς.** See note, *Ol.*, III. 5. — 3. **τὰς παρὰ τοῦ δεῖνος ἐλπίδας,** *the* HOPES *from* SOMEBODY (Mr. Such-an-one, cf. note, *Ol.*, III. 35), called *the hopes from the bema,* below, l. 17; the article points to familiar facts, and it is doubt- less a hit at some of the leading orators. — 44. 5. **οὐκ ἔξιμεν αὐτοί, κ. τ. λ.,** *shall we not go forth ourselves with some portion at least of soldiers who are our own citizens now, although we have not done it before?* Every word in this question is full of meaning, from the WE OURSELVES to the NOW, and the NOT BEFORE ; and the rapid series of interrogations expresses the intense ardor and earnestness of the speaker. — 8. **ἤρετό τις.** The question is rhetorically put, as if actually heard by the orator : "I heard some one ask." Heslop. — **τὰ σαθρά,** *the rotten parts.* The same word is used, *Ol.*, II. 21, and the same idea is there more fully developed. — 12. **οὐδέποτ' οὐδέν... μή.** C. 627, 713 ; Cu. 619, 620 ; G. 257, 283, 8 ; H. 843, 845. The emphatic denial is well expressed by Heslop : *there is no chance of our ever having anything done that should be done.* — 45. 13. **μέρος τι τῆς πόλεως** = μέρει τινι στρατιωτῶν οἰκείων, l. 6, above. — 14. **συναποσταλῇ**, *sent abroad with the rest of the army.* — **καὶ τὸ...συναγωνίζεται**, *the good-will of the gods and of Fortune too aids us in the struggle.* Cf. *Ol.*, I. 1 ; II. 2, and notes there. Kennedy and Heslop make εὐμενές the predicate of τὸ τῶν θεῶν. Better with Whiston to make τὸ εὐμενές refer to τῆς τυχῆς as well as τῶν θεῶν, and the subject of συναγωνίζεται. — 16. **ψήφισμα κενόν**, *an empty resolution.* Cf. §§ 19, 30 and notes there. — 18. **οἱ μὲν ἐχθροί, κ. τ. λ.**, *your enemies laugh at them while your friends are frightened to death at* (or *stand in mortal dread of*) *such expeditions.* — **ἀποστόλους** is the object of καταγελῶσιν as well as of τεθνᾶσι τῷ δέει = μάλα δεδίασι, or ὑπερφοβοῦνται. — 46. 20. **ἕνα ἄνδρα** is of course the general without an army. — 22. **ὑποσχέσθαι...ἔστιν**, *to make promises, however, and assertions, and to accuse this man and that* is *possible.* The allusion is to Chares, whose promises became a proverb. — 25. **ἀθλίων...ξένων**, *miserable unpaid mercenaries.* *Ol.*, II. 28. — 26. **οἱ δ᾽ ὑπὲρ...ὦσιν**, *while those who lie to you without scruple about what he may have done* (in the field) *are here* (in your presence). **ῥᾳδίως** limits ψευδόμενοι (Franke, Rehdantz, Heslop, Whiston), not ἐνθάδ᾽ ὦσιν (Westermann, Kennedy). — 27. **ὑμεῖς...προσδοκᾶν**, *and you keep voting* (present) *at random* (whatever you may chance to) *from what you hear, pray* (καί) *what ought we to expect ?* Heslop would express καί by an emphasis : *what* can *we expect ?*

H. How shall this state of things be brought to an end (47–50).

47–50. SEND OUT CITIZEN-SOLDIERS. THEN THE SAME MEN WILL BE AT ONCE SOLDIERS IN THE RANKS, EYE-WITNESSES OF THE CONDUCT OF YOUR GENERALS, AND JUDGES WHEN THEY RENDER UP THEIR ACCOUNTS. CEASE LISTENING TO FABRICATED REPORTS OF PHILIP'S DOINGS. THESE SILLY STORY-MONGERS ARE NOT HIS COUNSELLORS. TAKE FOR GRANTED THAT HE IS YOUR ENEMY, WHOM YOU MUST FIGHT AT HOME IF YOU WILL NOT MEET HIM ABROAD, AND ACT ACCORDINGLY.

47. P. 16, l. 2. **ὅταν ὑμεῖς, κ. τ. λ.**, they will cease, *whenever* YOU, *gentlemen of Athens, make* (appoint) *the same persons soldiers, and witnesses of the conduct of your generals, and on their return home judges of the accounts,* sc. of the generals (*Ol.*, I. 28). Rather a democratic constitution for an army ! But thoroughly consonant

with the ideas and the government of the Athenians, and not more democratic than were the 10,000 Greeks in their retreat, as described by Xenophon (*Anab.* passim), nor without parallels in the citizen-soldiers of the United States in the late war. The generals, as well as the civil functionaries (see *De Cor.*, passim) were ὑπεύθυνοι, and, before they could be discharged, were required to render an account primarily of moneys expended, but also of their conduct generally. *Dic. Antiq.*, Ἐυθύνη. — 8. τουθ'...αἰσχύνης, *to such a pitch of dishonor.* Cf. *Ol.*, II. 21. — 9. κρίνεται...θανάτου, *is tried before you for his life.* Sauppe cites instances from Æschines, Demosthenes, and Diodorus — Autocles, Cephisodotus, Leosthenes, Callistratus, and Chares several times. — 11. ἀγωνίσασθαι περὶ θανάτου, *to hazard his life in a struggle with the enemy.* — 12. τῶν ἀνδραποδιστῶν καὶ λωποδυτῶν, kidnappers and thieves (originally clothes-stealers in the baths) were punished with death. Lys. 13, 68 ; Xen. *Mem.*, I. 2, 62. — 12. τοῦ προσήκοντος, sc. the death of a soldier. — 14. κριθέντα, *by sentence of the law.* — 48. 15. ἡμῶν, al. ὑμῶν, but ἡμῶν is required by περιερχόμεθα. It is in emphatic contrast or comparison with στρατηγῶν, l. 9, and in emphatic continuation of νῦν δέ, l. 7 : *while among* us *some go about the agora and report that Philip is concerting with the Lacedæmonians the overthrow of Theban supremacy* (over other Bœotian cities, such as Orchomenus, Thespiæ, and Platæa. Cf. Grote, XI. 405), *and is attempting the dissolution of the republics* (of which Athens was the protector and Sparta the perpetual enemy throughout Greece). — μετὰ Λακεδαιμονίων precedes φασί for emphasis. — πράττειν, lit. practising, managing. — διασπᾶν may depend on φασί (Franke, Rehdantz, etc.), or on πράττειν (Westermann, Heslop, etc.). It makes little difference — without πράττειν, διασπᾶν may express what he is *attempting* to do. — ὡς βασιλέα, *to the king* of Persia, who was so important a personage in the early periods of Greek history that he needs no other designation, and βασιλεύς is even used of him without the article like a proper name. For ὡς = πρός, see C. 711 ; Cu. 450 ; G. 192 ; H. 621 ; and L. & S., *Lex.* — 19. ἐν Ἰλλυριοῖς, cf. *Ol.*, I. 13. — οἱ δὲ...περιερχόμεθα, *and the rest of us come round severally inventing stories.* Their whole political activity, as Rehdantz remarks, moved in a circle beginning with περιιόντες (l. 15) and ending with περιερχόμεθα. — 49. 20. ἐγὼ δ' οἶμαι, *but for my part, though I verily believe he is intoxicated with the greatness of his achievements and dreams many such things in his imagination...still I*

settled and abiding conviction. πεπεισμένος εἴην would have expressed his conviction from time to time as occasions might arise. Goodwin (Moods and Tenses, 62, R.) considers εἰλόμην to be used in a sense approaching that of the gnomic aor. so as to be followed by a subj. — 16. ἐβουλόμην ἄν, *I could have wished*, if it were possible, as it is not — supposition contrary to fact, with the condition omitted. C. 636 ; Cu. 544 ; G. 226, 2 ; H. 752. So ἄν εἶπον, l. 19. Render : *as I know that it is for your interest to hear the best advice, so I could have wished to know with equal certainty that it will be for the interest of him who has given the advice,* i. e. that it will be for my interest that I have given you the best advice. — 19. νῦν δέ, *but as it is, though it is uncertain what the consequences to myself will be, yet in the full conviction that these counsels will be for your interest, if you carry them into execution, I choose to give them.* See a similar apprehension of the difficulty and danger of free speech, with the same resolution notwithstanding, *Ol.,* I. 16 ; III. 21. — ἐπί denotes the point of view or ground of action both with ἀδήλοις...γενησομένοις and with τῷ...πεπεῖσθαι, and might be rendered *in* with both : *in* the uncertainty, and *in* the conviction ; but the ὅμως which follows ἐπ' ἀδήλοις justifies the rendering *although*, as above. — 22. νικῴη δ' ὅ τι, *and may that prevail, whatever it may be, which will be for the interest of you all.* Compare the conclusion of *Ol.,* I. and III.

SECOND PHILIPPIC.

INTRODUCTION.

A PERIOD of about eight years intervenes between the First Philippic and the Second, — the date of the former being B. C. 352 – 351, while the latter was delivered in 344 – 343. To this period belong the Oration De Libertate Rhodiorum (B. C. 351), in which Demosthenes advises the Athenians to forget all the bitterness of the Social War and protect the liberties of Rhodes, threatened by Artemisia, queen of Caria ; the Speech Contra Midiam (350) against his life-long personal enemy and persecutor Midias (the Clodius of Athenian history and of the life of Demosthenes), which, however, was not *delivered,* as the case was compromised ; the three Olynthiacs, which followed each other in rapid succession, Philippics all in reality, though not in name, and all spoken in the year 349 ; and the Oration De Pace (346), in which he dissuades the Athenians, justly offended with the perfidious policy and selfish ambition of Philip, from breaking the peace just made with him, called the Peace of Philocrates, since war with Philip now, besides being hasty, inconsistent, and liable to the reproach of bad faith, involved also war with the Amphictyonic league, of which Philip had recently become the agent and representative. During all this time, Midias, with the countenance of Eubulus, Demades, and other popular demagogues, was availing himself of every opportunity to insult Demosthenes, and even offer him personal violence ; and the latter part of the time our orator was engaged in a partly personal and partly public conflict with Æschines and the other ambassadors, whom he charges with selling the rights and liberties of their country to Philip in the embassies for the ratification of the peace; although the famous orations, or appeals to the country, of these rival orators were not made till after the Second Philippic. Meanwhile Philip has destroyed Olynthus, captured or received the surrender of the other Chalcidian cities, marched into Thrace, and stripped Cersobleptes of no small part of his dominions, taken a decisive part in the Sacred War, and brought it to a close in the utter ruin of the Phocian towns, partly flattered and bribed and partly compelled Athens to make with him a dishonorable peace (the Peace of Philocrates), and now, having been admitted to the Amphictyonic Council in the place of the ruined Phocians, he is even elected by that council to preside at the Pythian games instead of the humbled and disgraced Athenians.

The circumstances which gave occasion to the Second Philippic are thus clearly and concisely stated by Thirlwall in his History of Greece (Vol. II. p. 131, Amer. ed.): "The scanty notices remaining of the history of this period being chiefly rhetorical allusions, which are often extremely vague, and were seldom meant to convey the simple truth, do not permit us to follow Philip's movements step by step. We perceive, however, very clearly, that he was constantly endeavoring to extend his power and influence, either by arms or negotiation, on every side of his dominions. We hear of expeditions or intrigues towards the north and the south, the east and the west; and, though their immediate objects were widely remote from each other, they seem all to have tended towards one end, that of weakening and curbing Athens, which, if these projects had succeeded, would at length have found herself completely enclosed in the toils before she had received a wound. It is probable that Philip's eye embraced all these points at one view, and that he was continually prosecuting his designs in opposite quarters, though we happen to find them mentioned only in succession. It is to Peloponnesus that our attention is first directed, as the scene of a diplomatic contest which portended a fiercer struggle. Here Philip had succeeded, almost without an effort, to the sway which Thebes had won through the victories of Epaminondas; for Sparta, weakened as she was, was still an object of

jealousy to her neighbors, whose independence she viewed with
a malignant eye ; and since Thebes, having in turn sunk from
the height of her power, was no longer able to afford protection
to her Peloponnesian allies, they naturally transferred their
allegiance to the king of Macedonia, on whose aid even Thebes
had been forced to cast herself. We are not informed of any
new occasion of hostilities that arose between them and Sparta
immediately after the close of the Phocian War. Yet it appears
that they found, or thought themselves in danger, so as to be led
to cultivate Philip's friendship. He espoused their cause without reserve, declared himself the protector of Messenia, and
called upon the Spartans to renounce their claims upon her ;
and when his demand was rejected, as it seems to have been in
a somewhat contemptuous tone,* both supplied his allies with
troops and money, and announced his purpose of leading a
much larger force into Peloponnesus in person. (See this Oration, §§ 15 – 17.) It may easily be supposed that these favors
and promises rendered him highly popular throughout the confederacy, of which Messene, Megalopolis, and Argos were the
leading members, and that he was extolled as the friend of liberty, the champion of the oppressed. Demosthenes himself, in
a speech delivered about three years after the end of the war
(*De Falsa Leg.*, 296), mentions with indignation that many of the
Arcadian commonwealths had decreed brazen statues and crowns
in honor of Philip, and had resolved, if he should enter Peloponnesus, to admit him into their towns ; and that the Argives had
followed their example.

" These proceedings, of course, soon became known at Athens,
and excited no little anxiety there. An embassy was sent into
Peloponnesus, with Demosthenes at its head [and at his sugges-
tion], to counteract the progress of the Macedonian influence.
He went to Messene, and, it seems, to Argos. In one of his
extant speeches [the oration before us, §§ 20 – 25] he has given
us a specimen of the manner in which he endeavored to rouse

---

* Philip is *said* (Plutarch, De Garrul., 511, A.) to have written to the Spartans :
Αἰ ἐμβάλλω εἰς τὴν Λακονικὴν, ἀναστάτους ὑμᾶς ποιήσω. The laconic answer was,
Αἴκα.

the jealousy of the Peloponnesians against Philip. He referred to Philip's conduct in the case of Olynthus as a proof that no reliance could be placed on his professions, or even his acts of friendship, which were all meant to inveigle those who trusted him into bondage or ruin. . . . . He dwelt much on the bad faith which Philip had shown in his dealings with Athens, either in his promises about Amphipolis, or in those by which he had deceived the people through their ambassadors in the negotiations for peace. The natural and necessary hostility between a monarch, whether king or tyrant, and all free and legal governments, was also a topic by which the orator strove to alarm republican prejudices. · But though he affirms that he was heard with applause, he admits that his warnings had produced no practical effect, and that Philip continued after, as before, to enjoy the confidence of his Peloponnesian allies ; and some embassies which were afterwards sent with the same view, were attended with no better result. Philip did not let those attempts pass unnoticed. Even if he did not deem it necessary for his honor to repel the charge of perfidy which had been so publicly brought against him, he may have thought it a favorable opportunity for displaying and thereby strengthening his connection with Peloponnesus. He sent an embassy to Athens, which seems to have been headed by Python, whose eloquence could sustain a comparison with that of Demosthenes himself (Diod., XVI. 85) ; and it was no doubt at Philip's instigation that his envoys were accompanied by those of Messene and Argos. The Macedonians were instructed to expostulate on the groundless accusations which had been brought against their king, and formally to deny that he had ever broken his oath to the Athenians ; the Peloponnesians were to complain of the countenance which Athens had given to the attempts of Sparta against their liberty.

" This embassy gave occasion to the Second Philippic of Demosthenes, which seems to have been the speech with which he prefaced a motion for the answer which he proposed to give to the ambassadors. It is possible that more than one assembly was held on the business, — one, perhaps, to consider each subject [the complaints of Philip and those of the Peloponnesians], — and that on one of these occasions Python vindicated his master's conduct in a speech which Demosthenes afterwards describes as bold and vehement, though he himself met it with a reply which extorted tokens of approbation even from the ministers of Philip's allies. But this was evidently not the occasion of the Second Philippic. That is addressed to the people, not in reply to the foreigners, but to the Macedonian, Philippizing faction at home, and more particularly to Æschines, who, it seems, had recently taken Philip's part, and had supported Python's arguments with his testimony. Its main object is to excite the suspicion and resentment of the Athenians, on the one hand, against Philip, and, on the other, against the orators who had served as his instruments to overreach them. He contends that the motive which had induced Philip to prefer the interest of Thebes to that of Athens at the end of the war was not the presence of a force which restrained him, still less any regard to justice ; for he who maintained the independence of Messenia against Sparta could not consistently aid the Thebans in reducing the other Bœotian towns to subjection. The motive was, that he expected the one state, if its own interests were but secured, would be readily subservient to his designs against the liberties of Greece, while he knew that no prospect of selfish advantage would ever bribe Athens to resign her glorious inheritance, the foremost post of resistance to foreign attacks on the national independence. . . . . All this, however, is but subordinate and introductory to the concluding passage, in which the orator reminds his hearers of the disappointment they had suffered, and points their indignation against its authors. He does not name either Philocrates or Æschines, but alludes in a manner which could not be mistaken to the ribaldry with which the one had silenced his warnings, and to the solemn assurances or dexterous insinuations by which the other had quieted the people's apprehensions. The men who had thus involved the state in its present embarrassments ought, he says, to be charged with the task of defending its conduct against those who questioned it. At least, it was fit that the language by which they had caused so much mischief, which was not yet ended, should not be forgotten.

"It is to be regretted that the proposed reply.[to the demands of the ambassadors] has not been preserved ; it probably contained a manifesto which would have thrown some light on the history of this period. The tone of the speech leads us to suppose that it [the reply] made no material concession ; there is rather, as we shall see, reason to believe that it advanced some new claims ; yet it so far satisfied Philip and his allies as to avoid an open rupture."

Grote says (*His. Gr.*, XI. 615, note) : "Who these envoys were, or from whence they came, does not appear from the oration. Libanius, in his *Argument*, says that they came jointly from Philip, from the Argeians, and from the Messenians. Dionysius Hal. (ad Ammæum, p. 737) states that they came out of Peloponnesus. I cannot bring myself to believe, on the authority of Libanius, that there were any envoys present from Philip. The tenor of the discourse appears to contradict that supposition." Whiston accedes to the same opinion. Curtius (*His. Gr.*, V. 375) says : "Macedonian envoys arrived at Athens together with the Peloponnesian in order to support the cause of the latter, and at the same time to proffer complaints as to the uninterrupted insults heaped upon the king on the Attic orators' tribune." This last historian, however, supposes Python to have visited Athens somewhat later and at the head of another Macedonian embassy. The data are not sufficient to settle these details. But the authorities all agree in general in regard to the time, occasion, and object of this oration.

Demosthenes was now somewhere from thirty-eight to forty years of age, in the full maturity of his powers, and advancing towards the zenith of his influence. He had recently been sent as ambassador to the king of Macedon. He had just returned from an honorable and most important embassy to the Peloponnesian states. He was already not only the most admired orator, but the most trusted statesman of Athens. His reputation for patriotism and eloquence extended through all Greece.

"It was long since such an assembly of the citizens had been held at Athens. The city of Aristides seemed to have come to life again. The Peloponnesian envoys could not refrain from acknowledging the grandeur of the bearing of a civic community under such leaders ; and in so far Demosthenes actually gained his immediate object, that the dangerous hostilities in the peninsula were appeased, and that no opportunity was given to Philip for intervention." — CURTIUS, *His. Gr.*, V. p. 376.

ANALYSIS.

A. Exordium (§§ 1–5).

B. Main proposition, with the principal reasons for it (6–12).

C. Objections, or counter-propositions stated and answered (13–19).

D. Extract from speech to the Messenians, cited in confirmation and warning (20–27).

E. Answer (to the embassies) which the orator recommends (28). Omitted in the text.

F. Conclusion. Warning against bad advisers (28–37).

*speak, that ought to be and not a thing for which these speeches are
worth hearing.* — γιγνόμενον, l. 6, is not equivalent to πραττόμενον;
it does not refer to *action* in the field ; for, as Smead remarks, Demosthenes was not at this time in favor of war or belligerent measures ; on the contrary, it was only a year or two previous that he had
delivered his *Oration de Pace*, which was an argument for preserving
the peace.   But the reference, as the word and the circumstances
both show, is to the *bringing forth* of counsels and measures on the
bema ; and the complaint is that the orators only heap up invectives
against Philip, when they should bring forward definite plans for the
guidance of the people ; in other words, the times demanded, not
orators, but statesmen. — 6. ὡς ἔπος εἰπεῖν limits and softens the otherwise too strong and absolute negation expressed by οὐδέν. — 2. 8. εἰς
τοῦτο...ὥσθ', cf. εἰς τοῦθ' ὕβρεως...ὥστ', *Phil.* I. 37. — προηγμένα,
brought, lit. brought forward, as it were, to a *climax* or *pitch* of difficulty. Cf. *Phil.* I. 9, οἳ προελήλυθε ἀσελγείας. — τῇ πόλει, lit. *in
respect to the state.*   Render in idiomatic English : *all the affairs of
the state.* — 10. μᾶλλον καὶ φανερώτερον, *the more fully and the more
clearly.* — καὶ...παραβαίνοντα καὶ...ἐπιβουλεύοντα, *both of violating
the peace with you* (Athenians) *and of plotting against all the Greeks,*
or καί...καί = *not only...but also.* The emphasis is on the latter and
the more comprehensive view. — 13. χαλεπώτερον. The orators only
increase the difficulty and the perplexity unless they answer the real
question, τὸ τί χρὴ ποιεῖν, WHAT IS TO BE DONE ? — 3. 14. πάντας,
al. πάντες. If πάντες is the correct reading, it finds its syntax only
in the ἡμεῖς, l. 16, and the ὑμεῖς, l. 19, which are the two parts of
which it is the whole. If πάντας is the true reading, it is the subject of κωλύειν : *and the cause of this is that when* ALL *ought to check
those who seek to aggrandize themselves by deeds and by acts,* NOT *by
words only.* — 16. οἱ παριόντες, lit. we who come before you, is a frequent designation of the *orators.* — 17. καὶ γράφειν καὶ συμβουλεύειν
are appositives of τούτων : *we orators stand aloof from these things,*
viz. *moving resolutions and giving advice...but are continually re-
hearsing,* etc. That is, we are not statesmen, but mere orators. —
18. ὀκνοῦντες expresses the motive : *through fear of incurring your*
(lit. with you) *displeasure.* — 20. οἱ καθήμενοι is a designation for
the members of the ἐκκλησία as *sitting* and *hearing* in opposition to
the orators as rising (ἀναστάς, *Phil.* I. 1) and coming forward (παριόντες) to speak. Cf. *De Or.*, 169 : πᾶς ὁ δῆμος ἄνω καθῆτο, and *Dic.*

Antiq., art. Ἐκκλησία. — 20. **ὡς μὲν...παρεσκεύασθε,** *are better pre-pared than Philip to make fair speeches* (or just arguments), *and to understand another when he speaks, but to prevent him from doing these things upon which he is now intent you are wholly inactive* (take no steps whatever. Whiston.)

4. P. 19, l. 3. **ἐν οἷς, κ. τ. λ.** This clause is without a connec-tive, because it explains the preceding, like an appositive. The satire of the sentence is as keen as the logic is conclusive : *you suc-ceed best severally in that in which you severally find your occupation and about which you feel an interest,* viz. *he in deeds and you in words.* — **ἑκατέροις,** always of two parties, here, of course, refers to the Athenians and Philip. — 5. 8. **καὶ μὴ...ἡμᾶς,** *and how* (that) *they shall not proceed* (cf. note on **προηγμένα,** § 2) *still farther unperceived by us all.* — For **προελθόντα λήσει ἡμᾶς,** see C. 677 f ; Cu. 398, 590 ; G. 279, 2 ; H. 544, 799. — 10. **μηδ'...δυνησόμεθα,** *and how* (that) *a power shall not rise up against us so great that we shall be utterly un-able to resist it.* — With **μέγεθος δυνάμεως** compare **κάλλη...ἱερῶν,** *Ol.*, III. 25. — 14. **προαιρετέον** is followed by a dat. of the agent (C. 458 ; Cu. 434 ; G. 188, 4 ; H. 600), an acc. of the object (C. 682 ; Cu. 596, 2 ; G. 281 ; H. 804), and a gen. by virtue of the **προ-.**

It will be observed that this introduction is much longer than that of the First Philippic or of either of the Olynthiacs. The want of statesmanship in the other Athenian orators and of definite plans for decisive action in the people was not only Demosthenes's justification for his speech, but it was a vital point in regard to their counsels and conduct. Hence he dwells on it, and makes it at once his exordium and a part of his oration.

B. Main proposition, with the principal reasons for it (6–12).

6–12. PHILIP IS DOUBTLESS YOUR ENEMY, AND IS MAKING ALL HIS PREPARATIONS AGAINST *YOU.* AND WITH GOOD REASON ; FOR HE EXPECTS TO FIND IN THE THEBANS, MESSENIANS, AND ARGIVES WILLING DUPES AND SELFISH TOOLS OF HIS AMBITION ; BUT ALL YOUR ANTECEDENTS AND THE HISTORY OF YOUR ANCESTORS SHOW HIM THAT YOUR FRIENDSHIP CAN BE GAINED ONLY ON THE BASIS OF JUSTICE AND THE RIGHTS AND LIBERTIES OF THE GREEKS.

6. 15. **Πρῶτον μέν** have no formal correlative words. The first question, viz. what is the real character and relation of Philip, with the arguments and illustrations by which the answer is supported, occupy the oration as far as § 28. Then follow the still more prac-

tical questions, what is to be done, and what answer should be returned to the ambassadors. — 16. ὁρῶν, *although* he sees, or *while yet* he sees. The part. is concessive. — 17. μηδ'...παρασκευάζεσθαι. Observe the force of the middle voice and the emphasis on ὑμᾶς: *and that it is not against you that he is making all his preparations.* — 20. δι' οὕς = *propter quas*; δι' ὧν (l. 21) = per quas. Franke. The latter is the means; the former the cause or reason: *by reason of which I have come* (lit. it has come to me) *to expect the contrary, and by which I am led to think Philip an enemy.* — 22. βέλτιον προορᾶν. The present expresses character or habit: *to have more foresight.* For the justice of this claim, here so modestly put forth, see Introd., p. 54. — ἐὰν...προσθήσεσθε, *but if they who are confident and have trusted him* (have the more foresight), *you will give your adherence to them.* Al. προσθῆσθε, but the construction is changed. — 7. 24. ἐγὼ ...λογίζομαι, *well, then, I reason thus.* Rehdantz places a colon after λογίζομαι. — 26. πρῶτον μετὰ τὴν εἰρήνην. Immediately after ratifying the peace (of Philocrates, 346) at Pheræ he marched to Thermopylæ, and, joined by the Bœotians, overran Phocis, and put an end to the existence of the Phocians as a nation, having excluded them from a share in the peace with that intention. Grote, XI. 581, 582; Curtius, V. 329.

P. 20, l. 1. πῶς...ἐχρήσατο, *what use did he make of these* successes? — 2. τί δή ποτε, *why so, pray?* that is, why did he prefer to favor Thebes rather than Athens. Observe the rapid succession of questions and answers. — 3. ὅτι...ἐξετάζων, *because making his calculations with a view to his own aggrandizement and the subjection of everything to his own power.* — 8. 6. ὅτι τῇ μέν, κ. τ. λ., *that to a city like ours, on the one hand, and to a people of our character, he could offer no sufficient bribe, and he could do nothing by which you could be persuaded for the sake of your own separate interest to sacrifice any of the other Greeks to him.* — 10. ἀλλὰ καί, κ. τ. λ., *but both out of regard to* (lit. making account of) *justice and through fear of the dishonor attaching to the thing* and in the exercise *of a proper foresight* (after προσήκει, προορᾶσθαι is of course to be understood) *you will oppose him* (for the change of construction, cf. προσθήσεσθε, § 6) *if he undertake to pursue any such course just as much* (ὁμοίως...ὥσπερ) *as if you happened to be at war with him.* — 9. 14. τοὺς δὲ Θηβαίους, *but the Thebans, on the other hand, he believed* (just as the event proved), *in return for what he was doing for them* (lit. themselves, for it is represented from *their own* point of view), *would allow him to manage everything else to suit himself.* — 16. οὐχ ὅπως = οὐ λέγω ὅπως = *non modo non : would not only not oppose and check.* — 19. ταὐτὰ ὑπειληφώς expresses the *reason* for the favors he is showing them : *and now having* (i. e. because he has) *conceived the same opinion of the Messenians and the Argives he is conferring favors on them.* — 20. καθ' ὑμῶν ἐγκώμιον, *encomium on you,* — an unfrequent use of κατά (which with the gen. usually means *against,* cf. κατ' Ἀργείων, l. 26), yet not without parallel. Cf. *De Cor.,* 215. — 10. 21. κέκρισθε γάρ, *for by these acts* (of Philip) *you have been adjudged to be the only people of all* (Greece) *who would not for any price.* Philip's acts were a *public declaration* of his *judgment* to this effect. — 24. τὴν εἰς...εὔνοιαν, *your good-will towards the Greeks,* i. e. your patriotic regard for them. — 25. καὶ ταῦτ', κ. τ. λ., *and both these opinions, both this so favorable in regard to you and that so different in respect to the Argives and Thebes, he has very naturally formed, not only in view of the present, but also when he takes the previous history of the parties into the account.*

11. P. 21, l. 3. ὥστ'...βασιλεῖ, *so that* (i. e. so, provided that) *they would submit to the king.* For ὥστε expressing a fixed condition, see L. & S. 1, 5 ; Madv. 166 b. — 5. ἡνίκ', sc. before the battle of Platæa. — ὁ τούτων πρόγονος, *the ancestor of these* men, — this whole race of Macedonian kings, — a little spiteful. — 6. κῆρυξ, sent by Mardonius. The whole story, and the spirited answer of the Athenians, is given by Herodotus. VIII. 140–144. Whiston. — 9. λέγειν as present denotes the process = *to be telling;* εἰπεῖν as aorist emphasizes the impossibility that it should ever be fully *told.* — 11. ἔστι γάρ, *for really the deeds of* THOSE men *were too great for any one to speak them in words.* — ἔστι is emphatic. — τἀκείνων expresses distinction. — ὡς implies an ellipsis of οὕτω μεγάλα : lit. *greater than so great as,* etc. C. 711. — τοὺς μὲν...τοὺς δέ, *the former...the latter.* The Thebans joined the Persians and fought against the Greeks ; the Argives were neutral. Herod., VII. 150. — 12. 14. ἰδίᾳ, ant. to κοινῇ = *separately.* Cf. ἰδίας ὠφελείας, § 8. — 12. 14. οἶδεν, *he knows* in view of the above facts. — 16. ἡγεῖτ' οὖν, *therefore he believed.* — ἐπὶ τοῖς δικαίοις, lit. *on the basis of the right,* i. e. on condition that his aims are just. — 20. οὐ γάρ, *for it is not surely because he sees that they have more ships than we.* — γε not only emphasizes τριήρεις, but satirizes the absurdity of the idea. — 21. οὐδ'...ἀφέστηκεν, *nor*

is it because he has acquired an inland empire and renounced that of the sea-coast and of the ports, and so does not seek the friendship of a maritime state like Athens.

C. Objections or counter-propositions stated and answered (13–19).

13–19. DO YOU SAY, HE PREFERS THE FRIENDSHIP OF THE THEBANS TO OURS, BECAUSE HE REGARDS THEIR CLAIMS AS MORE JUST, OR BECAUSE HE WAS FORCED TO ESPOUSE THEIR CAUSE? HIS CONDUCT IS UTTERLY INCONSISTENT WITH BOTH THESE SUPPOSITIONS. HIS WHOLE COURSE OF ACTION HAS BEEN AGAINST US. HE KNOWS THIS, AND HE KNOWS THAT YOU ARE AWARE OF IT. THEREFORE HE HATES YOU, AND COURTS LESS DISCERNING AND MORE COMPLYING FRIENDS.

13. 26. Ἀλλὰ νὴ Δί', *yes but,* like Latin *ast,* or *at enim,* introduces an objection for the sake of answering it. Sometimes νὴ Δία precedes ἀλλά; in other passages γάρ follows νὴ Δία. See Heslop in loc. — πάντα...εἰδώς, *though he* (Philip) *knows all this,* sc. your power and his position.

P. 22, l. 1. τῷ...ἀξιοῦν, because the *claims of the Thebans are more just than yours.* The Thebans claimed Orchomenus and Coronea in Bœotia. Sparta claimed Messene on the same principle as a conquered dependency. But Philip assisted the independence of Messene, and thus cut himself off from consistently supporting the claims of Thebes over Orchomenus and Coronea, and yet did in fact compel them to submit to her supremacy. It is this inconsistency which is asserted in the sentence, ἀλλὰ τοῦτον, κ. τ. λ., *but this is just the plea of all others which it is impossible for him* NOW *to urge,* for it is utterly inconsistent with the course which he has just taken in regard to Sparta and Messene. — 5. τότε...παραδούς. At the close of the Sacred War Philip restored to the Thebans these towns, which had been in the hands of the Phocians since B. C. 354. — 14. 8. ἐβιάσθη is made emphatic by being placed before νὴ Δία, *yes, but he was* FORCED, *it may be said.* — 9. παρὰ γνώμην limits συνεχώρησε, *he yielded these points contrary to his intention.* — 10. ἐν μέσῳ ληφθείς, *because he was surrounded by.* — 11. καλῶς is often simply *well, very well, sehr wohl.* Here it is manifestly ironical. Whiston renders it *good!* Heslop, *admirable!* Kennedy, *excellent!* — 11. οὐκοῦν φασὶ μὲν, *so then they* SAY, *do they, that he is going to be suspicious towards the Thebans!* — 13. Ἐλάτειαν. Elatea was the metropolis of Phocis on the frontier of Locris. It was seventy-eight miles from

April 10th, 1886

Athens, and commanded the approach from Macedonia and Thessaly to
Bœotia and thus to Attica. Hence the alarm at Athens when, shortly
before the battle at Chæronea, news came that Philip had seized Elatea, and which our orator describes so graphically, *De Cor.*, § 169, seq.
The Thessalians led a detachment of Persians through Elatea, when
they invaded Greece. The walls of the city were dismantled at the
close of the Phocian War, and the rebuilding of them would be
regarded as friendly to the Phocians and unfriendly to the Thebans.
— 15. 14. ὁ δὲ ταῦτα, κ. τ. λ., yes, (δέ, lit. *but ;* it is corrective of
φασὶ μέν = this is not mere hearsay, it is matter of fact), *yes, but
these things he is* GOING *to do and he* WILL *be* GOING *to do* (that is, he
never will *do* them), *but he is not* GOING *to join with the Messenians
and the Argives against the Lacedæmonians, nay, he is actually* (καί)
sending in mercenaries, etc. — 18. τοὺς μὲν ὄντας, *he is for overthrow-
ing the Lacedæmonians, the certain* (τοὺς ὄντας) *enemies of the Thebans,*
(this does not look like mistrusting the Thebans !) *and is he now for
saving the Phocians, the very people whom he himself recently destroyed ?* The inconsistency is too palpable. The Thebans have just
destroyed Phocis ; will he now rebuild it in opposition to Thebes,
and that too at the very moment when he is seeking to overthrow
the Lacedæmonians, who are the confessed enemies of the Thebans
and friends of the Phocians ! The inconsistency is more definitely
pointed out in the next section. — 16. 21. καὶ τίς, *pray who can
believe this ?* — ἐγὼ μέν, κ. τ. λ., *for I for my part do not think that
Philip, if he either had been forced to act contrary to his will* (ἄκων
here = παρὰ γνώμην, l. 9) *before* (sc. when he was acting with the
Thebans against Phocis), *or if he was now giving up the Thebans.* —
25. κἀκεῖνα, the same as τὰ πρῶτα, l. 22. — 26. ἐκ = *from,* i. e. *in
view of,* or, *as an inference from : from his whole conduct* it is plain,
if one looks at it in the right light, that he is busily arranging (con-
cocting, Heslop) *everything against our state.*

17. P. 23, l. 1. καὶ τοῦτ᾿...συμβαίνει, *and this befalls him now at
least sure enough by a kind of necessity.* — νῦν γε δὴ is opposed to the
alleged compulsion of his *previous* conduct (ἐβιάσθη, § 14). — 3. ἄρχειν, κ. τ. λ., explanatory of λογίζεσθε, hence without a connective.
See note § 4. — τούτου is gen. of respect : *in regard to this.* — 4. ἀδικεῖ continues the explanation. With πολὺν ἤδη χρόνον it includes
the past with the present : *he has been wronging you for a long time
now* and is still doing it. — 5. οἷς γὰρ οὖσιν, *for it is by holding what*

is really yours that he has secured all the rest. οἷς is dat. by attraction to τούτοις, which is dat. of means.—18. 11. δικαίως ἄν...μισεῖν, *you would justly hate him.* Heslop encloses ἄν in brackets, and Schaefer says, delenda est. Many editors read, νομίζοι. — παρώξυνται, Anglice, *exasperated.* — 13. ποιήσας is opposed to πείσεσθαι, and τι may well be understood with it, *by doing something first = by striking the first blow.* — 13. ἐγρήγορεν...θεραπεύει. Observe the vividness of the asyndeton : *he is awake, he is on the alert, he courts against our city.* Rehdantz compares the German : Alles rennet, rettet, flüchtet. — ἐπὶ τῇ πόλει can be taken either with ἐφέστηκεν (Franke, Kennedy) or with θεραπεύει (Reiske, Dindorf, Whiston, Heslop, Rehdantz). — 19. 16. οὓς...προόψεσθαι, *who, by reason of their cupidity, he thinks, will be satisfied with the present state of things, while at the same time* (μὲν...δέ) *through dulness of understanding they will not foresee any of the consequences.* — σκαιότητα, lit. *lefthandedness.* Whiston renders it *obliquity ;* Rehdantz, *Thorheit.*. — 18. καίτοι... μετρίως, *yet surely men even of moderate intelligence.* — 20. ἔμοιγ᾽... συνέβη, *I had occasion to speak of,* sc. in the embassy to the Peloponnesus. See Introduction, p. 92 ; *De Cor.,* 79 ; Grote, XI. 614.

D. Extract from speech to the Messenians, cited in confirmation and warning (20 – 27).

20 – 27. LEARN WISDOM FROM THE EXPERIENCE OF THE OLYNTHIANS AND THE THESSALIANS, WHOM HE BLINDED BY GIFTS ONLY TO DESTROY OR ENSLAVE THEM. AVOID TOO CLOSE CONNECTIONS WITH DESPOTS. MISTRUST ALL KINGS AS THE NATURAL AND NECESSARY ENEMIES OF REPUBLICS.

20. This indirect way of warning his countrymen by a repetition of what the orator said originally to another people has been a favorite example with rhetoricians of the figure called *apostrophe* or *aversio.* See *Aquila Rom. De Fig.,* c. 9, quoted by Rehdantz. — 23. Πῶς ...δυσχερῶς, *with what vexation.* — 24. ἀκούειν...εἰ...λέγοι, *used to hear whenever any one said anything,* or *would hear if any one said anything.* — ἀκούειν = ἀκούοιεν ἄν, only somewhat more positive. The condition (εἰ...λέγοι) and the conclusion (ἀκούειν) both express repeated action. — 25. κατ᾽...χρόνους, *during those times.* — ὅτ᾽...ἀφίει, *when he proposed to give up Anthemus to them.* This was in B. C. 358 – 357. The district of Anthemus lay between Olynthus and Therma, afterwards Thessalonica (Grote, XI. 334). Whiston. Libanius calls it τὸ τῶν ταλαιπώρων Ὀλυνθίων.

P. 24, l. 1. **καὶ τὴν μέν, κ. τ. λ.**, *and took upon himself the enmity with us = our enmity.* Al. ὑμᾶς (Heslop) ; but most of the editions have ἡμᾶς, which is required in a speech to the Messenians: *us* Athenians. — **ἀνῄρητο...ἐδεδώκει.** The plup. follows the imp. to express the consequences which he *had thereby brought* upon himself : lit. *and had thereby* taken upon himself, etc. — 4. **λέγοντος ἄν.** λέγοντος denotes the condition = εἴ τις ἔλεγεν, and ἄν goes with πιστεῦσαι to express the conclusion : *or would have believed it if any one had told them.* — 6. **πόλυν**, sc. χρόνον, in reality it was for *all* time, as Wolf remarks ; but that was more than Demosthenes knew. — 8. **προδοθέντες, κ. τ. λ.** The bribery and treachery of Lasthenes and Euthycrates, citizens of Olynthus (hence ὑπ' ἀλλήλων), is often alluded to by Demosthenes. See *De Cor.*, § 48 and note there. — 10. **αὗται λίαν**, *these too close connections.* λίαν used as an adj. after αὗται, as it often is and any adverb may be after an article. In language and in sentiment this *gnome* of the Athenian orator reminds us of the advice of Washington to his countrymen to avoid "entangling alliances" with European powers. — 22. 11. **τί δ' οἱ Θετταλοί**, *and what the Thessalians?* i. e. what did they *expect?* προσεδόκων is to be supplied, as is shown by the preceding and following context ; see προσδοκᾶν, l. 3 above and l. 13 below. — 12. **τοὺς τυράννους**, the hereditary despots of Pheræ in Magnesia. — **Νίκαιαν**, Nicæa, a fortress which commanded the pass of Thermopylæ, was in the possession of the Phocians till it came into the hands of Philip about B. C. 346, and soon after the close of the Sacred War (B. C. 352) it was transferred to the Thessalians. Magnesia, a narrow strip of Thessaly between the mouth of the Peneus and the Pagasæan Bay (see Intr. to *Phil.* I. p. 51) was restored to the Thessalians by Philip about the same time. — 13. **προσδοκᾶν...αὐτοῖς**, *do you think they expected that the decemvirate now established would exist among them?* In *Phil.* III. 26, Philip is said to have established *tetrarchies* (not decarchies) in Thessaly. But the discrepancy is only apparent. He seems at the same time to have availed himself of the old division of the country into four districts (Thessaliotis, Phthiotis, Pelasgiotis, and Histiæotis), and revived the distinction of tetrarchies. But in each of these tetrarchies, or over the country as a whole (it is not agreed which), he also established a decemvirate, that is, a despotic or oligarchic government administered by ten men. Whiston well remarks that the Lacedæmonians had been in the habit of appointing

5 *

decemvirates in towns which they wished to keep under their control, and the unpopularity of these bodies in the Peloponnesus would
naturally excite a prejudice against the supposed author of such institutions elsewhere. It was therefore a good argumentum ad invi-
diam against Philip with the Messenians. — 15. πυλαίαν, strictly
the autumn meeting of the Amphictyonic council at Thermopylæ,
and then generally that council itself, or the right of sending depu-
ties to it. The Phocians had deprived the Thessalians of member-
ship in the Amphictyonic council, and Philip restored it to them
(ἀποδόντα). — 23. 17. ὑμεῖς δέ = so you ; thus the orator emphasizes the lesson which the Messenians should learn from the experience
of the Olynthians and Thessalians. They were now experiencing the
favors of Philip as those nations had done : pray that you may not
experience at length his deception and treachery as they did. — μέν
and δέ put in emphatic contrast the two parts of this experience. —
ἀπεύχεσθε = Lat. deprecate. — ἤδη...ἰδεῖν Heslop renders, awake to
see ; Whiston, see at last. — 24. 25. προσδεῖται, besides (προσ-) being merely mechanical (χειροποίητα) they also require the expenditure
of money. — ἔν δέ τι, κ. τ. λ., but one common safeguard the nature
(instinct, Whiston) of sensible men possesses in itself, — that does not
require to be manufactured, nor to be bought with money, — such is
the contrast suggested by μέν, l. 24, and δέ, l. 25. — τι = of a certain sort, indefinite here, but explained farther on.

P. 25, l. 1. πλήθεσι = πολιτείαις, republics. — 2. ἀπιστία. Compare Ol., I. 5 : ἄπιστον ταῖς πολιτείαις ἡ τυραννίς, and also the maxim
of the founders of our republic : "The price of liberty is eternal vigilance." — ταύτης ἀντέχεσθε, hold on to this against every assault (ἀντ-).
— 3. οὐδὲν μὴ, κ. τ. λ., idem quod οὐ μὴ δεινόν τι πάθητε. Franke :
if you continue (subj. pres.) to cherish this, you can be exposed to no
danger. — 5. καὶ τὰς προσηγορίας, not only its principles, but also
(or even) its titles, or in more idiomatic English, its very titles. This
speech at Messene was well worthy to be repeated in Athens, and is
equally deserving of remembrance and observance in modern times.
— 26. 10. ἀκούσαντες is concessive and ἐκεῖνοι is in emphatic contrast with ὑμεῖς, l. 17 : Those people, although they heard these words
and applauded the sentiments loudly and long (imperf. part.), and
although they heard many other speeches from the ambassadors both in
my presence and again after my departure to other cities, none the
more for all that, as it appears, will they shun the friendship of Philip,

nor his promises...but you, etc. — 16. τῷ λογισμῷ, *in their reason,* or *better judgment.* — 27. 17. οἱ καὶ συνιέντες, *who both understand your-selves.* By this compliment he gilds the bitter pill of reproof and warning. — 18. τῶν λεγόντων...ἡμῶν, gen. of source after ἀκούοντες, which is also followed by its direct object in the succeeding clauses : *and hear from us orators that you are plotted against.* — 19. περιστοι-χίζεσθε. See note on *Phil.* I. 9. — ἐκ τοῦ...ὑπομείναντες, *in conse-quence of doing* NOTHING *now, you will, before you are aware, as it seems to me, have to endure* EVERYTHING, *that is, the very worst.* Rehdantz follows Σ in reading ὥστε instead of ἐκ τοῦ, and Kennedy renders : *you, I fear, to escape present exertion, will come to ruin, ere you are aware.* — ἡ παραντίχ' ἡδονή, *the pleasure of the moment.* — ποθ' ὕστερον, *at some future day.*

E.   Answer (to the embassies) which the orator recommends (28).

28. YOU SHOULD DELIBERATE BY YOURSELVES HEREAFTER ON THE COURSE OF ACTION WHICH IT BEHOOVES YOU TO ADOPT.   I WILL NOW TELL YOU WHAT ANSWER YOU OUGHT TO RETURN BY THE AM-BASSADORS.

28. 25. ὕστερον, *after* the ambassadors have returned home. — ἃ δὲ...ἐψηφισμένοι, lit. *what answer having now returned* (i. e. by returning what answer) *you would have voted as you ought* = *what answer you ought to vote.* — ἀποκρινάμενοι denotes the manner or the condition, and ἂν εἴη' ἐψηφισμένοι the conclusion. Here, doubtless, the orator submitted a form of answer, a written document, which is not only not preserved, but the MSS. do not even indicate the place for it, although many of the editions have inserted its title, viz. ᾿ΑΠΟΚΡΙΣΙΣ. See notes on ΠΟΡΟΥ ᾿ΑΠΟΔΕΙΞΙΣ, *Phil.* I. 30. We cannot but wish with Thirlwall that the answer had been pre-served. See Introd., p. 95.

F.   Conclusion.   Warning against bad advisers (28–37).

28–37. JUSTICE WOULD REQUIRE YOU TO SUMMON BEFORE YOU THOSE AMBASSADORS WHO BROUGHT YOU SUCH FALSE AND FLATTER-ING REPORTS OF PHILIP, AND ALSO THE MEN WHO, AFTER THE RATI-FICATION OF THE PEACE, RIDICULED ME FOR MY GLOOMY FOREBOD-INGS, AND LET THEM FURNISH YOU THE ANSWER WHICH IS DE-MANDED BY THIS EMERGENCY OF THEIR OWN CREATION.   AND WHEN THOSE FOREBODINGS OF MINE PROVE TRUE, AS I FEAR THEY SOON WILL, VISIT YOUR RESENTMENT ON THEM, NOT ON ME.   MAY THE GODS AVERT SUCH CALAMITIES, ALTHOUGH THESE CORRUPT MEN THEREBY ESCAPE THEIR JUST DESERTS.

28. 26. **ἦν μέν οὖν δίκαιον,** *it were just now, in the first place, to summon,* etc., although you have not done so, nor do I expect you to do it now. The form implies that the thing was not done which it would have been right to do. *μέν = in the first place,* is correlative to **πάλιν,** p. 26, l. 6 = *then again.* — 27. **τοὺς ἐνεγκόντας,** Neoptolemus, Aristodemus, and Ctesiphon are named repeatedly in *De Fals. Leg.* — **τὰς ὑποσχέσεις.** Cf. § 23 ; *De Fals. Leg.,* 41. — **καλεῖν,** sc. in order to furnish the answer demanded by the present state of things and for which they are responsible.

29. P. 26, l. 2. **οὔτ' ἄν...πολεμοῦντες,** *and I know that you would not have ceased to carry on the war,* i. e. you would not have agreed to the peace of Philocrates. The construction of the sentence is just the same as if οἶδ' ὅτι were not used ; in other words, οἶδ' ὅτι is used quite like an adverb = *certainly.* C. 717 b ; H. 868 ; Madv. 193 r. —6. **καὶ πάλιν...καλεῖν,** *yes and then again* (it were right) (ἦν δίκαιον, p. 25, l. 26) *to summon another class.* — **γε** = *yes.* — **πάλιν,** correlative to **μέν,** p. 26, l. 6. — **ἑτέρους,** one of two, and being in the plural, one of two classes. The reference is to Philocrates and Æschines, who were members with Demosthenes of the second embassy specified below, l. 8. — **τοὺς** agrees with λέγοντας, l. 10. The skeleton of the sentence is this : *those who when I...was forewarning and protesting...said that I,* etc. — 7. **γεγονυίας...εἰρήνης,** *after the conclusion of the peace.* — **τῆς ὑστέρας...πρεσβείας,** *the second embassy,* viz. *that for the ratification of the peace ;* the first being for the negotiation of it, and Demosthenes being a member of both. — **ὕδωρ πίνων** denotes cause, — *being a water-drinker.* See *De Fals. Legat.,* 355, 25, where Demosthenes reports Philocrates as saying sarcastically : no wonder that Demosthenes and I do not think alike, for he drinks water, while I drink wine. It was a standing joke at Athens, that other men *spoke* by water (alluding to the clepsydra, or water-clock, which measured the speaker's time), but Demosthenes *composed* by water. — **εἰκότως,** *of course.* — 12. **εἰμί.** A marked instance of that singular mixture of direct and indirect quotation which the flexibility of the Greek language admits in so many different forms. — **τις** = *a sort of.* — 13. **ἐὰν παρέλθῃ,** *if he should pass* the straits of Thermopylæ, that pass being so important and so familiar as not to require specification. —14. **μὲν...δέ.** These particles mark the contrast between Θεσπιὰς καὶ Πλαταιάς and Θηβαίους ; instead of subjecting those Bœotian cities to Thebes, Æschines assures them that he would *fortify*

Thespiæ and Phatœæ, on the one hand, and, on the other, put a stop to the insolence of the Thebans. Those cities were as friendly to Athens as they were hostile to the Thebans, who, in 374 B. C., had destroyed the towns and dispersed the inhabitants. The best commentary on this passage is contained in *De Fals. Leg.*, 112 : "For this man (Æschines) said that he (Philip) would fortify Thespiæ and Platææ, and so far from destroying the Phocians he would humble the pride of the Thebans ; whereas in fact he has made the Thebans more powerful than they should be, and utterly destroyed the Phocians, and he has not fortified Thespiæ and Platææ, but has proceeded still further to enslave Orchomenus and Coronea (other Bœotian cities). — Χερρόνησον…διορύξει, *and will at his own expense dig a trench across the Chersonese*, making it an island, and thus protecting it against the Thracians. The distance was only four or five miles. The reader is familiar with the interest of Athens in the Chersonese, which was an ancient Athenian possession. — 16. Ὠρωπόν. Oropus, a fortified town near the northern coast of Attica, which had fallen into the hands of the Thebans, B. C. 366, would be highly acceptable to the Athenians, and together with Eubœa it would be an equivalent for Amphipolis, which they so much valued. Cf. Grote, XI. 573. — 18. οἶδ' ὅτι. See note above, l. 3. — 19. δεινοί. This word is used in Greek to express almost anything that is *remarkable.* Kennedy and Heslop here render it *famous.* — 31. 19. καὶ…αἴσχιστον, κ. τ. λ., *and, what is most disgraceful of all, in your confidence, you voted that this same peace should extend also to your posterity.* Smead renders πρὸς τὰς ἐλπίδας, *in regard to their hopes*, sc. of their posterity, and adds this comment, which is very just, whatever be the rendering of these difficult words : "Philip now had possession of many places heretofore belonging to the Athenians, and as it was expressly stipulated in the treaty that each should keep what he had and the same obligations extended to their children, it was virtually cutting off all hope of the future recovery of these places." Cf. Grote, XI. 575. — 22. οὕτω…ὑπήχθητε, *so perfectly were you led away.* — 32. 25. οὐχ ἵν'…Φιλίππου, *not that by falling into invective I may provoke retaliation upon myself before you, and afford my old adversaries a new pretext for getting something more from Philip.* So Whiston, and substantially Kennedy, Heslop, and others. Schaefer, Westermann, and Rehdantz make λόγον ποιήσω = λόγου τύχω, and render : *that I may get an equal hearing before you ;* but this does not seem to be justified by usage. ποιήσω seems to be used here in its proper sense of *make*, i. e. *cause*, or *bring upon*, lit. *make for myself*, i. e. *bring upon myself in like manner speech* (abuse) *before you*.

P. 27, l. 2. ὡς ἄλλως, lit. *quite otherwise*, sc. *than should be* = *to no purpose*. — 33. 4. καὶ οὐχί, κ. τ. λ., *and I could wish indeed that my conjectures may prove false ;* literally and in the Greek order: *by no means would I desire to be conjecturing rightly*. — 8. ἐφ᾽ ὑμᾶς ἐστίν, *are directed against you*. — τοῦ δεῖνος. Cf. *Phil*. I. 46 ; *Ol*. II. 31. It is gen. of source after ἀκούηθ: *hear from me nor from some one else*. — 34. 10. φοβοῦμαι δή, κ. τ. λ., *I fear then that, as your ambassadors have concealed. the purposes for which they know in their own consciences that they have been bribed, they who try to repair what these men have lost may chance to fall under your resentment.* — τοῖς πειρωμένοις, dat. of the agent with συμβῇ. — 14. ὡς τὰ πολλά, *generally*. — ἐνίους, *some people*, meaning, of course, the Athenians themselves. — 35. 16. ἕως...πράγματα, *while therefore the thing is in the future and in embryo*. Cf. *De Cor.*, 62 : τοῦ φυομένου καὶ συνισταμένου κακοῦ. — 19. τίς...προέσθαι, *who it was that persuaded you to abandon the Phocians and Thermopylæ*. The storm is already gathering which is to burst upon Æschines in the Oration on the Crown. Cf. *De Cor.*, 35. Observe the emphatic separation of Φωκέας from Πύλας. — 20. ὧν καταστὰς...κύριος, *by making himself master of which*, the part. denoting *means*, and κύριος being predicate after it. — 25. λυπήσει μὲν...γέγονε δέ. The emphasis is on the time : *the distress* (of the war that is sure to invade Attica) *will befall indeed* (in the future) *when it comes, but it has already begun* (in its origin and source)— *it began on that day*, sc. when Æschines deceived you by those false representations.

36. P. 28, l. 1. οὔτε γὰρ...Φωκέας, *for he would neither have conquered at sea, surely, and so would never have come to Attica with a fleet, nor would have marched with a land force past Thermopylæ and Phocis.* — κρατήσας and βαδίζων express two different *ways* or *means* of coming to Attica ; in English we overlook the logical relation and simply state the facts ; in other words, we use verbs where the Greek uses participles. The use of the people for the country (Φωκέας instead of Φωκίδα) is frequent in Greek. — 5. ἐν ὁμοίῳ πολέμῳ δι᾽ ὅν, *on a war like that on account of which*. — 37. 6. ὡς ὑπομνῆσαι, *for the purpose of admonition*. ὡς denotes the purpose more definitely. C. 671 e ; G. 266, N. 1 ; Madv. 151. — 7. ὡς...θεοί, *but*

that it should be exactly verified, avert it, all ye gods. Compare the conclusion of the *First Philippic* and the *First* and *Third Olynthiacs*, all of which end with a prayer, and especially that of the *De Corona*, which ends with a deprecation, in which, somewhat as here, a sharp distinction is drawn between the enemies of the country and the public welfare.

THIRD PHILIPPIC.

INTRODUCTION.

The third Philippic, or, as Dionysius of Halicarnassus (*Ad Amm.* 10) reckons it, the tenth Harangue against Philip, was delivered B. C. 341.* There is therefore an interval of only about two years between it and the second Philippic (B. C. 344 – 343). To this period belong the speeches De Haloneso (B. C. 343), which is now generally ascribed to Hegesippus, although Demosthenes is supposed to have delivered an oration on the same subject which is lost; the Orations of Demosthenes and Æschines *De Falsa Legatione* (343), which however were not spoken, but published as appeals to the people and are chiefly valuable as abounding in facts (or fictions) as the materials of history; and the Oration De Chersoneso (342), which, both in time and occasion, was closely connected with the third Philippic. Meanwhile Philip has taken Halonesus (a small island off the coast of Magnesia belonging to Athens), has made an unsuccessful attempt on Megara (defeated by the Athenians under Phocion), has invaded Epirus and annexed a portion of it to the dominions of his brother-in-law Alexander, but has been obliged to withdraw before an Athenian force sent to Ambracia and a league formed against him by the Athenian ambassadors Demosthenes, Hegesippus, and Lycurgus; has established the tyrants Philistides and Clitarchus in Oreus and Eretria, cities of Euboea; has driven Cersobleptes from his kingdom, and advanced far in conquest of Thrace; and he is now engaged in a hot dispute with Athens, occasioned by actual conflicts between his troops

* Heslop and Smead say, B. C. 342. But the more and better authorities (Grote, Thirlwall, Curtius, Franke, Whiston, Rehdantz) have it B. C. 341.

sent for the defence of Cardia and the Athenian forces sent under Diopeithes for the protection of the Chersonesus.

The peninsula known as the Thracian Chersonesus, stretching along the coast of the Hellespont (the modern Dardanelles) for a distance of fifty miles, so fertile and so highly cultivated in the heroic age that it is said by Thucydides (I. 11) to have furnished maintenance to the Grecian army during the siege of Troy, colonized in the time of the Pisistratidæ by Athenians under the older and the younger Miltiades (afterwards the conqueror at Marathon), recovered from the dominion of the Persians by Cimon, Miltiades' son, re-enforced by Pericles with a more numerous colony, and protected against the Thracians by fortifications and entrenchments across the isthmus, — this peninsula, thus dear to the hearts of the Athenian people by the ties of kindred and by association with the great men and great events of their early history, was of inestimable value to them materially and politically as commanding the straits on which Athens and the greater part of Greece depended for their main supply of corn, and also as guarding the approach to those Greek cities on the Hellespont (Selymbria, Perinthus, Byzantium, etc.), towards which, together with the Chersonesus, Philip was now looking with covetous eyes and advancing with stealthy but steady footsteps. While Athens sent Diopeithes with a body of mercenaries to protect her settlers and her possessions in this peninsula, Philip had taken under his protection Cardia, a city situated within the peninsula near the isthmus, which was unfriendly to Athens and which not only claimed to be independent, but was admitted by Æschines and the Athenian envoys as an ally of Philip to take part in the ratification of the peace of Philocrates. Under such circumstances, with hostile feelings and conflicting claims, conflict of forces was inevitable. The Macedonian troops on the one hand overran more or less of the Chersonese, and on the other Diopeithes made excursions out of the peninsula, and invaded portions of Thrace which were subject to Philip. Philip sent letters of complaint and remonstrance to Athens. His partisans there loudly demanded the recall and punishment of Diopeithes. A

H

strong feeling was raised against him, and it seemed for a time as if the Athenians would yield to the demands of Philip, until Demosthenes rose and by one of his most convincing and persuasive speeches, that On the Chersonesus, turned the tide in the opposite direction. In this speech he shows that the real question was not the guilt or innocence of Diopeithes, but whether Athens or Philip should possess the Chersonese and command the Hellespont, and urges the people, instead of recalling and punishing their general, to reinforce him, vote a war-tax, raise an army, and send ambassadors to the other Greeks to awaken them to a sense of the common danger and unite them against the common enemy. This speech produced the desired effect. Diopeithes retained his command, and continued to withstand the advance of Philip. And a few weeks later (so Curtius puts it ; Kennedy says, three months ; it is impossible to determine the interval between the two orations), moved perhaps by an embassy from the inhabitants of the Chersonesus (§ 73), Demosthenes followed up this speech by his third Philippic, in which he repeats his arguments and appeals, denounces Philip with still greater boldness and vehemence as the irreconcilable enemy of Athens and all Greece, demonstrates beyond dispute the justice of the charge by reviewing the history of his ceaseless encroachments, declares that the question of peace or war is no longer at their disposal, but the war is already begun, hurls his thunderbolts at the traitors and hirelings who have too long blinded the eyes of the people to his ambitious designs, and are ready to sell to him the liberties of their country, and summons them, in the role and spirit of their illustrious ancestors, to organize and lead Greeks, yes and barbarians, in a common, open, and determined resistance against the common enemy of liberty and of mankind. It is one of the clearest and strongest arguments and at the same time one of the most earnest and impassioned appeals among all the speeches of the great Athenian orator. Nor was it spoken in vain. Convinced and persuaded by it and animated with the spirit of its author, the Athenians now acted with a vigor worthy of their sires, expelled the tyrants whom Philip had established in the cities of Eubœa, sent a fleet to relieve Byzantium and the other cities on the Hellespont, and, for the time, completely baffled the plans of the Macedonian king. It was now, for the first time, that Demosthenes succeeded in inducing the people to restore the theoric fund to its original military use. Moreover, by his trierarchic law he distributed more equitably the military and naval taxes (*De Cor.* 104 – 106), and thus imparted new energy and efficiency to the naval power of the state. At the same time he went as envoy to Eubœa, to the Chersonese and to Byzantium, as he had before been to the Peloponnesus, to Ambracia, to Corcyra, Illyria, and Thessaly, everywhere reconciling Grecian cities and states among themselves and uniting them against Philip (*De Cor.* 87 – 89). In short, Demosthenes was the moving spirit of all the energetic measures of this interesting period in Athenian history. And his influence with his countrymen continued to be in the ascendency until, two or three years later (B. C. 338), he roused and rallied Athenians and Thebans to the final glorious though unsuccessful struggle in the fatal battle at Chæronea.

This was the last, the longest, and the greatest of all the orations of Demosthenes that were specially directed against Philip. Dionysius calls it the greatest of the Philippics (ἐν τῇ μεγίστῃ τῶν κατὰ Φιλίππου κατηγοριῶν, *De Thucyd.* VI. 947). Curtius (V. 394) speaks of it as the most powerful and the most successful of all the popular orations of Demosthenes. And ancient and modern critics have generally agreed in this opinion.

Two editions of this oration have come down to us. One of these is contained in the Paris Codex Σ,* wherein many sentences are omitted, which, however, are added in the margin by a later hand. The fuller edition is preserved in the other MSS., except one or two which want the additions or have them in the margin. In the abbreviated form of Σ the oration is for the most part intelligible and complete. At the same time the additions in the other MSS. are generally congruous and written in the style and spirit of Demosthenes. Various conjectures

---

* Cited as S by some editors. This MS. is usually remarkable for its brevity; and the difference is especially marked in the third Philippic.

NOTES.

A. The exordium, or rather the key-note of the oration, viz. the increasingly wretched state of Athenian affairs, and its cause, viz. the desire of the people to be flattered, and their unwillingness to hear the truth (1–5).

§§ 1–5. AFTER ALL THE SPEECHES THAT WE HAVE HEARD ABOUT CHASTISING PHILIP, AFFAIRS COULD HARDLY HAVE BEEN WORSE IF SPEAKERS AND HEARERS HAD CONSPIRED TOGETHER TO RUIN THE STATE. YOU HAVE TO BLAME FOR THIS YOUR ORATORS, WHO SPEAK ONLY TO PLEASE YOU, AND YOURSELVES, WHO WISH TO BE FLATTERED, AND ARE NOT WILLING TO HEAR THE TRUTH. GIVE TO ME THE FREEDOM OF SPEECH IN PUBLIC AFFAIRS WHICH IN OTHER MATTERS YOU EXTEND TO FOREIGNERS AND EVEN SLAVES, AND IT IS NOT YET TOO LATE TO REPAIR THESE EVILS.

1. Page 29, line 1. The exordium of the third Philippic bears a general resemblance to that of the second, but it is more earnest, more direct and outspoken, and more severe both on other orators and on the people. 2. ὀλίγου δεῖν = *almost.* C. 665 ; G. 172, N. 2 ; H. 575 ; *Lex.* s. v. Render : *in almost every assembly.* — περὶ ὧν = περὶ τούτων ἅ. ὧν is gen. by attraction ; otherwise it would be in the acc. with ὑμᾶς after ἀδικεῖ. — 3. τὴν εἰρήνην, *the peace* of Philocrates (B.˙C. 346), which was so notorious that specification was needless. — 4. οἶδ' ὅτι = *surely,* or *I am sure.* See note, *Phil.* II. 29. — ὑπηγμένα. Compare προηγμένα in a similar connection, *Phil.* II. 2. But ὑπηγμένα properly signifies, *led away under evil influences.* Cf. *Phil.* II. 31 : ὑπήχθητε. — ὑπηγμένα καὶ προειμένα may be rendered, *brought by neglect and corrupt influences,* not mere inadvertence, as the commentators generally have it. See *Lex.* s. v. — εἰς τοῦθ'...ὁρῶ introduces the conclusion of the long condition or concession which

is expressed by the circumstantial participles γιγνομένων, l. 1, and φησάντων, l. 5 : *although* (or *while*) *many speeches are being made… and although all would say…yet I see all your affairs brought…into such a state that*, etc. — 9. **εἰ καὶ λέγειν.** This explains, or rather is the thing which *he fears may be slanderous yet true*, and hence, like an object or an appositive, it has no connective. — 12. **οὐκ ἂν… διατεθῆναι,** *I do not think they could have been in a worse situation than they now are.* — 2. 14. **παρά** = *from.* Cf. note, *Phil.* I. 11 ; **διά,** l. 16 = *through.* — 15. **εὑρήσετε…προαιρουμένους,** *you will find* (that things have come into this state) *through the influence of those who prefer to please you* (court your favor) *rather than to give you the best advice.* — 17. **τινὲς μέν,** e. g. Eubulus and the party in power ; **ἕτεροι,** the opposition. — 18. **ἐν οἷς…φυλάττοντες,** *seeking to maintain a state of things in which they themselves enjoy reputation and possess power.* — 20. **τοὺς ἐπὶ…ὄντας,** *those who preside over public affairs;* the same with τινές above. — 21. **οὐδὲν…ὅπως βούλεται,** *labor only to make the state punish its own citizens* (lit. itself take satisfaction of itself) *and be wholly engrossed with this, while* (= and so) *Philip shall be at liberty to say and do whatever he pleases.*

3. P. 30, l. 3. **πολιτεῖαι** = πολιτεύματα, *politics of this kind are common among you* (lit. customary to you). — 7. **ὡδὶ,** *thus,* sc. as follows, explained in the next sentence, which therefore has no connective. — **ὑμεῖς,** emphatic and distinctive : *you* the people of Athens. So also παρ' ὑμῖν, l. 10. — **ἐπὶ μὲν τῶν ἄλλων,** *on all other subjects* except public affairs; opposed to ἐκ δὲ τοῦ συμβουλεύειν, l. 12 : *but from the counsels of state you have utterly banished it.* Cf. *Ol.*, III. 32. — **δούλοις** = *slaves, servants in general.* — **οἰκέτας** = *domestics, house-servants.* — 4. 13. **εἶθ' ὑμῖν, κ. τ. λ.,** *so then you* (still emphatic) *have experienced the consequences of this,* viz. *that in your popular assemblies you give yourselves airs* (lit. luxuriate) *and are flattered at hearing nothing but what is pleasant* (everything to please you) *while in your affairs and circumstances you are already in the extremest peril.* This passage is repeated almost verbatim from *De Chers.*, 34. — 19. **ἕτοιμος.** The subject and the copula are to be supplied from οὐχ ἔχω τι λέγω in the antithesis, the two clauses being closely linked together by μέν and δέ. — 5. 24. **τὸ χείριστον…βελτίω.** This passage also (as far as p. 31, l. 2) is repeated from *Phil.* I. 2, where see notes. The great Attic orator is as little afraid to repeat himself in different orations as the great epic poet was to repeat the same lines in successive books.

P. 31, l. 3. νῦν δέ, κ. τ. λ., *but now it is your sloth and indifference which Philip has conquered, but the state he has not conquered;* YOU *have not been worsted, nay, you have not even moved,* not even entered the field. Others render κεκίνησθε, *bestirred yourselves,* and others still make it passive, and render: *you have not even been moved* from your place.

B. Preliminary question: Is Philip at peace or at war with Athens? The latter proved by a review of his acts (6–20).

6–20. SOME OF YOUR ORATORS TELL YOU THAT SOME OF US ARE CAUSING WAR. IF IT IS IN OUR POWER TO MAINTAIN PEACE, I SAY, MAINTAIN IT. BUT IS THAT PEACE WHICH IS ALL ON OUR SIDE, WHILE HE CARRIES ON WAR AGAINST US? IS PEACE TO BE JUDGED OF BY WORDS AND NOT BY DEEDS? HE WOULD NEVER *DECLARE* WAR AGAINST US THOUGH HE WERE MARCHING TO THE PIRÆUS, ANY MORE THAN HE DECLARED WAR AGAINST OLYNTHUS AND PHOCIS TILL HE HAD DESTROYED THEM. EVER SINCE THE RATIFICATION OF THE PEACE HE HAS BEEN MAKING WAR UPON YOU BY HIS INVASION OF THE CHERSONESE, BY HIS ATTEMPT ON MEGARA, BY ESTABLISHING DESPOTIC GOVERNMENTS IN EUBŒA, BY HIS PRESENT ADVANCE INTO THRACE, BY HIS INTRIGUES IN THE PELOPONNESUS, AND BY THE WHOLE COURSE OF HIS OPERATIONS WITH HIS ARMIES.

6. This section and the following are omitted in the text of Σ, but inserted in the margin. — 10. ἔνιοι. Cf. *Phil.* II. 34, and note there. — ὥστε...καταλαμβάνοντος...ἀνέχεσθαι, *that at the very time when he is capturing cities...they allow certain persons to say...that it is some of us who are causing the war.* — 15. διορθοῦσθαι, *to set ourselves right in regard to this.* — 7. 16. ὡς ἀμυνούμεθα is the object of γράψας καὶ συμβουλεύσας, *for there is reason to fear that some time any one who has moved and advised a method of defence* (lit. how we shall defend ourselves) *may fall under the charge of having caused the war.* The Greek prefers such concrete forms of expression. — 19. διορίζομαι, *define, determine,* the original meaning of the Greek, as of these English words, being to *mark off a boundary.*—ἐφ᾽ ἡμῖν, *depends on us.* — περὶ τοῦ πότερον, *on the question whether.*—8. 23. καὶ τὸν...ἀξιῶ, *and I demand that he who says so should make a motion and take action* accordingly *and not prevaricate* (cheat the people). — 27. προβάλλει, *puts forward,* holds up before you. Σ reads προβάλλει; other MSS. προβάλλεται, which is used in the same sense, *Thuc.,* I. 37. — 27. τοῖς δ᾽ ἔργοις, κ. τ. λ., *while the measures which he him-*

self adopts are those of war. Thus may we preserve the emphasis of
the original.

P. 32, l. 3. **οὐ διαφέρομαι,** *I do not quarrel with that.* The word
is used in an emphatic sense to correspond with the emphasis on
φάσκειν : *I have no objection* to your *professing* to be at peace. —
5. **ἔπειτα...λέγει,** *in the next place he means peace towards him by
you and not towards you by him.* — **χρημάτων,** gen. of price : *this is
what he purchases with all the money he is lavishing.* — 10. 10. **εἰ
περιμενοῦμεν,** *if we mean to wait.* Heslop. — 13. **οἷς,** *by what he has
done,* dat. by attraction, its antecedent being dat. of means with
τεκμαίρεσθαι. — 11. 14. **τοῦτο μέν,** *to take one instance;* τοῦτο δέ,
l. 20, *to take another.* Whiston. This form of the acc. of specification is in apposition with the following sentence. — 17. **πάντα τὸν
ἄλλον, κ. τ. λ.,** *although always before if one* (whenever any one)
charged him with anything of the sort he used to complain of it. —
20. **εἰς Φωκέας,** strictly speaking, designates the name of the country, whereas ὡς πρὸς συμμάχους is a personal reference ; from which
mode of speaking arose the use of ὡς alone with names of *persons* in
nearly the same sense as εἰς with names of things. Donaldson's
Grammar quoted by Whiston. C. 711 c ; Cu. 450 ; G. 191, 3 ; H.
621. Cf. *Phil.* II. 36. — 22. **ἦριζον,** *were all the while contending,*
relative imperf. — 23. **πάροδον,** *his passage* through the straits of
Thermopylæ. — 12. 25. **ἔχει καταλαβών,** *he has seized and still holds.*
This combination illustrates the origin of the use of *have* as an auxiliary in the modern languages. — 26. **Ὠρείταις.** See below, § 59 seq.,
where he tells the story. It is dat. after ἔφη as well as after ἐπισκεψομένους, *he said to the miserable inhabitants of Oreus* (a city in Eubœa) *that in good-will he had sent soldiers to visit them,* sc. as physicians and friends visit the sick.

P. 33, l. 1. **πυνθάνεσθαι γάρ,** *for he heard in regard to them that
they were sick and afflicted with dissensions.* — **αὐτούς** would regularly be the subject of νοσοῦσι, but for emphasis is made the object with πυνθάνεσθαι. — νοσοῦσι is generic, and is explained by the
specific στασιάζουσι. Cf. *De Cor.*, 45 : αἱ δὲ πόλεις ἐνόσουν. — 2. **συμμάχων δ' εἶναι,** *and it was the part of allies,* pred. gen. of characteristic. — 13. 4. **εἶτ' οἴεσθ', κ. τ. λ.,** *so then you think, do you* (εἶτ' is
indignant and exclamatory), *that he chose to deceive rather than fore-
warn and overcome by force those people* (named above) *who would
have done him no harm* (if he *had* declared war), *though they might*

εὐσεβές, κ. τ. λ., *but whether one violates piety and justice in a small matter or in one of greater importance, it has the same force,* that is, he is a wrong-doer, and he has violated the same sacred principle. Cf. James ii. 10. Here as everywhere else we see the high-toned ethics of Demosthenes. — 4. **φέρε δή.** See note, *Phil.* I. 10. — 5. **βασιλεύς.** The king of Persia. — 6. **ὑμετέραν.** See Introd., p. 113. — 7. **καὶ ἐπιστέλλει ταῦτα,** *and writes this in his letters to us.* Introd., p. 113. — **τί ποιεῖ.** This rhetorical repetition (cf. *τί ἐποίει,* p. 33, l. 25) has great beauty and force, like a refrain in music. — 17. 8. **φησὶ μέν,** emphatic, — *he* SAYS, *to be sure.* Franke and Rehdantz read φής, *you say,* after Σ. But that would require the addition of ἐκεῖνον. — **τοσούτῳ,** lit. *by so much ;* dat. denoting the degree of difference. C. 468 ; Cu. 440 ; G. 188, 2 ; H. 610. Al. τοσούτου, gen. after δέω, which is the more common construction and the easier reading, but for that reason to be rejected. With either reading the meaning is : *I am so far from admitting that in so doing he is keeping the peace with you.* — 10. **Μεγάρων ἁπτόμενον,** *by his attack* (or *attempt*) *on Megara.* The series of participles of which this is the first denote the manner in which he has been breaking the peace, λύειν τὴν εἰρήνην. The attempt on Megara (B. C. 343) was defeated by a body of Athenian hoplites sent from Athens under Phocion. See a brief sketch of these several operations of Philip, Introd., p. 112 ; Grote, XI. 622. — 11. **ἐν Εὐβοίᾳ,** sc. Philistides in Oreus (B. C. 342) and Clitarchus in Eretria (343). Cf. *De Cor.,* 71, and below, § 57. — **νῦν ἐπὶ Θρᾴκην,** *and by his present advance into Thrace.* At the time of this oration (341) he was still carrying on those operations in Thrace, which ended in its complete subjugation. — 12. **καὶ τὰ ἐν Πελοποννήσῳ,** *by his intrigues in the Peloponnesus,* sc. with the Argives and Messenians. Cf. *Phil.* II. 15 seqq. ; Grote, XI. 611. — 13. **πράττει** expresses the *operations* he is carrying on, while ποιοῦντα has reference rather to the *effects* and results. Cf. note, *Ol.* III. 15. — 14. **φημί.** The ind. after ὥστε, l. 10, makes the *affirmation* more positive. — 15. **καί,** *even.* — **ἐφιστάντας.** Observe the force of ἐφ- : *setting up their engines against.* — 17. **προσάγωσιν,** *until they are actually bringing them to the walls.* Al. προσαγάγωσιν = *have actually brought.* — 19. **κἂν…τοξεύῃ,** *though he be not yet throwing a dart nor shooting an arrow.* In illustration of the rapidity and vividness of this passage Whiston quotes as applicable to it the language of Cicero, *De Orat.,* I. 161 : Tantus cursus verborum fuit, et sic evolavit

oratio, ut ejus vim atque incitationem adspexerim, vestigia ingres-
sumque vix viderim. — 18. 20. τίσιν...γένοιτο, *to what dangers then
would you be exposed if anything should happen,* i. e. if war should
come and you should be unfortunate. Euphemistic. See *Phil.* I. 12:
εἴ τι πάθοι. — 21. τῷ...φρονῆσαι, *to the alienation of the Hellespont,
to your enemy's becoming master of Megara and Eubœa, to the Peloponnesians' taking his side.* Observe the vivacity of the *interrogation* and the *asyndeton.* — 24. εἶτα. Compare εἶτα, § 13, above. —
19. 27. ὁρίζομαι, *from that day I date* (lit. *bound*) *his commencement
of hostilities.*

P. 35, l. 2. ὅταν βούλησθε is opposed to ἤδη : neglect to defend
yourselves *at once,* and you will not be able to do it *when you wish
to.* — 3. τοσοῦτον, acc. denoting the measure of difference, instead
of the dative. — καί...γε may here be rendered, *yes, and.* Cf. *Phil.*
II. 29 : *yes, and so much do I dissent from your other advisers that I
do not even think we ought* (δοκεῖ = it seems *good*) *to be inquiring
about the Chersonesus now nor Byzantium, but while* (μέν) *you should
lend aid to them and see to it that no harm befalls them, you ought to
be consulting for all the Greeks.* We have here an example of the
comprehensive and far-seeing statesmanship of Demosthenes. — 9. ἐξ
ὧν = *why,* the reasons by which I am led, lit. *out of* which, in consequence of which. — 12. εἰ μή...ἄρα, *if forsooth* (if then) *you will
not for others.* ἄρα, like εἶτα, points to the inconsistency and absurdity of the thing, and so is ironical. — 13. τετυφῶσθαι, *and am be-
sotted.* The old grammarians explain τετυφῶσθαι by ἐμβεβροντῆσθαι,
and derive it from Typho, Τυφῶν, the *thunder-struck* giant. But, as
Whiston says, a more natural derivation is from τῦφος, a smoke, mist,
or cloud, the accompaniments of storms and volcanic eruptions.

C. The main question, not the safety of the Chersonesus or Byzantium, but the rights and liberties of all Greece (21 – 35).

21 – 35. You have conceded to Philip the right never
granted to Athens, Sparta, Thebes, or any Grecian state,
much less to be granted to a barbarian, of doing what he
pleases. Review the history of his aggressions and wrongs,
and you will find that in thirteen years and less they exceed all which all the dominant Grecian powers have done
to the smaller states in a century. There are no bounds
either to his ambition or to his insolence.

21. 16. καὶ ἀπίστως...Ἕλληνες, *and that the Greeks are jealous*

and quarrelling among themselves. — 18. ἐξ ἐκείνου, *from what he
was.* ἐξ denotes origin. Cf. ἐκ μικροῦ καὶ ταπεινοῦ, l. 15. — ἢ νῦν...
ποιήσασθαι, *than that now, when he has already taken so many places,
he should subject the rest to his power.* — 22. 21. ἀλλ' is opposed to
the ὅτι μὲν...παραλείψω of the preceding section, and introduces the
point on which he wishes to dwell. — 22. ἅπαντας ἀνθρώπους, a
rhetorical exaggeration, like *all the world.* — ἀφ' ὑμῶν ἀρξαμένους,
beginning with you = *and you among the first.* — 23. ὑπὲρ οὗ, *in
regard to which,* i. e. which has been the cause or subject-matter of
all the wars, etc. — τὸν ἄλλον...χρόνον, *always before.* Cf. § 11 =
in all past time. — 25. τὸ ποιεῖν, κ. τ. λ., *the privilege of doing just
what he pleases, and fleecing and pillaging the Greeks one by one in the
manner he is doing* (οὑτωσί). Those expressive words, περικόπτειν and
λωποδυτεῖν, are sufficiently explained in the Lexicon. — 27. καταδου-
λοῦσθαι...ἐπιόντα, lit. to enslave their cities attacking them. ἐπιόντα
denoting the manner or means. Render, *and attacking and enslav-
ing their cities.*

23. P. 36, l. 1. προστάται denotes the *leading power* in Grecian
affairs, — the *hegemony,* as recent historians call it. In *Ol.* III. 24,
the Athenian hegemony is said to have lasted forty-five years ; but
there, he says, they ruled with the consent of the Greeks : τῶν Ἑλλήνων ἑκόντων. Here he wishes to include the period of unwilling subjection in order to aggravate by comparison the wrongs done by
Philip (§ 25), and so he adds the twenty-nine years of the Peloponnesian War. See note, *Ol.* III. 24. — ἑβδομήκοντα...τρία, sc. from
the close of the Persian War, B. C. 477, to the close of the Peloponnesian War, B. C. 405. — 2. τριάκοντα...δέοντα, *thirty wanting one,*
sc. from the end of the Peloponnesian War, B. C. 405, to their defeat
at Naxos by Chabrias, B. C. 376. — 3. ἴσχυσαν τι, *attained to some
considerable power.* Such is the force of the aorist. So ἄρξασι, l. 13
below = *when they had attained to the hegemony.* The battle of Leuctra,
won by the Thebans under Epaminondas, was B. C. 371. — οὐδὲ πολλοῦ δεῖ, *no, not by any means.* — 24. 9. τοῦτο μέν. Cf. note, § 11.
— ὑμῖν depends on πολεμεῖν, l. 12. The skeleton of the sentence is
as follows : *with you, for example, in the first place...all thought it
their duty to go to war, and again with the Lacedæmonians...all went
to war,* etc. — 10. οὐ μετρίως, *without due moderation ;* rendered
harshly by the commentators generally. It is an example of *litotes.*
— 11. καὶ...αὐτοῖς, *even those who had no fault to find with them.* —

constituted the tetrarchies. — κατὰ πόλεις perhaps, though not necessarily, implies a decemvirate (δεκαδαρχία) in *each city.* — δουλεύωσιν,
subj., instead of opt., to describe the present condition ; that they
might be, as they now are, subject, etc. — 27. 11. εἰς τὰς ἐπιστολάς.
This is the reading of Σ, and is entitled to the preference as the more
difficult reading. Al. ἐν ταῖς ἐπιστολαῖς. εἰς, of course, implies motion towards, *put into* his letters. — 13. καὶ οὐ γράφει μέν, *and he does
not write thus and not* DO *it.* See the famous passage in *De Cor.* 179,
in which οὐ μὲν...οὐ δέ thus alternate through several successive
clauses. — 14. ἀλλ᾽, κ. τ. λ., *nay, he is gone to the Hellespont, he had
previously come to Ambracia,* etc. The orator pictures the rapidity
of Philip's marches and conquests in his rapid and unconnected
clauses, so that we can see it. See a similar description in the proph-
ecy of Jeremiah xlviii. 1 seqq. — 17. ἡ βάρβαρος, sc. γῆ, which, as
Whiston observes, is also properly understood with ἡ Ἑλλάς : *neither
the Greek nor the barbarian world contains the ambition of the man.*
With this use of χωρεῖ compare John xxi. 25, where the hyperbole
is still stronger. — 28. 21. διορωρύγμεθα, *intrenched in separate cities.*
Ad rem. cf. *De Cor.* 61. — 23. οὐδέ is more emphatic than οὔτε =
no, nor to unite, nor to form any alliance for succor and friendship. —
29. 26. τὸν χρόνον...ἐγνωκώς, *each resolved to make the most of* (to
count as gain) *the time in which another is being destroyed.*

P. 38, l. 1. οὐχ ὅπως, *not seeking nor striving for the salvation of
the Greeks.* — 2. ἐπεὶ...ἀγνοεῖ, *for that like a course of fever or an attack
of some other disease he is coming even to him who now thinks himself
to be far removed,* none assuredly (γε, l. 2) *can be ignorant.* — 7. ἀλλ᾽
οὖν, *at any rate, they were wronged by genuine sons of Greece.* —
8. καὶ τὸν αὐτὸν τρόπον, *and one might have taken this in the same
way* (looked at it in the same light) *as he would if a legitimate son,
born heir to a large estate, should manage it badly or improperly,* viz.
he would say *that in this particular he was deserving of blame and
censure, but it would be impossible to say that he had no title and was
not heir to the property he was thus managing.* — 31. 14. ὑποβολι-
μαῖος, *a supposititious child,* the opposite of γνήσιος above. — 16. ἀλλ᾽
οὐχ, *but not so in regard to Philip and his conduct now, not so do they
feel in regard to Philip, who is not only not a Greek and no connection
of the Greeks, but not even a barbarian from a place which it is honorable to mention.* The repetition of negatives makes the denial very
emphatic. — ὀλέθρου Μακεδόνος, *a pestilent fellow of Macedon, a coun-*

try from which, etc.   So he calls Æschines ὄλεθρος γραμματεύς, *De Cor.,* 127.   The orator'. indignation, righteous as it is, in both cases carries him beyond the bounds of truth and justice.   Philip was generally conceded to have had Greek blood in his veins, and that of the family of Hercules.   He gives an ingenious but hardly a fair or honest turn to the fact that Macedonians were not found as slaves in Greece.   Rehdantz sees in πρότερον a suggestion of the shameful contrast now when the people who formerly were deemed unfit for slaves had become their masters ! — **32. 24. πόλεις.** The reference is particularly to the cities ·of Phocis which he had recently destroyed. — τίθησι is the technical word generally used of the person or people that *holds,* i. e. fixes, appoints, *presides over* the games.   "Two months after the surrender of the Phocians, Philip was nominated by the Amphictyonic Council President of the Pythian games in conjunction with the Thebans and Thessalians (B. C. 346).   The Athenians refused to send Theori on the occasion (*De Fals. Leg.* 128 ; Grote, XI. 602)." Heslop. — **25. τῶν Ἑλλήνων** is to be taken in connection with what has just been said of Philip as no Greek : that he who was not a Greek should preside over *the national festival of the* GREEKS, *and even, if not present in person, send his* SLAVES (that is, his agents, *slaves* in the eyes of Demosthenes and the Greeks) *to hold the games !* — this was intolerable insolence. — **26. κύριος δὲ Πυλῶν, κ. τ. λ.** The passage in brackets is omitted in Σ.   The force of the οὐ at the beginning of the section extends over all the clauses to καταστήσοντας, p. 39, l. 9, linking them all together in one question and thus making the enumeration of particulars more rapid and vivid : *does he not hold the Pythian games ?...and control Thermopylæ and the passes into Greece* (the people put for the country) *?...and possess the privilege of consulting the oracle first, to which not even all* GREEKS *have a claim, having thrust aside us* (the Athenians) *?* etc. This privilege of *pre-audience of the god,* on those days on which alone answers were given, had belonged to the Phocians, and was now, by vote of the Amphictyons, transferred to Philip.   The Delphians used to confer it on particular states or sovereigns as a reward for some special service.   Thus the Spartans received it ; also Crœsus, king of Lydia, for his magnificent presents and offerings.

33. P. 39, l. 5. **γράφει δέ,** *and write to the Thessalians how they ought to conduct their public affairs ?* The force of οὐ still continues. — **7. Πορθμόν.** Porthmus was the port of Eretria. — **τὸν δῆμον,**

to expel the democracy of the Eretrians. It was the partisans of the democratic form of government that were ex elled ; but these are artfully and yet naturally in view of the habitual use of the word at Athens called *the demus, the people.* See § 17 above, and below § 57 ; Grote, XI. 621. — 9. ἀλλ'...ἀνέχονται, *and yet the Greeks, although they see these things, endure it.* — 10. καὶ τὸν αὐτὸν τρόπον, *and they seem to me to look on just as they would at a hail-storm.* — 12. καθ' ἑαυτοὺς ἕκαστοι = ad se quisque, *praying that it may not come upon themselves severally.* See *De Cor.*, 45, where a similar idea is expressed in similar words : οὐκ ἐφ' ἑαυτοὺς ἑκάστων οἰομένων τὸ δεινὸν ἥξειν, and Sall. *Frag. His.*, I., which is manifestly an imitation, almost a translation of this passage : Qui videmini intenta mala, quasi fulmen, optare se quisque ne attingant, sed prohibere ne conari quidem. — 34. 13. οὐ μόνον δ' ἐφ' οἷς, *and not only does no one punish him for the outrages which all Greece is receiving at his hands, but none for the wrongs which each state is itself suffering.* — 16. οὐ Κορινθίων ...οὐχ Ἀχαιῶν. Here follow the specifications under the general charge, in which the reader will observe the emphatic position of the several states wronged and the rapid succession of questions in which the wrongs are enumerated. These words are gen. of the possessor : *of the Corinthians has he not gone against Ambracia and Leucas;* but the spirit of the passage is well expressed by Kennedy and Heslop : has he not wronged the Corinthians by attacking Ambracia and Leucas ? etc. These were Corinthian colonies on the northwest coast of Greece. See note, § 27. Naupactus is the modern Lepanto, so famous for the battle which checked the further advance of the Turks in the conquest of Europe. Echinus was a colony of Thebes on the northern coast of the Malian gulf in Thessaly. In reference to Cardia and the whole series of Philip's aggressions, see Introd., p. 112, seq. — 25. τί οἴεσθε...τί ποιήσειν, *and yet he who is using all so wantonly, what do you think when he has become master of each of us one by one, what think you he will do ?* The second τί is omitted in some MSS. and editions, but rests on good authority, and adds force to the interrogation.

D. The root of the mischief and danger is in the degeneracy and corruption of morals throughout Greece (36–46).

36–46. WHAT IS THE CAUSE OF ALL THIS ? THE GREEKS OF FORMER TIMES DETESTED TRAITORS AND HIRELINGS, AND PUNISHED THEM. YOU ENVY THEM, AND PUNISH THOSE WHO DENOUNCE THEM.

THE LATTER YOU SEE WITH YOUR OWN EYES. IN PROOF OF THE FORMER, REMEMBER THE INFAMY OF THE MAN WHO WAS OUTLAWED BY YOUR SIRES FOR BRINGING MEDIAN GOLD INTO THE PELOPONNE-SUS. HENCE, AS A NATURAL RESULT, GREECE WAS THEN FORMIDA-BLE TO THE BARBARIAN, NOT THE BARBARIAN TO THE GREEKS.

36. P. 40, l. 4. ἦν τι τότ', ἦν. Observe the favorite repetition, which we have so often seen in other orations, and emphasized by the ὦ ἄνδρες Ἀθηναῖοι by which it is followed: *there was a something then, there WAS, gentlemen of Athens, in the sentiments of the masses.* — 6. ἦγε, *kept Greece free.* — 7. ἡττᾶτο governs the same case of the same class of words as ἥττων, from which it is derived: *was over-come by* (lit. was less powerful than) *no battle on the sea or on the land.* It is the antithesis of ἐκράτησε : it conquered everything and could itself be conquered by nothing. — 8. νῦν δ' ἀπολωλός, *but the loss of which now has ruined and turned upside down all the affairs of the Greeks.* — 37. 12. χαλεπώτατον, *it was a most grievous thing to be convicted of receiving a bribe.* Observe the use of the imperfect in each of these clauses to express customary action. — 38. 14. τὸν οὖν καιρόν, κ. τ. λ., *hence the favorable moment for each several move-ment* (civil or military) *which fortune often provides could not be pur-chased,* etc. — πρίασθαι has for its object not only καιρόν, but ὁμόνοιαν, ἀπιστίαν, and τοιοῦτον οὐδέν. — 18. ὅλως = *in fine.* — 39. 20. ταῦτα and τούτων, of course, refer to the harmonious co-operation of the Greeks and their distrust of despots and barbarians mentioned above : *now these things have all been sold out till the market is as it were ex-hausted, and in exchange for these there have been imported things by which Greece has been ruined and made sick.* The figure of barter and sale is carried relentlessly through, and *Greece* ruined and sick unto death — GREECE (observe the emphatic position of ἡ Ἑλλάς) is the victim. — 22. ζῆλος...γέλως...μῖσος, i. e. *envy* of those whom our ancestors *hated* (ἐμίσουν), *laughter* at that which was then deemed most grievous and dreadful (χαλεπώτατον), and *hatred,* per-haps *punishment,* not of the criminals, but of the good citizen who exposed them. The three clauses in answer to the question here are carefully set over against the three which answer the question in § 37. The picture of moral degeneracy is all the blacker for being painted on so bright a background ; and the climax is reached *in any country* when the leading men envy those who have grown rich by corruption, laugh when they unblushingly confess the bribe, and,

instead of punishing iniquity, visit their anger and indignation upon
those who bring it to light ; and if the people love or are willing to
have it so, their ruin is inevitable. — 24. ἤρτηται, *result* (lit. depend)
from. — 40. 25. σωμάτων. The student hardly need be informed
that this is the regular word for *men* in the military sense. — 27. νῦν
ἅπασι, κ. τ. λ., *all* the Greek states *now possess in greater number
and abundance than they then did by far.*

41. P. 41, l. 4. προσδεῖσθε, *you have no need of my testimony in
addition* (προσ-) *to that of your own senses.* — 6. γράμματα here =
inscriptions. — 7. κατέθεντο…εἰς ἀκρόπολιν, *which they inscribed on
a bronze column and deposited in the Acropolis.* For this use of εἰς,
where we say *on* and *in*, see note § 27; C. 704; G. 191, N. 6; H. 618 a;
Madv. 79. — 42. 9. φησίν, *it says*, sc. the inscription, γράμματα.
— 9. Ζελείτης, *of Zelea,* a town of Mysia in Asia Minor, mentioned
by Homer. *Il.* II. 824. Cf. l. 17 below. — ἄτιμος, sc. ἔστω, *let
him be outlawed.* It is a civil technic, and the sense in which it is
here used is explained below, § 44, and is thus stated by Whiston :
let him be an outlaw, i. e. let him lose all the benefits which, though
a foreigner, he would have had at Athens by the *jus gentium,* or international law, and those to which, according to Æschines (*Cont.
Ctes.* 259), he was entitled as a *proxenus* of Athens. — 12. ὅτι…
ἤγαγεν. He was sent into Peloponnesus by Artaxerxes to stir up a
war against Athens. — 43. 14. τίς ἦν ποθ', *what must have been the
sentiment.* ποτέ as usual adds emphasis to the question. The time
is denoted by τότε. — 15. ἡ τί τὸ ἀξίωμα, *or rather what their con-
scious worth.* Kennedy and Heslop render ἀξίωμα, *dignity.* Whiston
renders it *spirit,* but very properly adds, that "the word is almost
untranslatable here. It implies a spirit of self-respect by which they
were induced to expect and demand (ἠξίουν) from themselves certain
actions and principles as alone worthy of their position." See also
Grote, VI. 233, note. — 16. Ζελείτην…δοῦλον βασιλέως…διακονῶν.
These are all circumstances which distinguish the case from the corruption of the present day at Athens and make it the more remarkable
that the Athenians should have punished it with such severity. —
20. ἀτίμους is plural because it follows αὐτὸν καὶ γένος (himself and
family) and agrees with both, while ἐχθρόν is singular because it precedes them, and agrees only with αὐτόν. ἀτίμους takes the gender of
αὐτόν. C. 490, 497; G. 138, N. 2; H. 511. — 44. 21. τοῦτο δ' ἐστίν,
and this is not the ἀτιμία commonly so called (which one would usually

call by that name). — 22. τῶν Ἀθηναίων κοινῶν, emphatic by position: ATHENIAN franchises. — 23. ἀλλ' ἐν τοῖς φονικοῖς, but it is
written in the laws relating to murder defining (lit. respecting) the
persons for whom he (the lawgiver) does not allow prosecution for murder: "and," says he, "let him die an outlaw." The argument is:
the ἀτιμία to which Arthmius was condemned could not be mere pri-
vation of civil rights, — what punishment would that have been to a
man of Zelea? — nay (ἀλλ'), he became ἄτιμος in the sense in which the
word is used in the φονικοί νόμοι, viz. out of the pale of all law, so
that he could be slain with impunity. So the orator explains himself in the following clause: this then is what he means, that he who
has killed a person of this class (ἄτιμον) is clear of bloodguiltiness.
The passage has occasioned much discussion, and the readings differ
considerably in different editions.

P. 42, l. 3. μὴ τοῦθ' ὑπολαμβάνουσιν. This participial clause
contains the condition: if they had not habitually cherished (imperf.
part.) this opinion, sc. that they must care for the safety of all the
Greeks, and not merely of Athens. — 4. οὕτω...ὥστε...ποιεῖν, with
such severity that they even made them stelites, that is, branded them on
pillars. The familiar distinction between κολάζειν and τιμωρεῖσθαι, as
drawn by Aristotle, viz. that the former is chastisement for the refor-
mation of the person chastised, while the latter is punishment for the
sake of the law and the state, is not always observed, and here both
words are used for emphasis. — 46. 7. οὐ γὰρ οὕτως, κ. τ. λ., for
YOU do not feel so towards such things as these nor towards anything
else. — 9. εἴπω, shall I tell you? lit. may I? Between ἀλλὰ πῶς
and εἴπω most of the MSS. and some editions insert two or three
lines which Σ omits, and which, as they manifestly disturb the connection, are omitted in this and in the majority of editions.

ΕΚ ΤΟΥ ΓΡΑΜΜΑΤΕΙΟΥ ΑΝΑΓΙΓΝΩΣΚΕΙ. These words,
found in many MSS. and most editions (in some bracketed), doubtless proceeded from some copyist who did not understand the immediately preceding context, and who supposed that here Demosthenes
read, or had read by the clerk, some document containing the resolutions, or the measures recommended by the orator. But this does not
accord with the preceding εἴπω, which in that case should have been
λέξω, nor with the fact that these recommendations follow in § 70
seqq.; nor indeed does the connection require this or any other inser-
tion. The reproof which the orator proceeds to administer to the

blindness and self-complacency of his countrymen, and the bribery of too many of them, is sufficient to explain the hesitation and the fear of their displeasure with which he introduces it.

E. Reproof of their blindness and self-complacency in regard to Philip, and the readiness of too many to receive his bribes (47–52).

47–52. YOU FOOLISHLY FLATTER YOURSELVES THAT YOU CAN OVERCOME PHILIP EVEN MORE EASILY THAN YOU DID THE LACEDÆMONIANS. BUT EVERYTHING HAS CHANGED AND ADVANCED SINCE THAT TIME, AND NOTHING SO MUCH AS THE MODE OF CARRYING ON WAR. THEN THE CAMPAIGN LASTED ONLY FOUR OR FIVE MONTHS. NOW PHILIP MAKES NO DIFFERENCE BETWEEN SUMMER AND WINTER. BESIDES THE LACEDÆMONIANS NEVER THOUGHT OF BUYING AN ADVANTAGE OR A CONQUEST, WHEREAS PHILIP ACCOMPLISHES MOST OF HIS ENDS BY THE HELP OF HIRELINGS AND TRAITORS.

47. 10. τοίνυν, *well then,* if you wish, I will tell you. — 11. ἄρα, cf. § 20, et passim. — 15. ὅμως...ἀνηρπάσθη, *yet our state resisted even them and was not destroyed* (swept away). — 16. ἁπάντων, *while everything, so to speak* (= almost everything), *has made great progress.* — 18. οὐδὲν ἡγοῦμαι πλέον, *I do not think anything has changed and advanced more than the* methods of carrying on *war.* — 48. 19. πρῶτον μέν is correlative to δέ, l. 24: *in the first place,* the comparative shortness of the campaign, *and,* secondly, the simplicity of the people who never thought of buying a victory—both necessitate corresponding changes in our action. — 20. ἀκούω. See note *Phil.* I. 23. — πάντας τοὺς ἄλλους, *and all the other Greeks.* — 21. τέτταρας μῆνας, κ. τ. λ., *for four months or five, just in the season.* Compare Thucydides's history of the very war here referred to, II. 47; III. 1, et al. With τὴν ὡραίαν, Franke compares *Or. Contr. Dion.* § 33 : ἐνταῦθα δ' ἐπιδημήσαντας παραχειμάζειν ἔδει καὶ περιμένειν τὴν ὡραίαν. — 22. ἐμβαλόντας ἄν, *would invade and ravage the country with heavy armed soldiers and national troops and then retire homewards again.* — 24. οὕτω...πολιτικῶς, *and so old-fashioned* were they or *rather so national in their ways.* πολιτικῶς, like πολιτικοῖς, l. 23, is opposed to that which is *foreign,* and here especially to the employment of mercenaries (ξένους, p. 43, l. 6), which had become so common in the time of Demosthenes ; the former might be rendered *Athenian,* as the latter might be rendered *Spartan.* — 25. χρημάτων. Kennedy compares the old lines of Ennius :

> Non cauponantes bellum sed belligerantes
> Ferro, non auro, vitam cernamus utrique.

P. 43, l. 1. **νόμιμόν τινα**, *but the war which they carried on was legitimate as it were and open.* τινά is an apology for the use of the epithet *νόμιμον* as applied to war. — **49.** 2. **δήπου**, *doubtless: but now you see doubtless that the traitors have caused the most of our disasters, and that nothing is done in fair field or fight.* —**τοὺς προδότας, κ. τ. λ.**, is opposed to *οὐδὲ χρημάτων, κ. τ. λ.*, and *οὐδὲν ἐκ παρατάξεως* (in battle array) to *νόμιμον…πόλεμον.* — 6. **ψιλοὺς…ξένους** opposed to *ὁπλίταις καὶ πολιτικοῖς στρατεύμασιν*, p. 42, l. 23, and governed by *ἐξηρτῆσθαι* with *στρατόπεδον* as an appositive: and *you hear of Philip marching where he pleases, not…but by attaching to himself skirmishers, cavalry, archers, mercenaries, — an army of that sort.* ἐξηρτῆσθαι is somewhat contemptuous ; compare our *hangers-on.* — **50.** 7. **ἐπὶ τούτοις**, *at the head of such troops as those.* Westermann and Franke take these words in the sense, which is frequent (and possible here), of, *besides this, præterea.* — 8. **νοσοῦντας.** The reader must have become familiar with our orator's fondness for this word to express the moral and political state of his countrymen, and especially their *dissensions among themselves* (ἐν αὑτοῖς). Cf. § 12 above ; *De Cor.* 45, et passim. Heslop renders : *suffering from internal disorders.* — 10. **ἐπιστήσας.** Cf. note § 17. — **καὶ σιωπῶ**, *and I pass over the fact that there is no difference between summer and winter, neither is there any season whatever exempt during which he rests* (intermits). — **θέρος** and **χειμῶνα** would regularly be nom. and subject of *διαφέρει*, but for emphasis they are attracted into the principal clause, and made the object of *σιωπῶ.* —**51.** 12. **μέντοι** is not adversative here, but affirmative, like *μὲν δή* (which is the reading here in some MSS.) = *certainly then.* This is the primitive meaning of the word = *μὲν τοι.* See Lex. : *certainly then, knowing these things all of you and taking them into consideration, you ought not,* etc. With the *pair* εἰδότας καὶ λογιζομένους here compare *ἐνθυμηθεῖητε καὶ λογίσαισθε, Phil.* I. 31, et passim. — 14. **εὐήθειαν**, *simplicity*, both of morals in not using bribes, and of warfare in their citizen soldiery and short campaigns. — 15. **ἐκτραχηλισθῆναι**, *plunge headlong into ruin.* The figure, which is too bold to be preserved in English, is drawn from a horse throwing his rider over his head. Cf. Xen. *Cyr.*, I. 4. 8 : ὁ ἵππος πίπτει εἰς γόνατα, καὶ μικροῦ κἀκεῖνον ἐξετραχήλισεν. The figure is carried out in βλέποντας. The word is also used, especially in the passive, in the sense of *breaking the neck* (Aristoph., *Nub.* 1501, et al.), and Rehdantz explains the metaphor thus here. Compare, however, *Ol.* II. 9 :

ἀνεχαίτισε, and *De Cor.* 138 : ὑποσκελίζειν. — 16. ὡς ἐκ πλείστου, *as long beforehand as possible.* For ὡς with the superl. see C. 553 ; Cu. 631 ; H. 664. For ἐκ with words denoting time, see note *Phil.* I. 1 : ἐκ τοῦ παρεληλυθότος χρόνου. — 17. ὅπως οἴκοθεν, κ. τ. λ., *seeing to it that he does not stir from home, and by no means* (οὐχὶ) *engage with him in a decisive battle.* The figure is well preserved in Heslop's rendering : *and not close with him in mortal struggle.* The omission of the connective increases the vividness. — 52. 20. ἄν περ = *if only.* Al. ἄνπερ. — 21. ἡ φύσις, one of the *many advantages,* subject of ὑπάρχει. — 22. ἧς...πολλήν, *much of which.* — 23. ἄλλα μυρία. The connective omitted. Render : *and a thousand others.* — εἰς δὲ ἀγῶνα is carefully and emphatically contrasted with πρὸς μὲν πόλεμον, l. 19 : *for* (lit. *towards*) *a war...but for* (lit. *into*) *a battle.* The prepositions are chosen to suit the nouns, though the obvious distinction cannot be expressed in concise and idiomatic English. Compare εἰς τὰ πράγματα and πρὸς τοὺς λόγους, *Ol.* III. 1.

F. The duty and necessity of punishing the agents and hirelings of Philip illustrated by numerous examples (53–62).

53–62. IT IS IMPOSSIBLE TO CONQUER YOUR ENEMIES ABROAD TILL YOU PUNISH THEIR MINISTERS AT HOME. LOOK AT THE SAD HISTORY OF OLYNTHUS, OF ERETRIA, OF OREUS ; AND SEE THE FATAL CONSEQUENCES OF LISTENING TO TRAITORS IN PREFERENCE TO PATRIOTIC ADVISERS.

53. 25. Οὐ μόνον...οὐδὲ...ἀλλά, *and you must not only cherish habitually these sentiments and not only oppose him constantly by deeds, the deeds of war, but on calculation and on principle you must begin to hate those among you who advocate his cause.* The force of μόνον extends to the second clause (οὐδὲ) as in *De Cor.* 2 and 107, and often. — μισῆσαι is what is sometimes called an ingressive aorist, like ἴσχυσαν, § 23, and ἄρξασι, 24 = begin to hate, conceive hatred. μισῆσαι enim est *odium concipere,* μισεῖν *odisse,* Franke. γιγνώσκειν and ἀμύνεσθαι, on the contrary, express continued action.

54. P. 44, l. 5. οὐ δυνήσεσθε. The inability which the orator foresees is, of course, a moral inability, as the next clause shows. The other MSS. add οὐδὲ βούλεσθε, which is omitted by Σ and most of the recent editions. — 7. μή τι δαιμόνιον, *that some supernatural power is driving the state to ruin.* The editors generally render τὶ δαιμόνιον, *some evil genius* or *evil spirit ;* and to this there is no objection, perhaps, if it only be remembered how different an idea the

words suggested to the old Greeks from that which we associate with
the words *evil spirit*. In classic Greek δαιμόνιον may mean a hostile
fate or a vengeful providence, but never exactly, as in N. T., an evil
spirit. See as an illustration the use of the word in Xenophon's
Memorabilia and Plato's *Apology*. See also L. & S. *Lex.* — 8. ὥστε
λοιδορίας, κ. τ. λ., *that for calumny, for envy, for jest, for any cause
whatever that may strike your fancy, you bid hirelings speak.* — οὐδ'
ἄν ἀρνηθεῖεν ὡς οὐκ. C. 713 d ; Cu. 617, Obs. 3 ; G. 283, 6 ; H. 838.
— 55. 12. καὶ οὐχί...δεινόν, *and this, bad as it is, is not by any means
the worst,* lit. not yet at all bad, sc. in comparison with what *yet
remains* to be said. — 14. τούτοις, *these men,* e. g. Æschines and
Philocrates, particularly Æschines, whom he had recently prosecuted
for misconduct of the embassy. Cf. *De Fal. Leg.*, and Introd. p. 112.
— 56. 18. Ἦσαν ἐν Ὀλύνθῳ, *there were in Olynthus some of the public men* (those engaged in the affairs of state) *who were Philip's crea-
tures, and who served him in everything, and some who were on the
patriotic side* (the side of the public good) *and labored to save their
fellow-citizens from slavery.* — Φιλίππου is gen. of the possessor after
ἦσαν, and τοῦ βελτίστου is substantially the same. — 22. ὧν προδο-
θέντων, gen. abs. denoting the cause : *by whose betrayal Olynthus was
destroyed.* Lasthenes, who was commander of cavalry, betrayed six
hundred men into an ambuscade, and Olynthus soon after fell into
the hands of Philip. Cf. § 66 below ; *De Cor.* 48 ; *Fals. Leg.* 266 ;
Thirl. *His.* II. 109, Amer. ed. — 24. καὶ ὅτ' ἦν, κ. τ. λ., *and who,
while the city still existed, were slandering and calumniating the patriotic counsellors to such a degree that the people of Olynthus were
persuaded even to banish Apollonides.* This Apollonides afterwards
became an Athenian citizen. Some question has arisen as to the
meaning of ἐκβαλεῖν, and the treatment of Apollonides, in regard to
which see Heslop ad loc., and Thirl. II. 109, 110.

57. P. 45, l. 1. τὸ ἔθος τοῦτο, *this habit* of listening to traitors
and enemies of the state. — 3. ἐπειδὴ ἀπαλλαγέντος, *when, after
Plutarch and his mercenaries were gotten rid of, the people was in possession of the city and of Porthmus, some were for bringing the government over to you and others to Philip.* The imperfect (ἦγον) denotes
attempt or *desire*. Plutarch, tyrant of Eretria, was at first supported
by the Athenians, but proving faithless to them in the battle at Ta-
mynæ (B. C. 354), was afterwards expelled by Phocion. — 6. ἀκούοντες δὲ τούτων, *and listening to the latter for the most part rather* (than

to the former). Al. τὰ πολλὰ, μᾶλλον δὲ τὰ πάντα, in most things or rather in everything. — 7. τελευτῶντες, *finally.* — 58. 9. καὶ γάρ τοι, *for you know.* — ὁ σύμμαχος αὐτοῖς, *their ally,* said in irony. Cf. § 33 above ; *De Or.* 295 ; Grote, XI. 622. — 12. καὶ μετὰ ταῦτα, *and since that he has expelled them* (the Eretrian democracy) *twice from the country, when at length they wished to save themselves,* sc. from the tyrants by the help of the Athenians. — 14. τότε μὲν...πάλιν δέ, *then* (= *once*)...*and again.* — 59. 16. τὰ πολλὰ implies that he passes over *the many,* that is, the most of the facts, and mentions only a *few.* — Φιλιστίδης. Cf. § 33 above ; *De Cor.* 48 ; Grote, XI. 621. — 17. ἔπραττε Φιλίππῳ, *was intriguing for Philip.* — 18. οἵπερ νῦν, *the very persons who now have possession of the government.* — 19. ταῦτ', sc. that they were partisans of Philip. — Εὐφραῖος, a pupil of Plato, was recommended by him to Perdiccas of Macedon, whose minister he was for some years. Heslop. — 21. ὅπως ἐλεύθεροι, sc. ἔπραττεν, *was laboring that.* Cf. πράττοντες ὅπως, § 56. — 60. 24. ἐνέδειξεν, *indicted him.* The technical term for a criminal process. Cf. *Dic. Antiq.*, Ἔνδειξις. — 27. καὶ χορηγὸν...καὶ πρυτανευόμενοι, *with Philip for their choragus and their prytanis.* These words, so full of meaning in the literary, civil, and religious life of the Athenians, and so well understood by classical scholars, have no exact equivalents in English ; *paymaster* and *president* perhaps come as near to them as any. παρ' ἐκείνου follows πρυτανευόμενοι in many MSS. and editions : *directed* (inspired) *from him.*

61. P. 46, l. 4. ἀποτυμπανίσαι, *and cudgelling* THEM *to death.* The allusion is borrowed from the beating of the tympanum. Observe the change of tense ; the *aid* to Euphræus should have been a *continued,* the *cudgelling* of the traitors a *finished* action. — τὸν δ' ἐπιτήδειον, *but they said that* HE *deserved to suffer this, and they rejoiced at it.* Sic Latine *idoneus* pro *dignus.* Schaefer. — 6. οἱ μὲν ἐπ', *they with all the liberty of action they desired.* — κατεσκευάζοντο, *and were arranging for the execution of the plot.* — 9. τὸν Εὐφραῖον. Cf. note on θέρος, § 50. — For the plural μεμνημένοι after εἴ τις, see C. 496 ; Cu. 362 ; G. 135, 3 ; H. 514 a. — 10. ὥστε and πρίν are both followed by the indic. to express the fact definitely *as* a fact. — 11. τοιούτου ...προσιόντος, *although an evil of such magnitude was approaching.* — 12. ῥῆξαι φωνήν. Compare *rumpere vocem* in Latin, and in English, *break silence.* — 12. διασκευασάμενοι, *fully prepared for action,* — *instructa acie.* — 13. οἱ πολέμιοι, *the enemy,* — always in a military

*much either from complaisance or through ignorance, but quietly sub-
mitting because they thought they were ruined in their main interests,
or, when they believed that all was lost.* — **65. 11. νὴ τὸν Δία καὶ
τὸν Ἀπόλλω.** Homer's heroes swear by the three principal deities,
Zeus, Apollo, and Athene, in a great emergency : *and verily by all
that is sacred I fear that this will be* YOUR *experience when upon reflec-
tion you see that you can do nothing.* — **15. κολακείᾳ...Φιλίππου,**
in flattery of (= *out of complaisance to*) *Philip.* Al. Φιλίππῳ. —
66. 15. καλήν γ᾽ οἱ πολλοί, *a beautiful return, indeed, have the people
of Oreus now received !* — **20. δουλεύουσί γε,** *yes, they are slaves, subject to the lash and the slaughter.* "Compare this with the choicest
of Mr. Burke's invectives of derision and pity upon the same subject,
— the sufferings of those who made peace with regicide France, — and
acknowledge the mighty effect of relying upon a single stroke to produce a great effect, if you have the master hand to give it." Lord
Brougham's Inaugural Discourse at Glasgow, quoted by Whiston. —
21. καλῶς, *beautifully did he spare the Olynthians !* — **67. 23. μωρία.**
The asyndeton which began with the previous section still continues.
— **24. κακῶς βουλευομένους,** *and while taking evil counsel...to think
you inhabit a city of such greatness that you will suffer nothing serious
whatever may happen.* There is no MS. authority for μηδὲν, but the
best editors insert it as required by Greek usage.

68. P. 48, l. 3. νὴ τὸν Δία, *yes, to be sure ! for we ought to have
done* SO AND SO *and not to have done* SO. νὴ τὸν Δία can hardly be
rendered into good English. Whiston renders : *but so it is by Zeus ;*
Kennedy : "*however* —"; Vömel : *Hercule vero.* — **4. πολλὰ ἄν,**
*many things might the Olynthians mention now, which, if they had
foreseen at the time, they would not have been ruined, many things
the people of Oreus.* The reader must often have observed our orator's
fondness for such rhetorical repetitions, making an impression somewhat like a refrain in verse. Cf. καλήν, § 66 ; οὐ, 34 and 32. —
69. 7. ἀλλὰ τί. The answer is self-evident, viz. none ; but it is
also illustrated and enforced by the apt and striking simile which follows. — **8. ἕως ἂν σῴζηται,** *so long as the vessel may perchance be
safe* (or *may be kept safe*). The passive of this verb is generally used
in the sense, *to be safe, to be well ;* but it is in the subj. with ἄν, and
I can hardly agree with Smead and the commentators generally that
"it has precisely the sense of the adj. with the copula, as below,
ἐσμὲν σῷοι." It suggests more the idea of a *process* (not merely a state),

and in this mood and with ἄν the further idea of contingency. —
ἄν τε μεῖζον, *whether the vessel be larger or smaller.* This clause
meets and answers the notion above that Athens is too *great* a city to
be destroyed. — 9. τότε is emphatic, and opposed to ἐπειδὰν δέ:
THEN, and not *when the sea has already overpowered it.* — 10. ἑξῆς,
in turn. — 11. σκοπεῖσθαι, *to be on the watch.* — μάταιος ἡ σπουδή.
The omission of the copula intensifies the conclusion: *vain the effort!*
Hardly allowable in English discourse, but not uncommon in Greek.
— 70. 13. καί introduces the application of the simile, as in *Ol.* I.
11 ; III. 18 ; *Phil.* I. 40 ; and τοίνυν emphasizes it, as οὕτως does in
Ol. I. 11 : *and we accordingly while we are safe.* The orator inge-
niously expresses the contingency in the illustration, ἕως ἂν σώζηται,
but here suggests no doubt of the present safety of the state, and
even goes on to magnify its resources and its dignity (ἀξίωμα, see
note § 43). — 15. τί ποιῶμεν. Instead of the formal application and
conclusion which the hearer expects, the orator, with an art which
has been much admired, or rather under a patriotic impulse which
seems natural and irrepressible, breaks out with, *what shall we do?* as
if that were the question which already filled the minds and hearts
of his hearers, and which they had long been wishing to ask. —
πάλαι...κάθηται, *some one sitting here this long time would be glad to
ask.* We should make the participle the principal verb in English,
and the verb a descriptive participle or substantive = *some one of
my hearers has been long wishing to ask.* — 16. ἐγὼ νὴ Δί᾿, *yes, indeed, and I will tell you, and will move a resolution also, so that if
you will you shall vote it;* that is, he is ready to do just what in the
beginning of his second Philippic he complains that the leading orators will not, viz. take the responsibility, be not only an orator but a
statesman, and not only tell the people what to do but put them in
the way of doing it. — 18. αὐτοὶ πρῶτον, sc. before exhorting others.
αὐτοί opposed to τοὺς ἄλλους, l. 23. — 20. λέγω, *I mean.* — 21. ἡμῖν
γε, *we Athenians at least must contend for liberty;* it is due to our
antecedents and our ancestry. — 25. πρέσβεις. After πρέσβεις, most
of the other MSS. and Σ, by a later hand, add : εἰς Πελοπόννησον,
εἰς Ῥόδον, εἰς Χίον, ὡς βασιλέα λέγω (οὐδὲ γὰρ τῶν ἐκείνῳ συμφερόντων
ἀφέστηκε τὸ μὴ τοῦτον πάντα καταστρέψασθαι): *send ambassadors to
Peloponnesus, to Rhodes, to Chios, to the king, I say (for it is not foreign to his interests even to prevent this man from conquering everything).* The passage is Demosthenic; but Becker has omitted it in

will never find those who will do it for him, and then, besides, I fear that there will come upon us the necessity of doing all at once every-thing that we do not wish. — οὐδὲ μὴ ποθ' εὔρη. C. 627 ; Cu. 620 ; G. 257 ; H. 845. — δέδοικα ὅπως μή. C. 625 ; Cu. 616, Obs. 3 ; G. 218 ; H. 742 a. — ἀνάγκη ποιεῖν. See the same construction, *Ol.* I. 15, where also the same fear is expressed in similar language.

76. P. 50, l. 4. ἐπανορθωθῆναι...γιγνομένων, *and I think that even now our affairs might yet be retrieved if these things were done.* The condition is expressed (with less contingency) by the participle, and the conclusion by the infinitive with ἄν. — 6. λεγέτω, pres. imper., *let him at once come forward and give it* (lit. let him *be* doing it forth-with). — ὅ τι δ' ὑμῖν. The oration, like so many others, concludes with a prayer for the blessing of heaven upon their deliberations : *and I pray all the gods that your determination, whatever it shall be, may have a happy issue.* This longest and most effective of all the popular orations of Demosthenes occupies only a little more than twenty pages in the Greek text, and only fifteen in Kennedy's trans-lation. It might easily have been delivered within the time (two hours) which Hon. Charles Francis Adams, in his recent address at the Commencement of Amherst College, declared should be the ex-treme limit of any oration or argument that would be effective.

Cambridge : Presswork by John Wilson & Son.

GREEK AND LATIN TEXT BOOKS.

————•————

ABBOTT'S LATIN PROSE. Latin Prose through English Idiom. Rules and Exercises on Latin Prose Composition. By the Rev. EDWIN A. ABBOTT, D.D., Head Master of the City of London School. With Additions by E. R. HUMPHREYS, A.M., LL.D. 18mo, cloth, 205 pages. $1.00.

The author's object is to prepare students for the study and composition of Latin Prose, by calling their attention first to the peculiarities of English idiom, and then to the methods of representing the English in the corresponding Latin idiom. A good deal of space has been given to the Prepositions. The Exercises are purposely unarranged, as connected examples are useless to test a pupil's knowledge.

Abbott's Latin Prose is the best book of the kind with which I am acquainted. It teaches the student to compose Latin, instead of translating stock sentences. — *Prof. Geo. O. Holbrooke, Trinity College, Hartford.*

Any book by the author of "English Lessons" and the "Shaksperian Grammar" I should expect to be good. This seems to me simply admirable, and is quite as valuable for the study of English as for the study of Latin. — *Prof. E. H. Griffin, Williams College, Williamstown.*

I feel sure the book will be widely used, as it deals with Latin Composition in the only right way. — *Prof. C. L. Smith, Harvard College.*

ARISTOPHANES' ACHARNIANS AND KNIGHTS.

The Acharnians and Knights of Aristophanes. Edited by W. C. GREEN, M.A., late Fellow of King's College, Cambridge. (*Catena Classicorum.*) 12mo, 210 pages. $1.35.

The text of this edition is mainly that of Dindorf. In the notes brevity has been studied, as short notes are more likely to be read, and, therefore, to be useful. Each play is preceded by an Introduction and an Argument.

I am exceedingly pleased with the Acharnians and Knights of Aristophanes, the new part in your *Catena Classicorum.* It is an excellent text-book. — *Prof. E. Jones, University of Michigan.*

5

ARISTOPHANES' BIRDS AND CLOUDS.

THE BIRDS OF ARISTOPHANES. With Notes and a Metrical Table, by C. C. FELTON, LL.D., President of Harvard University. New Edition, revised by W. W. GOODWIN, Elict Professor of Greek Literature in Harvard University. 12mo, 250 pages. $1.25.

THE CLOUDS OF ARISTOPHANES. With Notes and a Metrical Table, by C. C. FELTON, LL.D. New Edition, revised by Professor W. W. GOODWIN. 12mo, 250 pages. $1.25.

President Felton, by his tastes and his studies, was especially fitted for the difficult task of editing Aristophanes, and the notes of these two books show with what skill and thoroughness the congenial labor has been performed. Great care has been taken to explain the judicial expressions and the frequent allusions to the political and social life of Athens. In the new editions, revised by Professor Goodwin, the commentary has been enlarged by references to his Moods and Tenses of the Greek Verb.

CICERO PRO CLUENTIO. M. T. Ciceronis pro A. Cluentio Habito Oratio ad Judices. With English Notes, by AUSTIN STICKNEY, A.M., Professor of Latin in Trinity College, Hartford. Fourth Edition. 16mo, 155 pages. 90 cents.

The Notes are designed to supply the student with such information, in respect to the facts of the case and the scope of the argument, as is necessary to the proper understanding of the oration.

DEMOSTHENES' OLYNTHIACS AND PHILIPPICS. The Olynthiacs and Philippics of Demosthenes. With Introduction and Notes, for the use of Schools and Colleges, by W. S. TYLER, Williston Professor of Greek in Amherst College. 16mo, 256 pages. $1.25.

Separately. THE OLYNTHIACS. 98 pages. 75 cents.
THE PHILIPPICS. 158 pages. 90 cents.

The aim of the editor has been to help the student only where help was needed, to dispense with all *useless* comment, which includes all notes that are *certain not to be used*, and to condense the entire book within the smallest possible compass. The references are to the grammars of Hadley, Curtius, Goodwin, and Crosby. A notable feature of this edition are the general and special introductions, the analyses of the argument, and the summaries prefixed to each division.

We have just finished reading Professor Tyler's Olynthiacs and Philippics, and find the book very serviceable. The annotations are clear and scholarly, and the text is very correct. — *Professor D' Ooge, University of Michigan, Ann Arbor.*

The notes are compact and scholarly, the translations are concise and idiomatic, the difficulties are well explained; in short, the book seems to me, in every way, adapted to the young men and women who read these orations in our American colleges. — *Professor Kerr, University of Wisconsin, Madison.*

DEMOSTHENES ON THE CROWN. The De Corona of Demosthenes. With English Notes by the Rev. ARTHUR HOLMES, M.A., Senior Fellow of Clare College, Cambridge. Revised Edition, by W. S. TYLER, Williston Professor of Greek in Amherst College. 16mo, 304 pages. $1.50.

The text is preceded by an introduction, containing a concise statement of the history of the oration and an analysis of the argument. In the notes the American editor has omitted not a few of the English editor's citations from Greek authors, and whatever else seemed to be superfluous or sure to be neglected by college students and filled their place by references to American grammars and exact, yet idiomatic, translations of difficult passages.

I have already expressed to Professor Tyler my high appreciation of his *De Corona* of Demosthenes, and shall take pleasure in recommending it as the best edition for college use. — *Professor Harkness, Brown University, Providence.*

Professor Tyler's edition of Demosthenes' Oration on the Crown is a great improvement on the English one, both in its additions and its omissions. I know of nothing so well adapted to giving a student the fullest and clearest knowledge of this masterpiece of Greek literature. — *Professor Taylor Lewis, Union College Schenectady.*

ELTON'S GREEK HISTORIANS. Felton's Selections from Greek Historians, arranged in the Order of Events. New Edition, with Notes, by O. M. FERNALD, Professor of Greek in Williams College. With three maps. 12mo. $1.75.

In the new edition, some passages of the old " Selections " have been omitted in order to bring the work within a reasonable compass, though enough has been left for the historical reading of the freshman year in college. The extracts are taken from Diodorus Siculus, Herodotus, Thucydides, and Xenophon. The text has been thoroughly revised. The notes are entirely new, and include nothing of Prof. Felton's, except with acknowledgment. To the notes upon Herodotus has been prefixed a table of the peculiarities of the Ionic Dialect. The references are to Goodwin's and Hadley's grammars, and to Goodwin's Moods and Tenses.

FELTON'S MODERN GREEK. Selections from Modern Greek Writers in Prose and Poetry. With Notes by C. C. FELTON, LL.D., Eliot Professor of Greek Literature in Harvard University 12mo, 230 pages. $1.25.

The object of this volume is to exhibit the present state of the Greek language, as spoken and written by cultivated men, and as it appears in popular poems and ballads. The selections have been limited to a few authors, and to passages which refer to the history and condition of Greece, and which have an interest and value of themselves.

HERODOTUS. See Mather's Selections.

HORACE. The Works of Horace, with English Notes, by the Rev. A. J. MACLEANE, M.A. Revised and edited by R. H. CHASE, A.M. 12mo, 580 pages. $1.60.

This edition of Horace is substantially the same with Mr. Macleane's abridgment of his larger edition in the Bibliotheca Classica. The text is unaltered. Only such changes have been made in the notes as seemed necessary to adapt the book to the class room. Discussions respecting the various readings and disputed points have been omitted; the arguments of the Odes have been introduced from the larger work; and Dr. Beck's Introduction to the Metres has been appended to the notes.

ISOCRATES' PANEGYRICUS. The Panegyricus of Isocrates, from the text of Bremi, with English Notes by C. C. FELTON, LL.D. Third Edition, revised by Professor C. C. GOODWIN. 12mo, 155 pp. 90 cents.

The Panegyricus has been selected for publication, partly because it is an excellent specimen of the best manner of Isocrates, and partly because, by its plan, it presents a review of the history of Athens from the mythical ages down to the period following the treaty of Antalcidas, and is a convenient work to make the text-book for lessons in Greek history. The present edition is by Prof. Goodwin, who has added grammatical and other notes.

JUVENAL. Thirteen Satires of Juvenal. With English Notes by the Rev. A. J. MACLEANE, M.A., Trinity College, Cambridge. Abridged, with Additions, by the Rev. SAMUEL HART, M.A., Professor in Trinity College, Hartford. 16mo, 262 pages. $1.25.

Macleane's Commentary is highly valued among scholars, but its price has, for the most part, kept it out of the reach of our undergraduates. Professor Hart's abridgment has now put into their hands all that would be of use to them in the larger book. In addition, the editor has incorporated much that is useful from the notes of Heinrich, of Mayor, and of other commentators; and has inserted notes and comments of his own, including many explanations of peculiar construction, and a considerable body of grammatical references.

The work of the American editor is done with excellent judgment, and his additions to the notes will greatly increase their value for our students. — *Professor E. P. Crowell, Amherst College.*

I am happy to say that I have in use Professor Hart's edition of Juvenal, and find it a very useful, judicious, and scholarly manual, admirably adapted to the wants of the class. — *Professor L. Coleman, Lafayette College, Easton.*